David Aikman is a writer who is well-known around the world. I know him not only from his writings with *TIME* magazine and his many bestselling books but also as a friend and a man of integrity. David is a man committed to research-ing the backstories and understanding the spirit and the letter of the problems as well as the answers. He is truly an outstanding Christian leader in the realm of the media who writes what needs to be read. I happily commend him to you.

LOREN CUNNINGHAM
Founder of Youth With a Mission International
President of University of the Nations
Kailua-Kona, Hawaii

There is no subject more complicated—and more distorted by politics and the mainstream media   than the conflict in the Middle East. Yet David Aikman ad-justs the lens and brings this issue into sharp focus. Few people are as qualified as Aikman to give us such an accurate and balanced perspective. His Christian faith and his years as a journalist make this book a compelling read.

J. LEE GRADY
Editor, *Charisma* Magazine
Lake Mary, Florida

David Aikman's elegant, readable style of in-depth journalistic writing guides readers through the complexities of the world's biggest powderkeg in an eye-opening manner. Few journalistic writers today can come close to the breadth of international insight that Aikman brings to the craft of narrative reporting and historically informed journalism.

MICHAEL A. LONGINOW, PH.D.
Professor and Chair of Department of Journalism, Biola University
La Mirada, California

Like the biblical sons of Issachar "who understood the times" (1 Chron. 12:32), David Aikman regularly sheds light on the major people and trends of our times. He's brought his unique perspective to bear on topics such as modern-day China and the greatest evangelist of our era, Billy Graham. This newest work will undoubtedly break new ground on one of the most intractable struggles of our age: the conflict in the Middle East.

CHRIS MITCHELL
CBN News Bureau Chief
Jerusalem, Israel

DAVID AIKMAN

FORMER *TIME* MAGAZINE BUREAU CHIEF, JERUSALEM

THE MIRAGE OF PEACE

UNDERSTANDING THE NEVER-ENDING CONFLICT IN THE MIDDLE EAST

Regal

From Gospel Light
Ventura, California, U.S.A.

Published by Regal
From Gospel Light
Ventura, California, U.S.A.
www.regalbooks.com
Printed in the U.S.A.

All maps are from the United States Central Intelligence Agency.
www.cia.gov

Library of Congress Cataloging-in-Publication Data
Aikman, David, 1944-
The mirage of peace : understanding the never-ending conflict
in the middle east / David Aikman.
p. cm.
Includes bibliographical references.
ISBN 978-0-8307-4605-7 (hard cover)
1. Middle East—History—1979- 2. Middle East—Politics and government.
3. Politics and war—Middle East. I. Title.
DS63.1.A3437 2009
956.05—dc22
2009021909

1 2 3 4 5 6 7 8 9 10 11 12 13 14 15 / 15 14 13 12 11 10 09

Rights for publishing this book outside the U.S.A. or in non-English languages are
administered by Gospel Light Worldwide, an international not-for-profit ministry.
For additional information, please visit www.glww.org, email info@glww.org, or write to
Gospel Light Worldwide, 1957 Eastman Avenue, Ventura, CA 93003, U.S.A.

This book is dedicated to my two daughters,
Abbie and Amanda

CONTENTS

ROM.
Bucharest ★
UKR.
Krasnodar
RUSSIA
KAZAKHSTAN
Sevastopol'
Constanța
Sofia ★
BULGARIA
Varna
Black Sea
Gora El'brus
(highest point in
Europe, 5633 m)
Groznyy
KAZAKHSTAN
Aqtaü
(Aktau)
UZBEKISTAN
Nukus
Dasoguz
Buxoro
Thessaloniki
İstanbul
Bosporus
Samsun
Bat'umi
CAUCASUS MOUNTAINS
Caspian
Sea
(lowest point in
Europe, -28 m)
GREECE
Aegean
Sea
İzmir
Bursa
Ankara
Trabzon
DOĞU KARADENIZ DAĞLARI
GEORGIA
Tbilisi
ARMENIA
Erzurum
Yerevan
AZERBAIJAN
Baku
Sumqayit
Türkmenbaşy
Balkanabat
TURKMENISTAN
Türkmenabat
GARAGUM
Ashgabat
KOPPEH DAGH
Mary
Athens
Denizli
TURKEY
Kayseri
Van
Mount
Ararat
Tabriz
Urmia
Rasht
ALBURZ MTS.
Kūh-e Damāvand
Tehran
Balkanabat
Crete
Antalya
İçel
(Mersin)
Konya
Adana
Gaziantep
Diyarbakır
Mosul
Arbil
Zanjan
Qazvin
Qom
Arāk
Mashhad
Herāt
AFG.
CYPRUS
Nicosia ★
Latakia
Aleppo
SYRIA
Ḥimṣ
Kirkūk
Baghdad
Kermānshāh
ZAGROS MOUNTAINS
Eşfahān
IRAN
DASHT-E LŪT
Mediterranean Sea
Beirut
LEBANON
Haifa
Damascus
Golan
Heights
SYRIAN DESERT
IRAQ
Ahvāz
Kerman
Zāhedān
PAK.
Alexandria
Port
Said
Cairo
Al Iṣzah
Suez
Jerusalem
ISRAEL
West Bank
Amman
Dead Sea
(lowest point in Asia, -408 m)
JORDAN
Gaza Strip
SINAI
PENINSULA
Aqabah
An Nāṣirīyah
Al Baṣrah
Ābādān
Būshehr
Shīrāz
Bandar
ʿAbbās
Strait of
Hormuz
OMAN
Gulf of
Oman
QATTARA
DEPRESSION
WESTERN
DESERT
Asyūṭ
EGYPT
DESERT
Luxor
Aswān
Tropic of Cancer
Tabūk
HEJAZ
Ḥā'il
Ḥafar
al Bāṭin
Kuwait
KUWAIT
Al Jubayl
Ad Dammām
Dhahran
BAHRAIN
Manama
Doha
QATAR
Abu
Dhabi
Dubai
UNITED ARAB
EMIRATES
Muscat
Yanbu'
al Baḥr
Medina
Buraydah
Riyadh
SAUDI
ARABIA
OMAN
Administrative
Boundary
Ḥalā'ib
NUBIAN
DESERT
Jiddah
Mecca
Red
Sea
ASIR
RUB' AL KHALI
SUDAN
Omdurman
Khartoum
Wad
Madani
Port Sudan
Abha
Jizan
Salālah
Al Ghaydah
Arabian Sea
ERITREA
Massawa
Asmara ★
Sanaa
Ḥudaydah
YEMEN
Al Mukallā
Socotra
(YEMEN)
Addis Ababa
Dese
Lac'Assal
(lowest point in Africa, -155 m)
Aden
Gulf of Aden
Bab el
Mandeb
GREAT RIFT VALLEY
ETHIOPIA
DJIBOUTI
Djibouti
Berbera
Hargeysa
SOMALIA
Provisional
Administrative Line

Scale 1:21,000,000
Lambert Conformal Conic Projection,
standard parallels 12°N and 38°N
0   300 Kilometers
0   300 Miles

Boundary representation is
not necessarily authoritative.

Golan Heights is Israeli-occupied Syria.

West Bank and Gaza Strip are Israeli-occupied with current
status subject to the Israeli-Palestinian Interim Agreement —
permanent status to be determined through further negotiation.

Israel proclaimed Jerusalem as its capital in 1950, but the US, like
nearly all other countries, maintains its Embassy in Tel Aviv.

THE MIDDLE EAST

1

THE MIDDLE EAST:
A CENTRAL HUB OF WORLD AFFAIRS

Mahmoud Ahmadinejad . . . Al-Qaeda . . . Hezbollah . . . Hamas . . . Islamic radicalism . . . oil . . . *sharia* . . . terrorism . . . Iraq. Whenever the phrase "Middle East" looms over the horizon, so do a whole flock of Arabic names that conjure up a locust-plague of modern troubles. What is it about the Middle East that makes it so often seem like the worst locale on the planet? Why does it appear to be the only place in the world where there has supposedly been a "peace process" for decades but as much evidence of real peace as there is of marital bliss on a television episode of *Desperate Housewives*?

Is it the air, the water, the geography, the language, the culture, the religions? Is it a little bit of each, plus a generous splash of the burden of history—that shadow reigning over all our lives at birth through no fault of our parents or grandparents, or any ancestral link of whom we have ever heard?

Above all, the Middle East is a very complicated place. Anyone who would attempt to make sense of large parts of it in a single book might be considered arrogant or immodest, or even stark raving mad.

This, nevertheless, is what I am setting out to do in *The Mirage of Peace*. If I succeed in unearthing even a tiny bit of increased understanding of the complex issues that affect nations and regions here, or offer some small insight that illuminates a hitherto fuzzy patch of the global map, I shall be happy. I apologize in advance for all of the topics on which there has been neither time nor space enough to focus adequately, or even focus at all. I apologize for any mistakes that have crept into the text despite the most diligent efforts to keep them out. I apologize if I have offended anyone in the judgments and criticisms that one is forced to make quickly, and with inadequate qualification, in a book of an introductory nature such as this one.

First, an explanation of the area we commonly call today the "Middle East." Until the end of World War II, the region wasn't even called by this name. The geopolitical strategists in the foreign ministries and imperial chanceries of the major powers of Europe called it the "Near East." That term denoted a swatch of countries and states in the eastern Mediterranean, extending to the farthest south end of the Persian Gulf. Beyond the Near East lay the "Far East," that collection of exotic cultures and states on the Pacific Rim of Asia: China, Japan, Indochina, Southeast Asia. The transition to the term "Middle East" from "Near East" was not simply a switch in nomenclature. Although the region referred to by the two terms is generally the same, the lands that are included within them are by no means identical.

Specifically, the Near East meant Turkey—known in the nineteenth century as the Ottoman Empire—and Armenia, as well as the sheikhdoms and monarchies surrounding the Persian Gulf. It also included the Balkans, that grand crossroads of cultures and faiths and perennial venue of strife that lies between the Black Sea on the east and the Mediterranean on the west.

The Balkans dominated world headlines after the archduke of Austria-Hungary, Franz Ferdinand, was felled by an assassin's bullet in Sarajevo on June 28, 1914, unleashing the horrors of World War I. When that cruel episode of bloodletting ended in 1918, the Near East changed out of all recognition. Three of the great empires that had either vied for control of the region or sought to influence it for hundreds of years—the Austro-Hungarian Empire, the Ottoman Empire and the empire of Tsarist Russia—had collapsed. The victors of World War I—Britain, France and the United States—redrew the map of the Near East and, in so doing, helped set in motion the events that would lead to the region being called the Middle East today.

The term "Middle East" was, in fact, first popularized by an American: the naval historian and global strategist Alfred Thayer Mahan (1840-1914), whose theory of the importance of what he called "sea power"—meaning the power of national navies—propelled nations around the globe in the late nineteenth and early twentieth centuries to build up navies as instruments to wield long-range international power.[1] Kaiser Wilhelm II of Germany kept a copy of Mahan's book at his bedside on the imperial yacht, *Hohenzollern*.

Mahan first used the term "Middle East" in a 1902 article to refer to the area surrounding the Persian Gulf. When *The Times* of London ran an extended series of articles on the strategic significance of this region, it decided at the end of the series to drop quotation marks around the term "Middle East"—and we will now do likewise.

People who prefer the term the "Near East" don't give up easily. While waiting for an interview at an American embassy in, well, one of the Middle East countries, in the fall of 2007, I got into a friendly but forceful argument with an American diplomat who insisted on using the term "Near East." In this, her own government's bureaucracy supported her: the State Department bureau that handles this region of the world is called the Bureau of Near Eastern Affairs. Historians and archaeologists also support her view. Some of the most prestigious American universities have departments of "Near Eastern Studies" rather than of "Middle Eastern Studies."[2] Archaeologists and historians, particularly those interested in the ancient period of time, prefer the term "Near Eastern," perhaps because it sounds more academic, and hence less controversial, than "Middle Eastern."

U.S. diplomats, archaeologists and historians aside, the "Middle East" has become the accepted term in general usage. Commerce has played a role in making it so. The airline industry, under rules determined by the umbrella International Air Transport Association (IATA), which comprises 240 global airlines and 94 percent of the global airline industry, uses the collective term "Middle East" for fares and ticket taxes for the following countries: Bahrain, Egypt, Iran, Iraq, Israel, Jordan, Kuwait, Lebanon, Palestinian territories, Oman, Qatar, Saudi Arabia, Sudan, Syrian Arab Republic, United Arab Emirates and Yemen.

Many residents of the region object to the term "Middle East," which they say reflects a Eurocentric view of the world. And they are right. East, of course, means east of London and Paris, and certainly east of Washington, D.C. Nervous U.N. bureaucrats, fearful of offending anyone, have taken to using the term "West Asia." But in a sign that even the Arab world has come to acquiesce in the verbal formulations of an American naval historian, the name of the most influential London-based Arabic-language newspaper, *Asharq Alawsat*, owned by a Saudi Arab, is translated into English by the paper itself as "The Middle East." Like it or not, the Middle East is the commonly used and preferred term these days. After all, has anyone recently seen books with titles like *A History of West Asia*?

Now that we have examined the terminology and its history, the next question is which countries are included in this region that now is generally referred to as the Middle East. Certainly, the Middle East includes the Arab countries of Egypt, Sudan, Jordan, Syria, Iraq, Iran, Lebanon and, of course, Israel. But it also includes all the Arabian peninsula countries: Saudi Arabia, Kuwait, Qatar, the United Arab Emirates, Oman, Yemen and Bahrain. By a sort of cultural extension, it often refers to the Arab-speaking countries west of Egypt on the North African coast— Libya, Algeria, Tunisia and Morocco—even though those states consider themselves part of the *Maghreb* (literally "place of sunset" or "West/ Western" in Arabic).

But just like the IATA, I do *not* consider Turkey to be a Middle Eastern state. One simple reason is that Turks have considered themselves to be European. This has been the case ever since Mustafa Kemal, known as Atatürk (which means "the Father of the Turks"), founded Turkey in 1923 as a determinedly secular state. True, Turks are Muslims; they are not, however, Arabs. An equally valid reason for not including Turkey in the Middle East is the fact that the European Union is willing to at least consider Turkey's application for membership, signifying that European powers see validity to Turkey's view of itself as part of Europe. Obviously, Middle Eastern affairs impact Turkey tremendously, but that does not mean it is a part of that region.

So, if the Maghreb countries are not included, these are the countries making up the Middle East: Syria, Lebanon, Israel, Egypt, Sudan, Jordan, Iraq, Iran, Kuwait, Bahrain, Qatar, the United Arab Emirates, Saudi Arabia, Yemen and Oman. Some readers might wonder why Pakistan and Afghanistan are not on that list. And if the list were to include Pakistan and Afghanistan, then what about parts of central Asia that used to be part of the Soviet Union itself? A distinction, however, needs to be made between the region itself and the nearby countries that have connections with it or want to influence events within it.

The United States and Russia cannot, of course, be ignored when examining the situation in the Middle East. Russian leader Vladimir Putin has sought to play an increasingly influential role in the region as Russia's economy and self-confidence in international affairs has grown. The role of Pakistan, Afghanistan and Turkey will also be examined whenever understanding a particular point seems to require it. But none of these countries belongs in the category known as the Middle East.

When tackling a subject as controversial as the Middle East, it is inevitable that some readers will feel one or another aspect of the topic has been ignored or insufficiently dealt with. It would be impossible for a book like this to provide an encyclopedic amount of information about each country. Nor would that be useful, as a cascade of facts and details doesn't necessarily increase one's understanding of a region. And if there is one region of the world where wisdom and insight are really necessary, it's the Middle East.

Like it or not, the problems of the Middle East are here to stay. Like it or not, what is happening in the Middle East is going to impact the lives of all of us. And like it or not, that's going to be the case with or without American soldiers on the ground in the region, fighting for their lives, and by extension, for ours as well. For those who have a son or daughter, brother or sister, husband or wife fighting in Iraq, the impact is immediate and direct. But the events in the entire Middle East impact each of our lives in large and small ways, whether the effect is in how we in the free world must be vigilant against terrorists' attempts to bring violence and chaos into our lives or whether rising gas prices force us to consider changing our driving habits. What happens in the Middle East affects our daily lives in some way or another. Understanding the region and its conflicts is no longer a luxury and no longer the concern only of academics and dilettante travelers; it is absolutely vital for all of us.

Even a lifetime of study, though, would not uncover all the details needed to comprehend this complicated part of the world. This book will introduce the main issues, the main players both now and in history, and the important and relevant facts about the countries and the issues. Everyone knows that the policies and passions of the nations, political parties and religious communities of the Middle East are intense, contentious and often downright warlike. I hope this book doesn't leave any reader still wondering why this is so when he or she reaches the last page.

The people of the Middle East express a plethora of extremely strong views on all manner of subjects. I will try to show what those views are as fairly as I can. Achieving true objectivity is one of those unattainable ideals like trying to be equally kind to everyone. But I do believe it is possible to be truthful, and I am certain we should always try to be fair. Someone once asked me how journalists could be sure of being fair to all sides in their reporting. I replied that the test is to take an opinion you really do not like, express it in your own words, and then ask a person who holds that very opinion whether it is a fair expression of his or her view. If that person says yes, the journalist has been fair. By that criterion, I will try in this book to be fair to all parties, even to those whose views I clearly find odious.

Where to start? Well, not actually in the Middle East. The region is so much in our face that we need a dose of historical reality to put things in their true perspective. So let's start in what is often called "the eternal city": Rome.

Tourists to Rome usually visit the remarkable remains of the great civilization of classical Rome. Almost invariably, that includes the Colosseum, where gladiators fought each other and wild beasts. The heart of ancient Rome, however, was not the Colosseum; it was the Forum, the roughly rectangular area of land that was the site of public meetings, law courts and commerce, and lay between the Colosseum and the Capitoline Hill, the highest point in classical Rome. Running through the Forum from the top of the Capitoline Hill to the Colosseum was the Via Sacra, or Sacred Road, the route along which victorious generals paraded when they had been granted a "triumph" by the Senate or, in later times, by the emperor.

At the highest point of the Via Sacra stands a 15-meter tall victory arch to commemorate the triumphal procession in AD 71 of the Roman general and later Emperor Titus and his father, Vespasian. That triumph was to celebrate the victorious conclusion of one of the most intense military conflicts up to that point in Roman history: the suppression of the Jewish revolt in Jerusalem that had begun in AD 66. According to the Jewish historian Josephus (c. AD 37-100), a total of 1.1 million Jews died during the siege and final assault on Jerusalem. The Roman historian Tacitus (AD 55-120) reports a far smaller figure: 600,000. Whatever the case, the slaughter was horrendous.[3]

Josephus, a reluctant leader among the Jewish rebels, who had warned the rebels again and again that it was folly to challenge the might of the Roman Empire, was an eyewitness of both the early years of the conflict and the final assault on Jerusalem. He was captured a few years into the revolt but was well treated by Titus and accompanied the young general when he led three Roman legions in the final assault on Jerusalem. Josephus saw with his own eyes the burning and pillaging of the Jewish Temple and the carnage that took place after Roman legionaries broke through the city's outer wall and began to slaughter men, women and children. The savagery was undoubtedly the consequence of the severe casualties suffered by the Romans when, time after time, Jewish fighters had sallied forth from the embattled walls and massacred parties of soldiers who rashly approached too close to the city and became cut off from the main Roman army.

I have visited Rome and walked around the Roman forum, but I do not recall if ever I have had the Arch of Titus pointed out to me. As the briefest research indicates, it is one of the most handsome of Rome's many triumphal arches. Yet it is not its architectural design that has drawn the attention of so many people over the years. Rather, it is the marble reliefs on the inside of the arch.[4] The one on the south side is, by our standards, banal enough: the general, Titus, in a chariot, accompanied by the Goddess Victoria and the Goddess Roma, on his way to being crowned "triumphator," or conqueror.

On the inside of the northern base is a sculptural frieze showing another scene from that "triumph," and this is what has evoked the most interest: soldiers bearing prized treasures seized from the Jewish Temple. Clearly seen are the table of the showbread, on which offerings of bread to God were prescribed to be made, the trumpets that sounded the beginning of the Jewish new year, Rosh Hashanah, and the huge golden menorah, the seven-armed lamp that today is a symbol of both Judaism and the State of Israel. Josephus, who was also a witness of the AD 71 triumph, described these sacred items:

> Most of the spoils that were carried were heaped up indiscriminately, but more prominent than all the rest were those captured in the Temple in Jerusalem—a golden table weighing several hundredweight, and a lamp-stand similarly made of gold but differently constructed from those we normally use. The central shaft was fixed to a base, and from it extended slender branches like the prongs of a trident, and with the end of each one forged into a lamp: these numbered seven, signifying the honor paid to that number by the Jews. After these were carried the Jewish Law [i.e., the torah scrolls], the last of the spoils.[5]

Apart from the fierceness of the fighting and the brutality of the aftermath, the historical significance of the AD 70 sack of Jerusalem by the Romans is that it marked the beginning of the Jewish people's two-millennia exile from their homeland. Not all Jews were expelled from Roman Palestine after the capture of Jerusalem and the Temple. There were still many Jews living in Judea, and many of these were to join yet another revolt against Rome in AD 135. Jews, in fact, had been living in very large numbers outside their traditional homeland since the exile in Babylon in the sixth century BC. But the sacking of the Temple in Jerusalem is one of the great tragic events in Jewish history, and a central marker in the history of the entire Middle East.

Indeed, the Arch of Titus has become a grim symbol in Jewish history. When the State of Israel was founded in May 1948, a large delegation from the Roman Jewish community symbolically walked through the arch in the wrong direction; that is, not entering the Roman Forum as Titus did during his "triumph," but going away from it. Shortly afterward, the Menorah was chosen as the official insignia of the State of Israel, the design modeled after the sculptured depiction on the Arch of Titus of the lamp stand the Romans stole from the Temple in Jerusalem.

There are two larger points in all this. The first is that the Romans were not in doubt at all where the Jewish Temple was located; it was in the heart of Jerusalem, a city whose capture after fierce fighting, according to Josephus, cost the lives of more than one million people, no doubt including several thousand Roman soldiers. Yet, quite bizarrely, in the midst of negotiations for an Israeli-Palestinian settlement during the summer of 2000, when President Bill Clinton hosted Palestinian and Israeli delegations at Camp David, Yasser Arafat, the president of the Palestinian Authority, claimed that the Jewish Temple had not been in Jerusalem at all but in Nablus. It is nothing less than astonishing that a contemporary political leader could flatly overlook historical and archaeological evidence that has been around since the first century AD.

The second point is that the most magnificent of all Roman triumphal arches still standing today is a reminder of a profound fact: 2,000 years ago, when the Roman Empire—one of the greatest empires the world has ever known—was at the height of its power, the events in and around Jerusalem dominated world affairs. They still do.

The Romans have long since moved off the world stage, and the Jews more recently have returned to the lands tramped upon by the legions of Titus. They are not, however, the only people living in it.

2

ISRAEL AND THE PALESTINIANS

Pick up any newspaper or switch on any TV cable news program on any day of the year and there is a good chance you will hear a news item on the Israeli-Palestinian issue. It will probably be about the latest Israeli military action in Gaza or the West Bank against suspected terrorists; or some intransigent statement by Hamas, the Palestinian Islamic political organization; or yet another effort by the Israeli government and the Palestinian Authority to move forward what has been called "the peace process." There is, unfortunately, a likelihood that it will not be good news.

No conflict or issue in the modern history of diplomacy seems to have amassed such intensive international scrutiny or such relentless political and diplomatic efforts to solve it as the Israeli-Palestinian issue. As of August 2006 (the date of the most recent summary), the U.N. Security Council had passed 100 resolutions about the issue since Israel first became independent in 1948. The vast majority of the resolutions were critical of Israel. The General Assembly had published five resolutions, voting historically in 1947 for partition of Palestine, then under British Mandate control, into two states—one Jewish and one Arab. Since the 1947 votes (called U.N. General Assembly 181), the U.N. General Assembly has passed a further four. One of them became infamous, notably Number 3379, which, in 1975, equated Zionism with racism. Mercifully, that resolution was repealed by another resolution in 1991, called "U.N. GA 3379."

The Arab-Israeli dispute is the world's longest-lasting, most incurable and most festering diplomatic cold sore, to put it bluntly. The U.N. employs an official—B. Lynn Pascoe, the Under-Secretary for Political Affairs—who is an able American career diplomat who spends a great deal of his time trying to sort out problems of the Middle East. Much of that

time is devoted to the Arab-Israeli conflict. But the U.N. itself is also part of another international group called "The Quartet"—consisting of representatives of the European Union, the U.S., the U.N. and Russia—that is also trying to play a role in mediating the conflict. Since its establishment in 2002, The Quartet has pursued a diplomatic strategy called "The Road Map." Its designated representative in Israeli-Palestinian problem-solving is former British Prime Minister Tony Blair.

The Israeli-Palestinian issue, in its basic dimensions, is really pretty simple: It is the struggle between two different national groups, Israelis and Palestinians, over which of them should have control of a narrow piece of land at the eastern end of the Mediterranean. Before 1948, that land was called Palestine and had been ruled by Great Britain since 1917, after the British defeated the Ottoman Turks, who in turn had ruled it since 1517.

For most Palestinians, the land is still called "Palestine," though most of it became Israel after the Israeli War of Independence in 1948. All of it came under Israeli control after the Six-Day War of 1967.

From 1948 until September 13, 1993 (when the Israeli-Palestinian Declaration of Principles was signed on the White House Lawn by Israeli Prime Minister Yitzhak Rabin and Palestinian Liberation Organization [PLO] Chairman Yasser Arafat), the Palestinians, as represented by their principal leadership, the PLO, never even acknowledged the existence of Israel. Until 1979, neither did any other Arab country. The Camp David Accords of the previous year led to Egypt's official recognition of Israel—a sort of "cold peace"—and the Declaration of Principles of 1994 led to Jordan's establishment of diplomatic relations with Israel.

Why did Israel ever come into existence? The answer to that is pretty simple as well: anti-Semitism. The Jews of the world, exiled to many different countries after the Romans defeated the last of their revolts against Roman power—the revolt of Bar Kokhba in AD 135—had suffered terribly from persecution in the countries in which their communities existed. The worst of their persecution, for most of the time, occurred in Christian Europe, where the opprobrium of being, supposedly, "Christ-killers," was systematically pinned on them from the Middle Ages onward.

Why do Jews everywhere tend to detest the word "crusade"? It is because the first of a series of major murders of Jews took place during the First Crusade launched by Pope Urban II in 1095 to wrest the Holy Land from Muslim control. Jews in Muslim countries were seldom subjected to the kind of murderous pogroms that their co-religionists endured in Christian Europe; but under Islamic law—the *sharia*—they had to put up with the humiliation of *dhimmi* status (literally "protected," but in practice second-class citizens). On the whole, though, Muslim societies kept Jews suppressed but didn't persecute them systematically until relatively modern times, starting from the nineteenth century.

The Jews of Europe experienced significant improvement in their condition after the French Revolution (1789-1797). Most of the countries of Europe gradually adopted the Enlightenment notions of equality for all ethnic and religious groups.

Roots of Zionism

Many Jews in nineteenth-century Europe excelled in music and literature; and in the case of Benjamin Disraeli (1804-1881), a Jew converted to Anglican Christianity at the age of 13, in politics. Disraeli became the prime minister of Great Britain (in 1868, and then from 1874-1880). Some even began to trickle into Palestine out of response to a religious-inspired movement called *Hovevei Zion* ("Lovers of Zion"). Jews as a whole, however, continued to be vulnerable to volatile changes in public mood.

There was no example of this more vivid than the trial of Alfred Dreyfus (1859-1935) in France, in 1894. A major in the French army, Dreyfus was falsely convicted of espionage for the Germans and literally drummed out of the army in a ceremony where his officer's sword was symbolically broken over the knee of an attending officer. Until he was vindicated in a public campaign that uncovered the true spy, a certain Major Esterhazy, and demanded that the army be held responsible for repressing evidence that would have demonstrated his innocence, Dreyfus was the subject of a furious debate in the French media. The debate, in fact, divided France. Those resisting his vindication most vociferously rested much of their arguments on the alleged culpability of Jews for the general problems of society.

A thoughtful observer of the Dreyfus affair, as a journalist in France, was the Austrian-born, highly secular Jew, Theodor Herzl. Horrified, as many were, by the bigotry of much of France against Jews, Herzl (1860-1904) came to a radical conclusion about the safest possible solution for what Europeans often slightingly called "the Jewish problem." Jews everywhere, Herzl felt, needed an ultimate place of refuge, but where? Why, of course, in the ancient Jewish homeland of Israel in what Jews often called "Zion," meaning Jerusalem. Thus was born the political movement that became known as Zionism. A Zionist, henceforth, was anyone who advocated a political homeland for the Jews in Palestine, as that region of the Ottoman Empire containing Zion was called.

Herzl presided over Europe's First Zionist Congress in August 1897, in Basle, Switzerland. A few days after it was over, he wrote in his journal, "At Basle I founded the Jewish state. If I were to say this out loud today I would be greeted by universal laughter. In five years, perhaps, certainly in fifty years, everyone will perceive it."[1] He was off by one year, since the Jewish state of Israel declared its independence in 1948. In fact, even before Herzl launched political Zionism, Jews had fled to Palestine in relatively large numbers from 1881-1882, after anti-Jewish rioting (called "pogroms") had broken out in Russia. (Many Russians thought the Jews were disproportionately responsible for the incubation of anti-Russian, socialist and anarchist ideas and thus were indirectly responsible for the assassination of Tsar Alexander II in 1881.) That first wave of immigrants became known as the First Aliyah, or First Immigration. The word *aliyah* in Hebrew means "ascent," which all travelers have to do in order to reach Jerusalem in the Judean hills.

Zionism was actually opposed by many Jews, who thought that encouraging Jews to immigrate to Palestine would aggravate their situation in the countries where they lived. The Ottoman Empire, by the end of the nineteenth century, known as "the sick man" of major European powers, was also uncomfortable with Zionism, understanding that it would almost certainly provoke unrest among the Arabs living under its control. But Istanbul, the capital of Ottoman Turkey, was prodded into toleration of Jewish immigration by both the German Kaiser Wilhelm II, who saw himself as a peacemaker in the Middle East (and made a ceremonial visit to Jerusalem in 1898), and by Great Britain, the leading European imperial power of the era. From the late nineteenth century onward, there was an increasing sympathy for Zionism among British politicians.

More pogroms against Russian Jews by mobs of Russian extremist nationalists fueled the Second Aliyah (1904-1914). It also marked, as we shall see, the first signs of an organized local Arab hostility toward Zionism in Palestine.

Herzl died in 1904 and was succeeded by other Jewish leaders, of whom the most famous was to be Chaim Weizmann (1874-1922). World War I transformed Zionism from a marginal political movement to center stage in world politics. Weizmann, by now a respected scientist and a naturalized British citizen, had met the future British foreign secretary, Arthur Balfour, in 1906, and the two established a friendship that was to be significant for the future Jewish state of Israel.

After World War I broke out in the summer of 1914, the Ottoman Empire made the mistake (assisted by prewar British diplomatic blundering) of allying itself with the Germans. Though the Turks defeated British military expeditions early on in the war, in 1915, first at Kut in what is now Iraq, and then on the peninsula of Gallipoli that year and in 1916, they were forced on the defensive by overwhelming Allied military superiority, particularly after the U.S. entered World War I in April 1917.

British troops under General Edmund Allenby advanced into Palestine from Egypt and captured Jerusalem on December 9, 1917. A month before that momentous event, however, a political declaration of even greater significance had been made.[2] On November 2, 1917, the British Foreign Secretary, Sir Arthur Balfour, released a letter to Lord Rothschild, a leader of the British Jewish community, formally wedding British foreign policy to the aspirations of Zionism. "Her Majesty's government," Balfour wrote, in what was to become known ever after as the Balfour Declaration, "supports a National Homeland for the Jewish people in Palestine." The document had been cleared with American President Woodrow Wilson before its release. It said "a homeland" for the Jewish people, and not "a state," and it contained an important qualifying clause: "it being understood that the rights of non-Jewish populations in Palestine will be fully respected." In short, the British acknowledged, Zionism was a legitimate goal for Jews, but not at the expense of the people who lived there, namely the Arabs, or, as they were to become known, "the Palestinians."

After World War I, the League of Nations, which came into existence at the end of the conflict, formally conferred on the conquering power, Great Britain, "mandatory" authority to govern Palestine until such a time as its inhabitants could govern themselves. At first Britain was strongly supportive of Zionism. The first governor of Palestine, Sir Herbert Samuel, was himself a Jew. Leading British politicians, moreover, didn't conceal their own personal Zionism. In 1922, Winston Churchill, then Colonial Secretary, affirmed privately that he himself contemplated "the eventual establishment of a Jewish state."

An Identifying Marker for Arabs

By that time Jewish settlement in Palestine had provoked alarm among both Arab peasants dislodged from their land when Zionist agents purchased it, often from absentee landlords, and from Arab notables who clearly foresaw that the Jews might eventually uproot them.

Did the Arabs think of themselves at that time as "Palestinians"? American-Palestinian historian Rashid Khalidi says that the Arabs of Palestine began decisively to "imagine" themselves as Palestinians around 1922 or 1923, though he points out that as early as 1911, an Arab newspaper called *Filastin* ("Palestine" in Arabic) had been founded in Jaffa, the principal port on the coast of Palestine through which immigrant Jews arrived. Many Arabs living in the Ottoman-controlled territory thought of themselves as belonging to greater Syria. Yet whether wanting to be Syrians or simply Arabs belonging to Palestine, there is no question that the growing Jewish presence in the land aroused Arab opposition and contributed to the idea of "Palestinian" as the identifying marker of Arabs living in Palestine.

Israelis have sometimes disputed whether the term "Palestinian" has any real identity except as the emblem of Arabs opposed to a Jewish state. In 1969, the then-Israeli Prime Minister Golda Meir said in an interview with a British newspaper, "There is no such thing as Palestinians. They do not exist."[3] What she meant was that historically there had never been a country of "Palestine" with the name Palestine and a capital city. The Arabs living in Palestine had always been part of someone else's empire since the time when the Arab caliph Omar captured the city of Jerusalem from the Byzantine Empire in AD 638. In that respect, she was correct. But by the time Golda Meir was prime minister of Israel, the Arabs of Palestine who had fled during Israel's War of Independence, or by now

GAZA STRIP

WEST BANK

were ruled by Israel after Israel conquered the West Bank from Jordan, and the Gaza Strip from Egypt, during the 1967 Six-Day War, certainly thought of themselves as "Palestinian."

A national community doesn't need a long history as an established country to see itself as a "nation." After all, Americans fighting against the English crown in the 1770s had no trouble "imagining" themselves as "American." Khalidi's assertion that the Arabs living in Palestine were thinking of themselves as "Palestinians" at the beginning of the 1920s has merit. Even more significant is the fact that even before the outbreak of World War I, most editors and writers in Arabic newspapers printed in Palestine foresaw that the ongoing Jewish immigration was aimed at establishing an eventual Jewish state in Palestine.

The principal problem of the Palestinians in their relations with the Jews migrating to Palestine was the quality of their political leaders in Palestine. Almost without exception these have defined "Palestinian" as a state that implies there cannot also be another state that is Jewish adjacent to it within the boundaries of Palestine. The British administration ruling Palestine under the Mandate tried to enlist Arab participation in a governing council. While the Jewish community in Palestine—about 82,000 by 1922—was eager to be accepted as partners with the British colonial rulers, the Arabs were not. The British gambled that they might be able to co-opt the political leadership of the Arabs by appointing one of the most outspoken opponents of the Jews as a recognized Arab leader. They appointed Haj Muhammed Amin al-Husseini, the Grand Mufti of Jerusalem, in 1921. After that year, al-Husseini continued to be the most prominent Palestinian leader inciting opposition to, and hatred of, the Jews.

In 1929, al-Husseini fomented Palestine-wide riots that led to 133 Jews being murdered, including 67 in the Jewish community of Hebron who numbered several hundred. (Jews have been present in Hebron, one of the four holy cities of Judaism, for at least 800 years.)

During 1936-1939, there was a revolt against the British and the Jews led by Arab guerrilla units. The revolt had been egged on by Husseini, who formed the Arab Higher Committee in 1936 to coordinate a strike that year and to plan other moves against both Jews and British. The British managed to suppress the revolt, but it led to a full-scale British government enquiry, called the Peel Commission, on what to do about Palestine. In November 1937 the Commissioners, arriving in Palestine in top hats, black morning suit coats and striped pants, interviewed both Jewish and Arab representatives in its investigations. One Palestinian leader, when interviewed, said, "Palestine is a term the Zionists invented. . . . Our country was for centuries part of Syria."[4]

Rejection of Partition of States

The Peel Commission concluded that there was so much animosity between the Arab and Jewish communities in Palestine that the country would have to be partitioned. The Jewish leadership of Palestine, represented by World Zionist Organization, reluctantly agreed with this proposal; the Arab representatives flatly refused. In effect, they rejected the notion of a country that they could call "Palestine," because the British offered it as part of a package that would also lead to the creation of a Jewish state. So intense was the animosity of the Arabs toward the Jews that the Arabs testifying before the Peel Commission would not even sit in the same room as the Jews.

There was deep tragedy in the Arabs' rejection of the offer of a state—albeit less than the whole of Palestine that they wanted. Their rejection of the Peel Commission plan amounted to an insistence that the Jews could not have their own state either. This all but guaranteed that if the Jews were to obtain their long-cherished ideal of a state, they would have to fight for it, and in the process, either they would be defeated and lose everything, or the Arabs would be defeated and be worse off than before the British made the original proposal for a partition.

To placate the Arabs, the Peel Commission recommended that Jewish immigration into Palestine should be limited to 25,000 over a five-year period projected from 1939-1944. Of course, war interrupted all of these plans, but the limitation on immigration of Jews from Europe just as Hitler was setting in motion plans for the Holocaust was a tragedy ensuring that millions of Jews would die in Europe's gas chambers.

Confirming the worst of Palestinian Arab hatred for the Jews, al-Husseini spent the war years in Germany conferring with Hitler, plotting an anti-Jewish alliance of Germans and Arabs, and propagandizing hatred for the Allies. In 1946, at Nuremburg, al-Husseini was convicted in absentia as a war criminal. He succeeded in escaping from Germany to Egypt, where in 1948, he was elected chairman of the Palestine National Council. He died in Beirut in 1974.

Militant Jewish Attacks and Arab Reprisals

After World War II, the British attempted to keep a lid on tensions in Palestine by stopping all Jewish immigration into the country. The Jews of Europe who had survived deportation and the death camps were festering by the thousands in "displaced persons camps," makeshift refugee camps throughout Europe. Many of them sought passage to Palestine in ships illegally chartered for that purpose. Many ships were intercepted by Britain's Royal Navy and the passengers sent to internment camps in Cyprus.

Meanwhile, in Palestine itself, Britain was facing what was to become, in retrospect, its Vietnam: 100,000 British soldiers were unable to suppress a growing guerrilla movement for Jewish independence. Some Jewish groups, notably the Irgun and Lehi, adopted terrorist tactics. In July 1946, the Irgun exploded a bomb beneath a wing of Jerusalem's King David Hotel, then the headquarters of the British administration. Some 91 people died, including British, Arabs and Jews.

Meanwhile, Palestine's Jewish community, now numbering about 600,000, was coming under increasing attack from irregular Arab forces fighting on behalf of Palestine's Arab community, which numbered approximately 1.2 million. There were atrocities on both sides. On April 9, 1948, Jewish forces attached to the *Irgun* and *Lehi,* not part of the mainstream political leadership of the Jews, massacred between 107 and 120 Arabs in the village of Deir Yassin, near Jerusalem. Four days later, 79 Jewish nurses and doctors were murdered in a convoy of medical vehicles descending to Jerusalem from the Mount Scopus Jewish hospital. The difference in the massacres was that the mainstream Jewish leadership condemned the atrocities committed by Jews, but the Palestinian Arab leadership was bloodthirsty in approving atrocities committed by Arabs. When it was obvious there was going to be wholesale war to determine whether the partition would be implemented, Arab League Secretary Azzam Pasha declared, "This will be a war of extermination and a momentous massacre which will be spoken of like the Mongolian massacres and the crusades."[5]

At the U.N., anguish at the situation in Palestine was extreme. The British had told that organization in 1947 that they could not be responsible for the chaos likely to develop in the country after their scheduled departure in May 1948. On November 29, 1947, the U.N. General Assembly voted on a resolution to partition Palestine into Jewish and Arab zones that had been drawn up to represent as closely as possible where the Arabs were a majority of the population and where the Jews were. The Jews of Palestine accepted partition and lobbied hard for it among U.N. member states. The leadership of the Palestinian Arabs, and indeed of the entire Arab world, rejected partition. Nevertheless, the resolution passed by a vote of 33-13 with 10 abstentions, more than the required two-thirds majority.

War of Independence

Between November 1947 and the departure of the British the following May, Arab irregular forces fought with increasing intensity against Jewish settlements throughout Palestine, especially where those settlements were relatively isolated and vulnerable. Sometimes the British acted to defend the Jews; sometimes they did not. But after the Union Jack was pulled down for the last time over British headquarters, at midnight on May 15 (the Mandate was formally ended on May 15, 1948), the Jews of Palestine knew they were in a battle not only to determine how to share Palestine with the Arabs, but whether they would survive there as a community at all.

On the previous morning of May 14, in the Tel Aviv Museum, the leader of the Jewish community in Palestine, David Ben-Gurion, formally proclaimed Israel independent. Within 24 hours, regular armies of five Arab states were invading Palestine with the definite intention of strangling the Jewish state in its infancy. The Jordanians concentrated on Jerusalem and the road between that city and Tel Aviv. By the end of May, they had captured the Old City and forced all the Jewish civilians to leave. The Egyptians bombed Tel Aviv from the air and sent armored columns up toward the city. The Syrians and the Iraqis had little success in the north of Palestine, trying to overrun Jewish positions in Galilee.

Though many had predicted that the Yishuv (Hebrew name for the Jewish community in Palestine) would be overrun by better-equipped Arab regular armies, the statistics on the ground quickly revealed that this was unlikely. The largest of the Arab armies, from Jordan, was only 10,000 strong; and on May 15, the total of the invading Arab forces was around 26,000. After the war broke, Israel's founding Prime Minister, David Ben-Gurion, ordered universal adult male conscription. Thus, by July 1948, the Arabs numbered around 40,000, and the Israeli forces around 63,000. A year later that figure had doubled. Despite two cease-fires in the summer and fall of 1948, the war resumed until the Israeli Defense Forces, as Israel's disparate military units of Haganah, Irgun, Lehi, and Palmach (a special command unit) were renamed, went on the offensive everywhere, driving all the Arab armies out.

The Jews were better organized, better led and far more highly motivated than their Arab opponents; after all, if they did not prevail, they feared they would probably all be killed. As it was, some 6,000 Jews died in the War of Independence, a figure that represented 1 percent of the total Jewish population in Palestine at that time. By the time fighting had ended and separate armistices were signed between Israel and all her Arab adversaries in 1949, Israel had improved considerably on the borders assigned to it by the U.N. partition resolution. The new borders, internationally recognized, became known as the "green line" of Israel as recognized by the international community. Israel's territory now comprised about 78 percent of British Mandate Palestine. The biggest chunk of the territory it did not acquire was the double bulge, named "Judea and Samaria" by the Israelis and "the West Bank" by Arab and other observers, which was taken over by Jordan and formally annexed by that country in 1950.

For the Palestinians, Israel's War of Independence has been dubbed since 1948 as *El Naqba*, "the catastrophe." This is because in the course of the fighting an estimated 750,000 Palestinians either fled or were forced out of their homes, fleeing to the Arab states that had invaded Israel.

There is still huge controversy over why the Palestinians fled. The Palestinian story is that the Israelis forced them out at gunpoint. The Israelis admit to a few instances of direct coercion by their own troops, but claim that in most cases the Palestinians fled either at the urging of neighboring Arab states to avoid being caught in the fighting or because they themselves believed the war would go favorably for the Arabs. Unquestionably, many Arabs fled because they feared that they might encounter a Deir Yassin on a much larger scale. They appeared to believe at the time that they would be able to return to their own homes. Jews living in Arab countries, meanwhile, had their own *"naqba,"* suffering murders, pogroms and mass exile from many Arab countries in which they had lived for centuries before 1948. The number of Jews who had to leave Arab countries under fear or direct pressure was very similar to the Palestinians who fled Palestine: about 750,000.

Settling In or Just Settling?

The glaring difference in this population "exchange" is that the Jews who immigrated to Israel from the Arab world were fully absorbed into the life of the new nation within a few years. In 1952, there were about 500,000 immigrants to Israel living in tents or makeshift housing; but by the mid-1950s, the tent cities that had sprung up to absorb hundreds of thousands of new Jewish immigrants had disappeared. By contrast, the Palestinians in most of the Arab states to which they had fled were not allowed to become citizens and were given no assistance at all in being absorbed. Only Jordan, from early on, gave full citizenship rights to Palestinians.

The total number of Palestinians in the world is estimated to be 10 or 11 million people, including about 3.6 million formally described by the U.N. as "Palestinian refugees." This figure comprises the original 750,000 or so and their descendants. In proximity to Israel are about 2.34 million Palestinians living in the West Bank, and about 1.48 million in Gaza. Hundreds of thousands of Palestinians are still living in the grimy refugee camps set up six decades ago in Jordan, Lebanon and Syria. The remainder comprise a diaspora of Palestinians scattered throughout the Arab world and other foreign countries.

After the armistice in 1949, Israel found itself with a population of 156,000 Arabs within its "green line" borders, that is, the borders of Israel recognized internationally at the formal termination of hostilities. Relations with the newly established Israeli government were tense at first, mostly because the Israeli authorities were uncertain of their Arab citizens' loyalties. In fact, for some of Israel's Arabs, martial law was maintained until 1966. Israel's Arabs today—comprising 1.4 million, or 20 percent of the total Israeli population of 6.2 million—eventually were given full citizenship rights except that of serving in Israel's military, and they comprise a significant presence in Israel's parliament, the Knesset. There are currently 12 Arab members of the Knesset, and they are often outspoken critics of the Jewish government, even to the point of supporting Palestinian positions when the Palestinians have opposed Israel. Israel's Arabs are entitled to travel on Israeli passports, but many of them now describe themselves not as Israelis, but as Palestinians.

Israel's Military: A Societal Glue

The population of Israel today is 7,337,000, according to figures released by Israel's Central Bureau of Statistics (CBS). Some 5,542,000 of the population (75.5 percent) are Jewish Israelis and 1,477,000 (20.1 percent) are Israeli Arabs.[6] The remainder are some 318,000 immigrants and their offspring who are not registered as Jews by the Interior Ministry. These include approximately 200,000 foreign workers, many of them from Asian countries like China, the Philippines and Thailand.

The Jews of Israel today comprise an astonishingly varied reflection of the global society in which Jews have settled. Physically, Israelis vary from blonds you might expect to see in Scandinavia to people with skin so dark you would immediately assume the person you were seeing was African. And you would be right. Thousands of Ethiopian Jews immigrated to Israel in the 1970s and 1980s and are highly visible in Israel, especially in the Israeli army. Israelis reflect in their physical attributes the repeated waves of immigrants who have entered the country since it first became established. There are Jews from Europe, Russia, Africa and the Arab world.

Though there have been tensions among the ethnic communities—notably between the European-origin Ashkenazi Jews who formed Israel's initial leadership, and the Arab world Sephardic Jews who migrated to the country after its founding—taken as a whole, Israeli society has been astonishingly successful at integrating its immigrant newcomers. The key socialization device is service in the country's military, which requires a duty of three years for men and two years for women. The very real probability that every generation of Israelis will be called upon to fight a war in defense of the country makes this duty soberingly real for mothers and siblings of the nation's soldiers.

At the same time, Israel is seemingly split socially into tribes of citizen groups: the ultra-religious *Haredim* with their beards, long black frock coats and black homburgs or black fur hats; the ultra-secular cavorting in miniskirts and bikinis at raves on Mediterranean beaches; the Russians with brilliant computer expertise or great talent in classical music; the Ethiopians, edgy about the degree of their social acceptance in Israel; the Ashkenazi elite of north Tel Aviv, with their easy travel to far-flung parts of the world. It is a veritable phantasmagoria of human variety. (An excellent account of Israel's diversity is Donna Rosenthals's *The Israelis: Ordinary People in an Extraordinary Land.*[7])

Israel's political system, a parliamentary democracy, is a confusing kaleidoscope of parties, sometimes with only one or two members that represent this diversity. The Knesset, or parliament, has 120 members; but there were no fewer than 18 parties in the seventeenth Knesset before the 2009 elections. A party must acquire at least 1.5 percent of the total electoral vote before it is allowed a seat in the Knesset. In addition, the strict proportional representation system of voting ensures that almost every conceivable political viewpoint is represented within the Knesset and that it is very difficult for any one party by itself to acquire a majority of 61 seats. Voters vote not for an individual member of the Knesset, as in the U.K. or the U.S., but for a party "list," and the number of seats awarded each party is precisely proportionate to the number of votes nationwide that the party received.

The parties combine and recombine with other parties to form shifting coalitions of alliances and Israeli governments that sometimes seem—and are—filled with internal contradictions. In January 2007, for the first time, an Arab, Raleb Majadele, was appointed a government minister. Israel's leftist parties criticized the move because the government at that time included a far-right nationalist party called Yisrael Beiteinu, and some right-wing Knesset members criticized the appointment because they feared it would water down Israel's Jewishness.

Israeli politics brings together in the Knesset chamber 120 people with views ranging from Jewish religious nationalist to Marxist, from Palestinian secular nationalist to right-wing Jewish nationalism. There is often a lot of shouting as Knesset members heckle each other or harangue government ministers (who have to be Knesset members). Yet, when the country faces the threat of foreign attack, citizens tend to fall into line patriotically and support the military leadership of the country.

The 1967 Six-Day War

The fact is that Israel has gone to war in its own defense more frequently than any other nation on earth. It had barely recovered from the trauma of the Independence War before Egyptian president Gamal Abdel Nasser, in 1956, flexing his muscles in the name of pan-Arabism, nationalized the Suez Canal and threatened to cut off Israel's trade with the outside world. In conjunction with British and French forces that allied themselves with Israel to attempt to take back the Canal, Israeli forces advanced across the Sinai Peninsula to the edge of the Canal itself but were forced to abandon their positions and withdraw under pressure from the Americans.

In 1967, a far more serious threat surfaced, again from Egypt, when Nasser blocked the Straits of Tiran, Israel's sea access to the port of Eilat, on the Red Sea, and at the same time allied himself with Syria and Jordan in a three-pronged alliance ranged against Israel. Nasser made it clear that he actually intended a war of annihilation against Israel. "If war comes," he said, before the war broke out, "it will be Israel's destruction."[8] On May 27, 1967, he added, "Our basic objective will be the destruction of Israel. The Arab people want to fight." Nasser's belligerence followed a similar threat on May 20, by Syrian president Hafez al-Assad. He said, "I, as a military man, believe that the time has come to enter into a battle of annihilation."[9]

Israel mobilized all its reserves, which essentially closed down the normal economic production of the country, and waited.

The U.N. seemed unable to resolve the standoff. The U.S. was reluctant to see a new war break out in the Middle East and made it clear to the Israelis that Washington disapproved of any military action initiated by Israel. Israel ignored the advice. In one of those strategic decisions that changed history, Israel's Air Force took off from its bases on June 5, 1967, swept in low over the Mediterranean coast of Egypt and totally annihilated the Egyptian air force on the ground. It then attacked bases in Syria, and after Jordan initiated shelling of Israeli Jerusalem and other points in Israel, attacked Jordan too. The end result of what was called the Six-Day War, one of the most decisive military victories in modern history, was the complete defeat of Egypt and Syria, the Israeli capture of the West Bank from Jordan, the capture of the Gaza Strip from Egypt, the capture of a significant portion of the Golan Heights from Syria and of the entire Sinai Peninsula from Egypt up to the Suez Canal.

It seemed like a smashing success for Israel; and indeed, the year 1967 was something of a watershed for worldwide Jewish pride in the Jewish state. But the military decisiveness of the victory concealed at first the complexity of the political dilemma it had created.

Israel's defense minister Moshe Dayan assumed that Arab states, having been totally smacked down in their desire to annihilate Israel, would now be willing to make peace with it. But they weren't. At a meeting in Khartoum, Sudan, in August 1967, an eight-nation gathering of the Arab League came out with the "three noes" formula: no peace with Israel, no recognition of Israel, no negotiations with Israel.

The Israeli military occupation of the West Bank, though intended to leave as much of the municipal administration of West Bank towns as possible in the hands of Jordan-appointed Palestinian officials, in fact became irksome for ordinary Palestinians. This was because the constraints on daily life for Palestinians who wished to travel from one part of the territories (the West Bank and the Gaza Strip) to another were onerous. Palestinians had to acquire I.D. cards from the Israeli authorities and needed permission of the Israelis to perform a multitude of professional tasks. In addition, Israeli military checkpoints became annoying obstacles to ordinary travel in the Palestinian territories, even to relatively short distances.

Above all, the military authorities were different: they were Jews. Though many of the Israeli military administrators were reasonable and wise, there were—and still are—instances of arrogance and bullying on the part of some of the ordinary Israeli soldiers assigned to maintain security in what Israelis came to refer to as "the territories."

Palestinian Nationalism on the Rise

It was natural for the Palestinians to look around for a champion of growing national resentments. Before long, the Palestine Liberation Organization (PLO) would come to be seen by many ordinary Palestinians as their champion, the flag-wavers for Palestinian nationalism.

The PLO had been founded in 1964 on the initiative of Egyptian president Gamal Abdel Nasser at what was then the Intercontinental Hotel (today the Seven Arches Hotel) on Jerusalem's Mount of Olives. Jordan at that time controlled the Old City of Jerusalem and the eastern part of it, since the Green Line definition of the territory of Israel stopped in the Western half of Jerusalem.

One of Nasser's hopes in promoting the establishment of the PLO was that it would be a useful tool of Egyptian diplomacy, especially in promoting Nasser's brand of pan-Arabism. But by February 1969 a Palestinian called Yasser Arafat had emerged as the leader of the PLO, moving it out of the diplomatic shadow of Egypt and President Nasser's pan-Arab ambitions, and turning it into a genuinely independent political force in its own right.

The New Face of the PLO

Yasser Arafat was born to Palestinian parents in Cairo, graduated in engineering from Cairo University and migrated, in 1957, to Kuwait, where he became closely associated with other Palestinians working there. Sometime in the late 1950s, Arafat formed Fatah, an organization whose name was a reverse acronym of the Arabic name *Harakat al-Tahrir al-Watani al-Filastini,* which means "The Palestinian National Liberation Movement." Fatah was the backbone of the PLO, and the powerbase upon which Arafat was able to control it.

In 1968, the PLO under Arafat tried—unsuccessfully—to foment anti-Israeli insurrections on the West Bank, but by its guerrilla raids across the Jordan River provoked Israel into attacking its bases in Jordan. In March 1968, at Karameh, a Palestinian refugee camp in Jordan, the PLO put up a stout resistance against attacking Israeli units and thus created its own myth of a militant organization continuing to fight against Israel despite Israel's overwhelming military superiority vis-à-vis the Arabs.

The PLO in the late 1960s and early 1970s embarked on a series of terrorist adventures and airliner hijackings that seemed for a while to cause an overlap of the words "Palestinian" and "terrorist." The Palestine National Charter that the PLO published in 1968 revealed that it not only sought the total destruction of Israel with military violence as the primary means of accomplishing it, but that it was ideologically on the side of the Soviet Union in that country's Cold War confrontation with the U.S.

Including Fatah, the PLO was an umbrella of many different Palestinian revolutionary organizations—the Popular Front for the Liberation of Palestine, the Popular Democratic Front for the Liberation of Palestine and el-Saiqa. The PLO pronounced itself "secular," meaning that it deemed the Islamic faith to be secondary to Palestinian national aspirations, and

"democratic," meaning that it subscribed to the methods of political control elaborated in the Communist Party-run people's democracies of Eastern Europe, i.e., dictatorial. Given its take-no-prisoners attitude toward
Israel, it was not surprising that the Israeli government made it illegal for
any of its citizens to have contact with PLO representatives, either within
Israel and the Palestinian territories ruled by Israel, or overseas.

The 1973 Yom Kippur War

Israel was subjected to a fourth war of survival against the Arab world when
Syria and Egypt joined forces to make a surprise attack on it on October 8,
1973. It became known in Israel as the Yom Kippur War, because it broke
out on the holiest day of the Jewish year. The country completely shut
down, with no public or private transportation in operation, and no TV or
radio broadcasts. In fact, many Israeli soldiers and reservists were fasting,
and the difficulty of communicating what was happening on the nation's
borders made mobilization cumbersome and difficult to coordinate.

Egyptian president Anwar Sadat had launched the surprise attack to
try to restore Egypt's national prestige after its humiliation by Israel in
the Six-Day War. Israeli positions on the Sinai side of the Suez Canal were
quickly overrun by Egyptian troops. In the north, Syrian troops at one
point were prevented from breaking through from the Golan into Galilee
by only three Israeli tanks holding out against them before reserves could
arrive. In a famous incident during the war, Defense Minister Moshe
Dayan told Prime Minister Golda Meir that the "Third Temple" was in
danger. His meaning: Israel's very survival as a state was at stake.

But the Israelis rallied. They were resupplied by an American airlift of
military supplies and, in a daring counter-punch against the Egyptians,
succeeded in crossing the Suez Canal into Egypt and cutting off the Egyptian Third Army. At this point, both Washington and Moscow intervened
to impose a cease-fire. After a tense three days of threat and counter-threat
during October 22-25, 1973, among the Americans, Soviets, Egyptians,
Syrians and Israelis, a cease-fire came into effect and the Egyptians sur-
prised the Israelis by being willing to enter into direct talks with Israeli
military commanders.

President Sadat, who had succeeded Egyptian president Nasser on the
latter's death in 1970, did indeed accomplish his objective of restoring
Egypt's national pride. Even though Egypt ended the conflict in a much
worse military position than before it started it, its successes against Israel

in the early days of the war created the impression that Egypt had punctured the "myth" of Israeli military invincibility. That sense of Egyptian euphoria enabled Sadat to align his country with the U.S., instead of with Egypt's previous patron, the Soviet Union. More dramatically, it gave Sadat the prestige he needed among his own people to fly to Israel in 1977 on a mission of peace and reconciliation. He was rapturously received by the Israelis, who had been profoundly hurt by the decades of rejection of their state by all Arab neighbors. Still, to move beyond symbolic gestures to concrete diplomatic results took at least two more years.

"Peace" at Camp David

One key landmark in the journey was the decision by U.S. president Carter, in September 1978, to invite President Sadat of Egypt and Prime Minister Begin of Israel to an unprecedented 12-day diplomatic retreat at the presidential retreat of Camp David in Maryland. The agreements that came out of the negotiations led directly to the signing in 1979 of an Egypt-Israel peace treaty, the establishment of diplomatic relations between Israel and Egypt and the return to Egypt of the Sinai Peninsula, which Israel had occupied since 1967.

Sadat thought he was also negotiating for "autonomy" of the Palestinians under Israeli military administration, but his Israeli counterpart at Camp David, Prime Minister Menachem Begin, had a different notion of "autonomy." Begin actively promoted a policy inherited from the prime ministers of the Labor Party who had succeeded him (Levi Eshkol, Golda Meir, and Yitzhak Rabin) of establishing Israeli communities, often called "settlements," in the West Bank and Gaza, i.e., in territory whose final disposition was in doubt. This "settlement policy" was again and again to be a bone in the throat of Palestinians wanting to negotiate a peace with Israel and was frequently criticized by the U.S. Begin had no real concept of Palestinian political autonomy on a national level; he imagined that it would operate at the local and municipal levels only.

The Rise of Radical Islam

Meanwhile, among Palestinians, the "secular" aspirations touted by the PLO were being increasingly eclipsed by the rise of Islamic radicalism in the territories that Israel controlled. The Six-Day War had effectively demonstrated the impotence of Arab secular nationalism when faced with the Israeli military superiority. In addition, the success of the Ayatollah

Khomeini in mobilizing the Iranian masses to overthrow America's ally, the Shah of Iran, in 1979, gave renewed hope to Palestinians who thought the only possibility of a successful anti-Israeli uprising lay in embracing a socially dictatorial interpretation of Islam.

In the early 1980s, there were signs that radical Islam was making inroads among Palestinian intellectuals. Islamic students began winning elections in the hitherto secular West Bank University of Bir Zeit, in El Bireh, just north of Jerusalem.

But the fact of a powerful Islamic political force among the Palestinians didn't become evident until 1987. In that year, a traffic accident in Gaza involving an Israeli military truck and Palestinian civilians—in which four Palestinians were killed—touched off a storm of rioting and stone-throwing, and soon a territories-wide uprising against Israeli military presence.

Hamas Takes the Lead

Within months, a Palestinian Islamic movement called Hamas (an acronym for Islamic Resistance Movement) had surfaced and in Gaza emerged as a more credible and efficient organizer of civil Palestinian life under Israeli military rule than the PLO had been. Hamas considered itself the Palestinian branch of the Muslim Brotherhood, a radical Islamic movement that had been started in Egypt.

A second Palestinian Islamic group called Islamic Jihad also got started at about the same time. Demonstrations against Israeli troops were spontaneous and, in general, were not orchestrated by the PLO leadership then based in Tunisia. The insurgency was to become dubbed by Palestinians in general as the "First Intifadeh." But Hamas and Islamic Jihad within five years morphed into terrorist groups that employed suicide bombings as a tool of resistance to the Israelis.

Hamas has an organizational founding document, or charter, (see Appendix) that is so extreme in its pronouncements, not just toward Israel, but toward Jews in general, that it makes the PLO Covenant, or Palestine National Charter, read like a mild debating club statement. The Hamas Charter accepts as historically valid the anti-Jewish rants of a notorious forgery called the *Protocols of the Elders of Zion*, a document based on a French nineteenth-century historical satire that was converted into a document blaming Jews for everything wrong in the world.

The *Protocols* began to have an influence in Europe and the Arab world only when the secret police of Russia's last tsar, Nicholas II, deployed it as "proof" that much of the unrest occurring within Russia at the end of the nineteenth century and the beginning of the twentieth had been fomented by Jews.

The Hamas Charter accepts as "true" absolutely paranoid interpretations of history that would be ridiculous except for the fact that many people in the Palestinian territories of Gaza and the West Bank, especially in Gaza, seem to believe them. Typical assertions by the Hamas Charter include that the Jews "were behind the French Revolution, the Communist revolution and most of the revolutions we have heard and hear about, here and there. With their money they formed secret societies, such as Freemasons, Rotary Clubs, the Lions and other such 'clubs' in different parts of the world for the purpose of sabotaging societies and achieving Zionist interests."[10] More ominously than the almost comic-book historical assertions are the prescriptions for how to solve the Palestinian issue. "There is no solution for the Palestinian question," declaims the Charter, "except through Jihad. Initiatives, proposals and international conferences are all a waste of time and vain endeavors."[11]

How had the Palestinian diaspora provided such ready soil for the fiery pronouncements of Hamas?

After fleeing their homes in Palestine as the Israelis consolidated control over Israel, those Palestinians who left rapidly filled up refugee camps in Syria, Lebanon, Egypt and Jordan.

Wealthier Palestinian families had lost all their land in Israel, but they had not necessarily become impoverished. With what money they were able to gather in exile, they succeeded in providing education for the next generation of Palestinians, not only in the Arab countries but also in many Western countries. As a result, the Palestinians not only quickly became among the best educated of communities in the Arab world, but they also occupied excellent jobs in various parts of it. They were engineers, financial experts, physicians and corporate officers. Well-traveled and often multilingual, they struck many observers as the "Jews" of the Arab world—sometimes rootless, often stateless and subject to endless humiliations at airport immigration lines throughout the world. They nevertheless demonstrated talent and enterprise in whatever community in which they found themselves.

The problem was that Arab states didn't want to absorb them as citizens, unlike the Israelis who had so successfully absorbed Jews from different parts of the Middle East and the world. In addition, their own leadership hopscotched its way from Arab capital to Arab capital in the tireless pursuit of a Palestinian "nation" that other Arab and, indeed, non-Arab Muslim countries could support. Inevitably, the PLO wore out its welcome in many Arab states.

The PLO in Lebanon

The first major crisis involving the PLO and an Arab state was in Jordan, in September 1970. PLO military units in some parts of the country were acting as though Jordan didn't really exist; the PLO was a state within a state. PLO fighters were strutting through Amman and other cities, ignoring or intimidating Jordanian police, molesting women. Fearing that his regime itself faced direct threat, Jordan's King Hussein ordered his army, composed largely of Bedouin troops, to attack the PLO and drive them out of Jordan. The crisis for the PLO became known as "Black September," and gave its name to a terrorist unit that killed 11 Israeli athletes at the Olympic games in Munich in September 1972.

Ousted from Jordan, the PLO leadership moved to Lebanon, where before long the PLO was conducting itself with the same arrogance toward Lebanese civilians that it had shown towards Jordanians. The PLO encamped itself in largely Shiite or Christian Lebanese villages in the south of Lebanon, from where its guerrillas periodically shelled or rocketed Israeli towns or sent in terrorist units to attack Israeli civilians. I recall visiting a PLO military position in Nabatiyeh, southern Lebanon, in the summer of 1980. A well-turned-out officer in green fatigues offered me a cup of tea and joked that it was "Fatah whiskey." He seemed as self-confident as a local police chief might have been. A few yards away from his headquarters was a well-camouflaged artillery piece that had been used to lob shells into Israel in the previous weeks.

During the 1970s, Israel periodically responded to PLO rocket or artillery strikes on its northern towns by making military incursions into Lebanon to "punish" the PLO, but it took repeated shelling of Israeli towns on Israel's Lebanese border before Israel, in June 1982, launched a full-scale invasion of Lebanon with the intention, if possible, of ousting the PLO once and for all from the country.

Massacre in Beirut

The invasion of Lebanon in 1982 was Israel's first war that had not been precipitated by a threat to its existence from outside its borders. Within a few days of its outbreak on June 6, 1982, Israeli military units had advanced to the outskirts of Beirut. As the Israeli army surrounded the Lebanese capital and began shelling and bombing Palestinian positions within it, Israel became increasingly seen in the U.S. and international media no longer as an underdog whose very survival was threatened but as a regional bully. That impression was reinforced when Israeli troops controlling access to Beirut permitted Christian militia forces to enter the Sabra and Chatila Palestinian refugee camps and murder hundreds of Palestinian civilians.

An Israeli commission of inquiry into the massacre concluded that Defense Minister Ariel Sharon (later to be prime minister) was responsible for not having restrained the Christian militias. In an unmistakable way, Israel had been drawn into Lebanon's own internal political crisis and, in spite of itself, had been exploited by various parties in the settlement of internal Lebanese scores. The PLO, after weeks of being battered by the Israeli army, was compelled to leave Lebanon in August 1982 and set up its headquarters in Tunisia. Hundreds of thousands of Palestinian civilians, however, remained behind in the squalid refugee camps they had inhabited since 1948.

The Rise of Hezbollah

One unintended consequence of the Israeli invasion of Lebanon was the rise of a new element on the Lebanese political scene: an Islamic political party composed of Shiite Lebanese Muslims and called Hezbollah ("party of God"). As the Israeli military presence in Lebanon dragged on for years, Hezbollah, trained and funded by Iran, developed a disciplined and effective guerrilla force that inflicted painful weekly casualties on the Israeli Defense Forces attempting to maintain, for years after the invasion of 1982, a security zone in the southern part of the country below the Litani River. Palestinian refugees still lived in teeming camps in Lebanon, but the Palestinian political leadership—the PLO in Beirut—must have looked on in frustration as Hezbollah proved much more capable of taking on the Israelis in Lebanon than the PLO had been.

After their ouster from Beirut, the PLO struggled to provide leadership over Palestinians in the territories ruled by Israel. Israeli air force jets at one point bombed the PLO headquarters in Tunis, and on another occasion successfully landed a commando team that assassinated Arafat's number two, Abu Jihad, in 1988. But events elsewhere were impinging on the freedom of action of the PLO. Nowhere was this more the case than in the Arabian Gulf. In August 1990, the Iraqi Army, under orders of Saddam Hussein, invaded and occupied the Arabian Gulf state of Kuwait, on Iraq's southern border.

At this point, PLO Chairman Yasser Arafat made perhaps the worst blunder of his career. Without thinking through how the rest of the world would respond to Saddam's occupation of Kuwait, Arafat publicly allied himself with the Iraqi tyrant. It was a cruel blow for Palestinian expatriates, for they immediately became scapegoats for other Arabs offended by Iraq's action. The Iraqi invasion was condemned at the U.N. and throughout the Arab world, and was reversed only after a large international coalition force, under U.S. command, organized a counterattack to liberate Kuwait in January and February 1991. Arafat's decision to take Saddam's side during the crisis provoked ugly reprisals against the Palestinians in Kuwait after the Iraqis were dislodged.

Only the Arab states and—before the end of the Cold War in 1991—the Soviet Union and its East European allies wanted to deal directly with the PLO. Israel had laws against its own citizens' doing so. The U.S. regarded the PLO as a terrorist organization and made its first diplomatic overtures toward the PLO only in 1988 in Tunisia, when Secretary of State Shultz decided that one of Arafat's many convoluted statements constituted a placatory gesture of conciliation toward Israel. This, Secretary Shultz considered, justified the U.S. now dealing openly on a diplomatic level with the PLO.

When Shultz's successor, Secretary of State James Baker, convened a post-Gulf War diplomatic conference in Madrid, in October 1991, Israel itself was still unwilling to meet with PLO representatives. Palestinian delegates attended the international conference in a "private" capacity as Palestinians who were "prominent" in the territories controlled by Israel. It was a transparent fiction; everybody knew that the PLO was telling the delegates what positions to take.

The Madrid conference was sufficiently broad in its Arab participant list to give Arafat "cover" to begin talking to Israel in an indirect way. After it was over, Israeli and Palestinian "multilateral groups" began discussing issues of water usage, arms control, security and the status of Palestinian refugees. The groups were called "multilateral" because their meetings took place in Washington, London, and other cities and were hosted by various countries that had attended the Madrid conference.

The Oslo Accords

A remarkable and, for many years, very promising breakthrough in Israeli-Palestinian relations was achieved in Norway in the summer of 1993. Meeting in complete secrecy under the protection of the Norwegian government, two small teams of Israelis and Palestinians—initially it was only two Israeli left-wing academics—began the process of breaking the diplomatic logjam between the two national groups (Israelis and Palestinians). The result of intense but, on the whole, remarkably cordial discussions, was a Declaration of Principles, signed in Washington on the White House Lawn on September 13, 1993.

Though the U.S. had not even known about the Israeli-Palestinian talks in Norway until they were completed, it was obvious that the U.S., as Israel's chief international protector, would have to be brought into the agreement. As a select audience of VIPs, including former Presidents Carter and Bush, and the widow of assassinated president of Egypt, Anwar Sadat, looked on in applause, Israel's Prime Minister Yitzhak Rabin publicly shook hands on the rostrum with PLO Chairman Yasser Arafat. Behind them both, his broad arms extended like an eagle gathering up its offspring, was a grinning President Bill Clinton. The following year, in Oslo, Norway, Arafat, Rabin and Foreign Minister Shimon Peres each was awarded the Nobel Peace Prize for the achievement.

The Oslo Accords, as they were often popularly known, made rapid initial progress. The Israelis first withdrew from Jericho and then began moving completely out of Palestinian urban communities on the West Bank. They withdrew from Gaza, which witnessed the return of Yasser Arafat to Palestinian soil to a rapturous welcome in 2004. In the initial peace euphoria that infected both communities, Israelis began traveling as consumers and tourists in large numbers to West Bank towns and cities. Jericho developed a casino (open only to Israelis and other non-Palestinians), which did a booming business for a few years.

But there were ominous thunderstorms afoot. Hamas, which had utterly repudiated the Oslo accords, early in 1994, began actively trying to sabotage them. In April 1994, the first of a series of Palestinian suicide bombs began ripping through the flesh of Israeli civilians on buses in Tel Aviv and Jerusalem.

There was virulent opposition to the accords from some in Israel as well. In November 1995, after attending a peace rally in Tel Aviv, Prime Minister Rabin was shot and killed by an Israel extremist nationalist,

Yigal Amir, a student at Tel Aviv's Bar-Ilan University, who considered the Oslo Accords a betrayal of Israel's national patrimony. It seemed as if extremists on both sides, Israeli and Palestinian, were trying to sabotage peace between the two communities.

The suicide bombings, most claimed by Hamas, but some by a group called Palestinian Islamic Jihad, increased in intensity, killing hundreds of Israelis between April 1994 and two years later. By that time, Israeli public opinion was becoming increasingly disenchanted by any conciliatory approach to the Palestinians, and in the election of June 1996, the country voted in Likud Party leader Binyamin Netanyahu as its new prime minister. A conservative on both economic and security issues, "Bibi," as he was universally known, spoke perfect American English acquired while a high school student in the U.S., and held a hawkish overall view of Arab intentions. He began dragging his feet on further Israeli withdrawals and, though at the Wye River Plantation in Maryland, a conference site of the Aspen Institute, he agreed to a whole new series of redeployments of Israeli forces of the West Bank, his attitude toward terrorism was uncompromising and tough. Under his prime ministership the rate of suicide bombings declined.

Netanyahu's tough approach on terrorism couldn't overcome his unpopularity in other areas, and in July 1999, he was succeeded by Labor Party prime minister Ehud Barak. At one time the most decorated soldier in the Israeli army, Barak had once commanded a team of commandos that had raided PLO headquarters in Beirut. His disguise during the approach had been to be dressed as a woman.

More Attempts at Reconciliation

Barak, in keeping with the more dovish traditional attitude of Israel's Labor Party, was willing to make major concessions in order to try to complete what Rabin had started in 1993. Accepting an invitation from President Clinton to sit down with PLO Chairman Arafat at Camp David, in July 2000, Barak seemed, for a while, to be willing to go farther than any previous Israeli leader since Rabin in meeting the demands of the Palestinians for peace with Israel.

Though none of the negotiating positions was officially recorded—both sides agreed that there would be no agreement until all details were agreed upon—in practice Barak offered to return, after a period of time, 93 to 95 percent of the West Bank to the Palestinians, to turn over the entirety of East Jerusalem to them and to give them total sovereignty over the Haram al-Sharif (the "Noble Sanctuary" or Temple Mount as the Jews called it), on which were located the two mosques the Dome of the Rock and the El-Aqsa Mosque. On the issues so important to Palestinians—the status of Palestinian refugees—the Clinton-Ross team proposed an international fund of $30 billion to assist in resettlement or to compensate the refugees.

Arafat neither accepted the proposals nor offered any counterproposals, but simply decided to return to the West Bank, prompting President Clinton to blame him publicly after the summit for being responsible for the failure of the meeting. The efforts by the Clinton team to keep the negotiations going in spite of the failure of the official summit were accepted by both Israeli and Palestinian negotiators, and in the last three weeks of the Clinton administration, in January 2001, Arafat was at the White House yet again. According to negotiator Ross, who was in the Oval Office during the meeting, Arafat accepted all the proposals the Americans had offered and then added oral qualifications that essentially negated them. Ross commented two years later, "These were ideas that were comprehensive, unprecedented, stretched very far, represented a culmination of an effort in our best judgment as to what each side could accept after thousands of hours of debate, discussion with each side."[12]

Why did Arafat balk? One theory is that he was literally worried that he might be murdered if he accepted terms from the Israelis that were less than the Palestinian maximum position. He hinted at as much in conversations with the Arab media. Another theory is that, after years of mortal struggle with Israel, he could not bring himself to call off what he had almost all the time considered a life-or-death struggle.

By September 28, 2000, Ariel Sharon, then leader of the opposition Likud Party in the Israeli Knesset, made a well-publicized visit to the Temple Mount. Even though the visit was coordinated beforehand with Palestinian officials and personally approved by Yasser Arafat, Palestinian youths protested it by throwing stones at the Israeli security forces guarding Sharon. The following day, there was full-scale rioting in Jerusalem and other West Bank municipalities. Thus was started what became known as the Second Intifadeh, or "Al-Aqsa Intifadeh," the bloodiest confrontation yet between Palestinians and Israelis.

Suicide Bombings and Targeted Assassinations

Prominent in the unrest were numerous suicide bombings directed against Israeli civilian targets. Within four years, some 1,000 Israelis and 4,000

Palestinians had been killed, and Israel's sense of self-confidence was severely shaken. The Israelis killed were overwhelmingly civilians, whereas the Palestinians killed were almost all either stone-throwers or activists helping the intifadeh. Tourism, an important money-earner for Israel, plunged, as American tourists in particular worried about their safety while visiting the country. (American Christian tour groups were noticeably less likely to cancel than Jewish groups, a fact that many Israelis noticed and appreciated.)

The Israelis responded brusquely to the Palestinian escalation, not only by temporarily reoccupying the West Bank urban areas, but also by deciding to build a "barrier" separating the "Green Line" borders of Israel from the West Bank. The barrier, for some of its length an actual concrete wall cutting through towns and fields, was detested by most Palestinians, who successfully brought legal action in the Israeli Supreme Court, in some instances, to change its pathway. But as a security device it worked; Palestinian suicide bombings dropped dramatically after construction was started, though efforts by Hamas and Islamic Jihad to initiate them did not cease.

For its part, Israel began a deliberate program of "targeted" assassinations of Hamas and other leaders, sometimes using snipers, sometimes helicopter gunships armed with missiles, sometimes triggering explosives inside cell phones known to be in the hands of Hamas operatives. Sheikh Ahmed Yassin, the founder of Hamas and a paraplegic since a sporting accident at the age of 12, was killed in one such "targeted" assassination by a missile fired from an Israeli helicopter gunship in March 2004.

Road Map for Peace

Worried that the escalation of the violence might lead to a complete collapse of diplomacy in the region, President Bush made a speech in June 2002, announcing for the first time that Washington actually supported the eventual creation of a Palestinian state. At the same time, a group of major powers and international organizations that became known as "The Quartet"—the U.S., Russia, the E.U., and the U.N.—announced the unfolding of a "Road Map" for peace in the Israeli-Palestinian question. Terrorist violence would have to cease, but Israel also would have to make public statements unequivocally committing itself to a two-state solution to the Palestinian issue. It would also have to withdraw some of the "settlements" that had been established within the West Bank since 2001.

The Road Map, officially launched in 2003, essentially languished for the next four years because of a lack of energy and interest in Israeli-Palestinian negotiations on the part of the Bush administration. President Clinton had struggled almost frenetically to push the Israeli-Palestinian negotiating process toward a lasting agreement. Even as late as January 2001, just before the inauguration of his successor, Clinton and his administration's Middle East envoy, Dennis Ross, had bent over backwards to keep the Palestinians in the game. Yasser Arafat, in fact, visited the White House during the Clinton administration 23 times, far more frequently than any other foreign leader.

For incoming Republican President George W. Bush, that ostentatious red-carpet treatment for a figure many Americans regarded as an emblem of terrorism and violence seemed to be the wrong signal to send to the watching world. At his first National Security Council meeting as President, in January 2001, Bush made it clear—and his then National Security Council advisor, Condoleezza Rice, apparently agreed—he would prefer to let Israeli-Palestinian affairs just fester on their own for a while rather than absorb the energies and risk the prestige of the United States in trying to solve them.

But international crises and diplomacy have a way of shouldering their way into public attention past the best laid plans to neglect them. What the Russian writer Aleksandr Solzhenitsyn once called "the pitiless crowbar of events" undermined the Bush administration's early resolution. The Al-Qaeda attack on September 11, 2001, happened, the U.S. invaded Afghanistan, and in March 2003, it invaded Iraq. But fighting against determined urban guerrillas, who were often Arab-world international jihadists, proved extremely difficult.

By the second term of the Bush administration, the U.S. war in Iraq had become increasingly unpopular around the world. The U.S. needed to show a face to the world that was not so resolutely eager to fight a war on Arab soil. Bush's staunch British ally, Prime Minister Tony Blair, who had agreed to go to war in Iraq with the U.S. in 2003, was under strong pressure from Arab states, his European Union partners and reportedly even Russia to push the U.S. into trying once again to resolve the Israeli-Palestinian issue. Pro-Western conservative Arab states in the Gulf—Saudi Arabia, Kuwait, the United Arab Emirates—were nervous about discontent among their own people with Israel's apparent reluctance to offer the Palestinians satisfactory terms for their own statehood. That nervousness eventually was passed up the chain of alliances to Washington itself.

By 2007, Bush realized that Washington was now under enormous international pressure to *appear* to be doing something to try to solve the Israeli-Palestinian crisis. He allowed his second-term Secretary of State, Condoleezza Rice, to make new American diplomatic probes into the region. Between 2005 and 2007, she made no fewer than eight visits to the Middle East. The culmination of this new flurry of shuttle diplomacy was a major conference that Rice convened in November 2007, in Annapolis, Maryland. Though it was only a one-day affair, Rice succeeded in corralling attendance from senior representatives of the U.N., the Quartet, Russia, China, Japan and no fewer than 40 Arab states. The trophy guests, however, were Israeli prime minister Ehud Olmert and Palestinian Authority president Mahmoud Abbas (who succeeded Arafat on the latter's death in 2004). Abbas had been elected in his own right president of the Palestinian National Authority in January 2005.

As a demonstration of diplomatic event coordination, Annapolis was a great success. The Madrid conference of 1991 had been the last occasion when Israeli and Arab diplomats from several countries had even sat in the same room. The presence of so many Arab diplomats and leaders from the Middle East was also a sign that the U.S. had succeeded in gaining major global approval for a renewed Israeli-Palestinian diplomacy.

But clearly, not everyone was even listening to the speeches. When Israel's Prime Minister Olmert was making his own remarks, Prince Saud al-Faisal, the Saudi Arabian foreign minister, ostentatiously removed his translation earphones from his ears.[13] Though negotiations did indeed resume, by the time of President Bush's visit to Israel in January 2008, no breakthrough had been accomplished. Bush revisited the Jewish state in May 2008, on the occasion of its sixtieth anniversary; but though he was enthusiastically applauded after his speech in the Israeli parliament, the Knesset, his remarks were criticized by many Arab leaders and news organizations as being too supportive of Israel.

There was widespread approval in the Arab world of the U.S. presidential election of Democratic candidate Senator Barack Obama in November 2008. Palestinian president Abbas issued a rather stilted congratulatory statement that said, "President Abbas congratulates U.S. president-elect Barack Obama in his name and the name of the Palestinian people, and hopes he will speed up efforts to achieve peace, particularly since a resolution of the Palestinian problem and the Israeli-Arab conflict is key to world peace." Arab League Secretary-General Amr

Moussa said, "I stress the importance of the message that Mr. Obama has never ceased to send, which is we all need change and that is what we do expect from the new leader of the United States. We need an American policy based on honest brokership."[14]

3

SYRIA AND LEBANON

Probably no two Arab countries in the Middle East share a common border but have so little else in common than Syria and Lebanon. Syria is a large swath of land the size of North Dakota, with stark climatic and geographical contrasts and a population of 19 million people. In the far west, a thin lowland strip borders the Mediterranean. The climate there is moderate and temperate. A long ridge of high ground stretching from Turkey to the border with Lebanon divides this region from a drier, more arid zone that stretches eastward into real desert. Lebanon, by contrast, is a thin wraith of a country that is smaller in land area than Connecticut and has a population of only 4.1 million people. In Lebanon you can snow-ski in the mountains and water-ski in the Mediterranean on the same day. The climate, for much of the year, is as balmy as Southern California.

But it is more than climate and geography that make Lebanon and Syria so different from each other. Syria is a totalitarian Stalinist autocracy whose ruler, Bashar al-Assad, inherited his political dictatorship from his father, just as North Korea's Kim Jong-il inherited *his* power from the regime's founder Kim Il-sung. Syria's current political stability has been bought at the price of a relentless tyranny. Lebanon is a cosmopolitan, sophisticated and parliamentary democracy state, one of the freest of all Arab states, according to Freedom House.[1] It is more Westernized than any state in the Middle East except Israel, yet it is a fragile jigsaw puzzle of different religious communities that seem to teeter permanently on the brink—and sometimes lurch into the brink—of civil war. The only problem for little Lebanon is that its far bigger and more powerful neighbor has dominated its political life for several decades.

Ancient Syria

But let's look at Syria first. Syria's significance throughout history derived from its strategic location at the crossroads of trade, culture and conquest in the Middle East. Syrians are justifiably proud of having hosted, back in 1400 BC, the Canaanite civilization of Ugarit, whose cuneiform script, recorded on clay tablets, was the world's first genuine alphabet and the ancestral alphabet of Phoenician, Hebrew and Aramaic. It was from Phoenician that both the Greek and Latin scripts evolved. But Syria also hosts perhaps the greatest collection of early writing samples discovered in the past 100 years, a gigantic collection of 15,000 cuneiform tablets in the Sumerian script at a place called Ebla, located about 60 miles northeast of Ugarit.

Syria was conquered by successive waves of the Middle East's historic migrations and in turn served as the headquarters of some of the great empires that came to power in the region. Alexander the Great (356-323 BC), in his world-conquering foray into Asia, pried Syria loose from the clutches of the Persian Empire to which it had previously belonged. A successor regime of Alexander's empire called the Seleucids (312-63 BC) had a dubious claim to fame in that, trying to suppress the practice of Judaism in Judea, which the Seleucids controlled, they provoked the revolt of the Maccabees (164-63 BC), a Jewish national liberation movement whose leaders were to rule Judea as an autonomous Jewish kingdom until the Romans took over in 63 BC.

The Maccabees—aside from saving monotheism from an assault by Greek pagans who wanted the Jews to worship Zeus and other pagan deities—made one unique contribution to Jewish life, the celebration of Hanukkah. According to the Jewish Talmud,

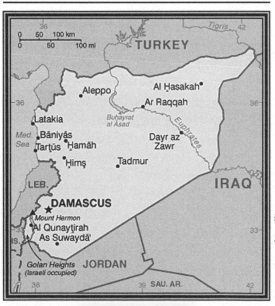

Source: Central Intelligence Agency

SYRIA

when the Temple in Jerusalem was being reconsecrated after the defeat of the Seleucids in 165 BC, one day's supply of olive oil needed for the Temple's sacred candle lasted, miraculously, for eight days, enough time to harvest and consecrate additional supplies of olive oil.

Syria was ruled from Rome until AD 330, when the Emperor Constantine divided the Roman Empire into two and made Byzantium (now Istanbul, in Turkey) the capital of the eastern half. Syria, of course, played a significant role in the early days of Christianity, for, according to Acts 9:3-5, it was on the road to Damascus that St. Paul was converted. In the Byzantine Empire, Syria continued to be an important center of Christian life. But Byzantium had been weakened by decades of warfare with the Persian Empire, and when warriors of the new desert faith of Islam swept north from Arabia, Damascus was one of the first great cities to fall to the Arabs, in AD 636.

For nearly a century, Syria's capital of Damascus was the center of the Arab Umayyad dynasty. The Umayyad Mosque in modern Damascus is one of the great Muslim pilgrimage centers of the modern Middle East and is an impressive example of early Muslim Arab culture. After AD 750, the Umayyad dynasty in Damascus had succumbed to an Islamic power-shift and the ascendancy of the Abbasids and their new empire based in Baghdad.

Syria was overrun by the Crusaders in the twelfth century, and by the Mongols in the thirteenth. In 1400, an even more fearsome conqueror swept in from Samarkand in Central Asia: Timur (who is known more familiarly in English as Tamburlaine), a warrior of Turkic and Mongolian ethnic origin whose atrocities against civilians were on a genocidal scale. Syria went into decline for more than a century.

It began to revive only after the newest Islamic power to rise to imperial status in the Middle East, the Ottomans, the ancestors of modern Turks, took control of Damascus and Jerusalem in 1517, and incorporated virtually all of the Arab world into the Ottoman Empire, based in Istanbul.

Eclectic Demographics

Modern Syria grew out of administrative divisions of the Ottoman Empire that were called *sanjaks*. Several different *sanjaks* covered the area of the countries that are now Syria, Lebanon, Israel and Jordan. Even the word "Syria" was an invention of Europeans in the nineteenth century, a time when foreign visitors to that part of the Ottoman Empire frequently remarked that there was no such thing as a sense of being "Syrian." In 1853, the British statesman Lord Shaftesbury said that Syria was "a country without a nation," and a few decades later the British female Middle East explorer, Gertrude Bell, said that Syria probably contained "the most fractured population in the world."[2]

"Fractured" is accurate. The majority of the Syrian population—some 74 percent—are Arabs of Sunni Muslim origin. But there are several other large minority communities. Some 9 percent of the population are Kurds, an ethnic community numbering at least 25 million who speak a language close to Farsi (Persian) and are spread over an area that includes at least four countries in the region: Turkey 11.4-14.4 million; Iraq 4-6 million; Iran 4.8-6.6 million; and Syria 1.74 million. In Damascus, there is a statue of the most famous Kurd in history, Salah ad-Din, or Saladin, who defeated the Crusaders in 1187.

There are also about 1.7 million Turks in Syria, and about 800,000 Druze, some 4 percent of the population. The Druze, like the Kurds, are spread over several countries, including Israel and Lebanon, and describe themselves as "Unitarians, Monotheists," but are so removed from traditional Islamic beliefs—they believe in reincarnation—that the Druze of Israel, though speakers of Arabic, do not even consider themselves Arab, and many Muslims don't think the Druze are co-religionists.

About 10 percent of Syria's population is Christian, some 55 percent of whom are of the Chalcedonian Antiochan Orthodox, 18 percent being Catholics. The 10 percent figure may have temporarily swelled considerably because of the presence of an estimated 1.5 million refugees from Iraq currently in Syria. Most of these are Iraqi Christians. There is a small Christian town in Syria, Malula, where the altar of the St. Serge Church dates back to the fourth century AD and the villagers still speak the Aramaic language that Jesus spoke. (I visited Malul in 2007 and had the strange and wonderful experience of hearing the Lord's Prayer spoken in fluent Aramaic by one of the townsfolk.)

Modern Political History

Perhaps the most important minority of all in Syria is the Alawi, or Alawites, who comprise about 12.5 percent of the population. The Alawites claim to belong to the "Twelver" branch of Shia Islam, but their belief system is a hodge-podge of different religious streams, including even Gnosticism and Phoenician paganism. Historically, some prominent Muslim scholars have considered them to be not Muslim at all. Ibn Taymiyya

(1268-1328), who is revered and often quoted by Islamists like Osama bin Laden, wrote of the Alawites (for whom another name has been "Nusayris"), "The Nusayris are more infidel than Jews or Christians, even more infidel than many polytheists."[3]

The Alawites might have remained one of the many obscure, minor Middle Eastern sects but for one thing: the Assad family dynastic dictatorship that has ruled Syria for nearly four decades is an Alawite family, and Alawites dominate the Syrian army, security apparatus and political system in numbers that are quite disproportionate to their percentage of the population.

In 1936, Hafez al-Assad's grandfather himself wrote a letter to the French, who then administered Syria, asking them not to leave the country. If they did, he said, the Alawites would be oppressed or massacred by the Sunni Muslims who formed the majority of the Arab population of Syria. Sulayman al-Assad wrote, "The spirit of hatred and fanaticism embedded in the hearts of the Arab Muslims against everything that is non-Muslim has been perpetually nurtured by the Islamic religion."[4] But one aspect of Alawite teachings—the fact that the contents of their sacred books have never been published—proved problematic for Hafez al-Assad four years after he had seized power. The problem was, Syria's constitution stated that the country's president had to be a Muslim.

So in 1974, Imam Sadr, a religious leader of the "Twelver" branch of Shiites in Lebanon, was asked by Hafez to proclaim in a religious ruling that the Alawites were indeed an authentic Islamic community. The good imam obliged. Unfortunately, however, in the convoluted story of Arab internal squabbles, Musa al-Sadr turned against Syria in 1976, after it invaded Lebanon with some 20,000 troops to prevent the Lebanese Christians being completely swamped in Lebanon's just-started civil war. In 1978, Musa al-Sadr visited Libya, then and now ruled by President Muammar Gaddafi, and simply disappeared. Killed, kidnapped, or still in jail in Libya? Nobody knows, but the imam's disappearance remains a point of contention between Libya and Lebanon.

But we are getting ahead of ourselves.

After World War I

The great turning point in the modern history of Syria, as indeed for most of the current states of the Middle East, was the watershed of World War I (1914-1918). Even Osama bin Laden has picked on that date as catastrophic for the Arab Muslims of the Middle East, and for good reason. The end of World War I brought about the defeat of the Ottoman Turks in 1918 by the British. In anticipation of the eventual defeat of the Turks, there had been a secret agreement between Britain and France over which chunks of the old Ottoman Empire each would take when the war ended. That accord, the Sykes-Picot Agreement of 1916, essentially drew a horizontal line through a map of the Middle East. The French would have control of the northern part of the map, over areas that would eventually become Syria and Lebanon, and the British would control Palestine, Transjordan and what was to become Iraq.

It's a fascinating, but complicated story, and we don't need to get too embroiled in the details.[5] In a nutshell, however, the French insisted on taking control of the former Ottoman *sanjaks* comprising modern Syria and Lebanon. The British were to be awarded Palestine by the League of Nations, for they had already conquered Palestine at the end of 1918. In the classic colonial pattern, the French, in the domains they controlled, favored certain ethnic minorities, including the Alawites, whom they recruited in large numbers for the colonial military.

The French finally left Syria in 1946, and the country acquired sovereign independence. Yet, if the Syrians hoped that prosperity and tranquility would follow the departure of their colonial rulers, they were cruelly disappointed. There were multiple coups in Syria between 1946 and a decade later, and Syria had the dubious distinction of experiencing the first military coup in the Arab world on April 11, 1949. A Kurdish general in the Syrian army called Husni al-Za'im (1897-1949) seized power in a bloodless putsch, but was himself deposed four months later and then executed. Syria, between 1949 and the coming to power of the elder Assad in 1970, was to experience a total of 21 coups, almost all of them generating bloodshed, and almost all of them because the political structure of Syria was not robust enough to resolve political differences through a peaceful political process.

The first of those coups, by General al-Za'im, revealed a virus that was to manifest itself repeatedly in Syrian political life, an allergic reaction to the very existence of Israel. General al-Za'im's coup was the first of many Syrian coups carried out by Syrian military figures dissatisfied with the previous regime's inability to defeat the Jewish state. Syria had joined in the first such Arab collective effort to strangle Israel at its birth in 1948, when five Arab armies invaded the newly declared independent country only to be defeated decisively in the conflict.

The coup that really changed the political structure of Syria, however, took place in 1963. In that year, the Ba'ath Party, among whom a significant number of senior members were frustrated Alawites, seized power. The party had its origins in the 1940s under French rule, when a Syrian of Orthodox Christian background, Michel Aflaq (1910-1989), who had studied at the Sorbonne, struggled to define a new ideology for Arabs. Like many Arabs of Christian background, Aflaq mistrusted the political doctrines of Islam. He thus developed an ideology characterized by the desire to promote both "Arab socialism" and "pan-Arabism," the latter being a movement that sought to unite all the Arabs under a single political entity.

In the 1950s, the ideology of pan-Arabism resonated in much of the Arab world. Egypt's ruler Gamal Abdel Nasser rose to power on the dreams of a postcolonial vision of pan-Arab socialism, close to but not identical with Soviet-style Marxism-Leninism. Nasser, and before him Aflaq, thought this ideology would enable Arab states both to unite and to resist the hegemony of the Western nations who had so dominated the Middle East since Napoleon's invasion of Egypt in 1798.

In 1958, the dream of a pan-Arab national state culminated in the creation of a political union of Egypt and Syria, which was called the "United Arab Republic." Egypt continued to be called by that name until 1971, but the Syrians quickly tired of playing second fiddle to the Egyptians, and after yet another coup in Damascus in 1961, withdrew from the union. Two years later, in 1963, Ba'ath Party conspirators in Syria seized power and began to establish a nationwide network of party cells from the ground up. Three years after that, there was an internal purge of Ba'ath Party leaders initiated by Alawites in the leadership. After Syria's defeat by Israel in the Six-Day War of 1967, however, the feeling that Ba'ath leaders had betrayed the country led to yet another coup. In December 1970, Air Force general Hafez al-Assad seized power and began to turn Syria into a totalitarian state whose government bureaucracy closely overlapped with that of the Ba'ath Party.

Syria's Reigning Dynasty

Today, nearly four decades later, Ba'ath Party membership in Syria constitutes about 10 percent of the entire population and is the *sine qua non* of career advancement. In the year 2005, 997 of the nation's 1,370 judges were Ba'ath Party members. The secretary-general of the Party is also the president of the country, in today's instance, of course, being Hafez al-

Assad's son, Bashar al-Assad. The Party's leader is the Regional and National secretary of the Party, and is elected by the Party's Regional Command, a sort of politburo, which in turn is elected by the party congress, which meets every four years. But to indicate how seamlessly Hafez al-Assad orchestrated the intertwining of state and Party functions during the 30 years that he was in power, it needs only to be noted that he was elected by the compliant People's Council, not a Ba'ath Party structure at all, but Syria's state parliament. In this legislature, 167 seats are automatically assigned to one group, the National Progressive Front. And within *that* parliamentary conglomeration, the 800-pound gorilla is the Arab Socialist Ba'ath Party, which holds 134 seats in the People's Council.

Hafez al-Assad ruled over Syria with an iron fist from 1970 until his death in June 2000. He survived several different secretaries of state of the U.S. who diligently visited him and waited for a meeting with the great leader. He had a habit of lecturing them, and other visiting foreign diplomats, for hours at a time on his view of the history of the Middle East. It certainly contained some bizarre theories. He liked to startle visitors by telling them that Jesus Christ was "a Syrian Jew."[6]

But al-Assad's most serious challenge politically was not with American secretaries of state, but with Muslims. Starting in 1976, Assad faced a serious challenge to Ba'ath Party power by Islamic radicals led by the Muslim Brotherhood, an Islamic group founded by an Egyptian in 1928, which had spread to many countries in the Muslim world. The Muslim Brotherhood organized urban demonstrations against the regime, took over whole sections of Syrian cities, and assassinated several senior Ba'ath Party officials and military officers. In June 1980, Assad himself was nearly murdered in a grenade and machine-gun attack on his motorcade. The country was on the brink of civil war.

In a decisive and ruthless suppression of Muslim Brotherhood supporters who had taken over the city of Hama, Syria's fourth-largest city, in February 1982, the Syrian army shelled the city without mercy for three weeks, crushing the rebellion and killing, in the process, between 15,000 and 25,000 of the inhabitants. In the same year, membership in the Muslim Brotherhood was made a capital offense in Syria, and the organization was driven completely underground. It remains so to this day, though there are obvious signs of an increase in Muslim piety at street level. Women increasingly wear the *hijab* in public, and more and more men wear beards.

For all the signs of a resurgent Islamic commitment, in many respects, Syria is an Arab version of Eastern Europe's "people's democracies" of the Cold War era of, say, the 1970s. The Eastern European analogy is physically apparent at first glance as you ride into Damascus from the airport. Your taxi passes regiment after regiment of run-down, drab-looking, shabby apartment blocks. There is sparse traffic on the roads, and a very large number of the cars that travel show signs of road damage and are dirty. There is a look of sullen uniformity in much of Damascus that makes it resemble nothing so much as an Arab version of Minsk, the capital of the former Soviet republic of Belarus, at the height of the Soviet Union. Of Minsk it used to be said, cynically, that it was simply "East Berlin, without the charm."

Damascus could not honestly be called a charming city, with its chaotic traffic and drab-looking edifices, though some of its broader boulevards do bring to mind its days of glory as a capital of the Arab world under the Ummayad Dynasty and its more recent past as part of French colonial rule in the Middle East. It's important to note, however, that ordinary Syrians can be charming and hospitable, a stark contrast to the grim visage the Syrian government displays toward the rest of the world.

When Hafez al-Assad died in June 2000, there was a scramble to make the political succession as smooth as possible. In the manner of a medieval oriental potentate, he had seized power in 1970 not just for his fellow Alawites, but also for his own family. His eldest son, Basil, had been groomed to succeed his father, but the fast-living young man died in a car wreck in 1994. The next in line was a second son, Bashar, who had until then been living quietly in London as an ophthalmologist. Bashar was summoned back to Damascus for some quick dictator-in-waiting training, and when his father died in June 2000, the only minor formality was a needed constitutional change to enable the new president to take office at the age of 34, and not 36, as the Syrian constitution required. The constitutional amendment was passed effortlessly, and Bashar took over the reins of power.

Portraits of Bashar stare out from slightly fading photographs in stores and businesses throughout Syria, reminding everyone that this is a one-party state presided over by a dictator. When Hafez al-Assad was alive, he festooned city and countryside with heroic statues of himself pointing, Lenin-style, to the future. Most of the statues are still in place. Bashar, a more introverted personality, has not duplicated his father's cult of personality. One reason may be that, educated for part of his medical studies in Great Britain, and married to an Arab wife who was born and raised in London, he is just a tad uncomfortable with the role of a modern Middle Eastern potentate. With his long neck and rather small head, a moustache that isn't quite as thick as some Middle Eastern leaders like, he calls to mind nothing so much as a slightly befuddled polar bear.

Shortly after he came to power on his father's death—it's easy to say, "acceded to the throne"—Bashar seemed to promise something similar to a Gorbachev-style *perestroika* for Syria. He relaxed restrictions on the In-ternet, which blossomed from a mere 30,000 users in 2000 to possibly more than 1 million users now; released within a few weeks 600 political prisoners; and ruled over a remarkable period of free expression in Syria, from the summer of 2000 to the winter of 2001, which became known as the "Damascus Spring."[7] "Salons" of free discussion sprang up in Damas-cus and several other cities, and within weeks there emerged the "Mani-festo of the Ninety-nine," a document signed by professionals and intellectuals calling upon the government to end censorship, to free polit-ical prisoners and to establish the rule of law. This was followed by the "Manifesto of the One Thousand," which made even more far-reaching demands: an end to the 1963 Emergency Law authorizing the Syrian Ba'ath Party's draconian control of politics, democratic elections, human rights guarantees for women and an independent judiciary.

One of the initiators of the "Damascus Spring" was two-term member of parliament Riad Seif. He started his reform initiatives within weeks af-ter the death of Hafez al-Assad, and convened one group of the newly as-sembled intellectuals as the Forum for National Dialogue. When the regime seemed to be leaving him alone, he went one step further. He an-nounced that he would be forming a new political party, the Movement for Social Peace. This, apparently, was one step too much for the government. When some 600 people showed up for a lecture that Seif delivered by loud-speaker in early September 2001, the *Mukhabarat*, Syria's security and in-telligence apparatus, pounced. Seif was arrested the following day and sentenced to five years in prison. Though he was released in 2006, he has been under steady police surveillance since then.

According to Robin Wright, a long-time and experienced reporter in the Middle East, and author of an excellent book on the region, *Dreams and Shadows: The Future of the Middle East*, Seif's heroic efforts to campaign for reform and democracy in Syria are dwarfed by a man she met in exile in Lebanon, and whom many consider the Nelson Mandela of the country.

He is Riad al-Turk, 79 years old as of 2009, who was imprisoned for the first time in 1952 for opposing the military regime. He opposed Syria's union with Egypt in 1958, for which he was again jailed and tortured. Finally, he was arrested in 1980 and held for 18 years in a windowless cell, being frequently beaten and tortured.[8] Though he was released in 1998, al-Turk became vocal in the "Damascus Spring" movement and was arrested for the fourth time in the late summer of 2001 and sentenced to two more years in prison. After an international outcry at this savage treatment of an old man, al-Turk was released after 15 months and allowed to leave the country.

Al-Turk evolved over his long life as a political dissident from young Communist youth leader to a genuine social democrat. He turned against Marxism-Leninism after the Soviet invasion of Afghanistan in 1979. He is today a supporter of liberal democracy and is against political violence. It might be speculated that many Syrians share his views: they have seen plenty of Stalinism, thank you; they don't want Islamist fascism; and they certainly don't want violence. Syria's opposition leaders, however, are mostly men in their sixties and seventies who can still recall the distant past when Syria had a functioning political democracy. Most young people have grown up knowing only the swaddling clothes of the Ba'ath Party and the al-Assad dynastic dictatorship. Their main concern tends to be finding a job after completion of university education.

In addition, Bashar al-Assad has deftly used the widespread unpopularity in Syria of the U.S. invasion of Iraq to make outspoken advocacy of democracy both unpopular and dangerous. Despite the ban on the Muslim Brotherhood from 1983 onwards, Bashar has tried hard to bridge the gap between the secularism of the Ba'ath party and the revivalist sentiment of serious Syrian Muslims, channeling generous government funding into the construction of mosques in Syria. Barry Rubin, one keen observer of Syria, thinks that in practicing this careful hedging of his political bets, Bashar al-Assad has managed to create a unique "Arab nationalist-Islamist synthesis" that enables his regime to cultivate a sort of perpetual hostility towards the U.S. and the West. Rubin provocatively suggests, "Iran's president Ahmadinejad in 2006 [when Israel was fighting a war against Hezbollah in Lebanon] is a resurrected Nasser from 1966, threatening the West, confidently predicting that Israel will be wiped off the map, and toying with war as a way of achieving a quick, easy victory. Bashar is not a brash young man of gangly frame and failed moustache but a champion of resistance."[9]

Without question, the regime freely cultivates hatred of Israel and the Jews.[10] When I visited Damascus in November 2007, I saw prominently displayed in a bookstore in central Damascus a copy in English of the notorious anti-Semitic forgery, *Protocols of the Elders of Zion*. Hanging over the counter was a magazine praising Lebanon's Shiite Muslim leader Hassan Nasrallah. The head of the militaristic and virulently anti-Jewish and anti-Israeli political movement Hezbollah, Nasrallah has depended on Iran for Hezbollah's military equipment and training, and on Syria for permission to acquire it.

Lebanon—the Switzerland of the Arab World

It's easy to travel from Damascus to the Lebanese capital of Beirut, a distance by road of only 53 miles. I took a taxi there one early Saturday morning, and within 20 minutes of leaving downtown Damascus, the Chevy Caprice was flying along the road at 90 MPH, heading toward Lebanon. We arrived at the border a mere 40 minutes after leaving Damascus. Border formalities for entering Lebanon were simple, thanks to the smooth handling of Lebanese immigration bureaucrats by my Lebanese driver. I was at the downtown hotel in Beirut little more than an hour later. I might as well have been in a different universe.

Signs of Lebanese cosmopolitanism were apparent as soon as the road from Syria dipped down into the Bekaa Valley of Lebanon. Mercedes sedans were both more numerous and in much better shape than the cars of Damascus. New construction was proceeding apace in the towns close to the border, and billboards for Marlboro and the French cigarette Gitanes greeted us as the road climbed up toward the central mountain range of Lebanon, Mount Lebanon. More billboards flashed by, with sexy women advertizing jeans. As the road finally made its way down to the Lebanese coast, the country's wealth was apparent: elegant villas with lush

Source: Central Intelligence Agency.

LEBANON

gardens jostled the roadside, and the drabness of Syrian provinciality was quickly forgotten.

Lebanon's per capita income is approximately $11,300, nearly three times that of Syria at $4,000. For many years, in the 1960s, considered the "Switzerland" of the Arab world, and Beirut the "Paris of the Orient," Lebanon's sophisticated banking and commercial operations attracted investment and businessmen from all over the region. But then came the country's disastrous civil war, a tragic clash of ethnic communities that devastated the nation during 1975-1990 and cost an estimated 100,000 lives.

Lebanon is unique among countries in the Middle East in that it is the only Arabic-speaking country that once had a Christian ethnic majority. When the French took over the former Ottoman *sanjaks* of Syria and Lebanon in the 1920s, they presided over an ethnic mix of communities as diverse as Syria's—Sunni Muslim, Druze, Alawites and Christians—but with the distinction that Maronite Christians were the largest community. The Maronites were a branch of Eastern Orthodoxy whose scriptures were in the Syriac language and who had fled to the mountains of Lebanon to escape the Arab invasion. After several hundred years and "rediscovery" by the European crusaders, they linked up with the Roman Catholic church, with whom they have had a relationship ever since.

As early as the nineteenth century, the French saw themselves as guardians of the Maronite Christians of Lebanon who were often the victims of oppression in the Ottoman Empire, and so when the League of Nations confirmed France's mandate to rule Lebanon in the 1920s, Lebanon's Christians at first identified warmly and eagerly with French culture, religion and politics. It was under the French that the last official census of Lebanon was conducted—in 1932—and the Lebanese way of ordering the politics of their national life was pretty much set in stone. According to this census, some 54 percent of the country was Christian, and the remainder of the population belonged to the Sunni Muslim, Shiite Muslim, Druze communities and others.

When France recognized Lebanese independence in 1943, the country ruled itself according to a principle known as "confessionalism," an arrangement referred to as the National Pact. Officially, even today, there are 18 designated ethnic-religious communities that are recognized by the state as having rights to certain positions in the government bureaucracy and the military. But the most important feature of "confessionalism" is that the president of the country, though selected by the parliament, must come from the Maronite Christian community. The prime minister must be a Sunni Muslim, and the speaker of parliament must come from the Shiite community. The seats in the 128-member parliament are divided equally into Christian and Muslim segments.

As long as everyone agreed that the Maronites were a majority of Lebanese, this system worked, more or less. The U.S. became directly involved in Lebanese affairs for the first time in 1958, when President Eisenhower sent in the marines to help the pro-Western Lebanese president, Camille Chamoun, remain in power. Lebanon's Muslim community was agitating to join the pan-Arab community that Egyptian president Gamal Abdel Nasser was promoting in the form of the United Arab Republic. Some Sunni Muslim activists in Lebanon wanted the country to abandon its close ties with the West. The presence of the marines forestalled any possible pro-Nasser coup, and after a few months, the crisis subsided and the marines left.

By the 1970s, it was becoming clear that the largest ethnic community in Lebanon was no longer Christian—which it had been in 1900—nor Sunni Muslim, but Shiite Muslim. More importantly, the Shiites were trying to assert their new demographic power in the politics of the Lebanese state. Adding to this combustible political mix was the new wild card of Palestinian activism. There had been several hundred thousand Palestinian refugees who had fled to Lebanon during Israel's 1948 War of Independence. What turned them into an aggressive component of Lebanese politics was the ejection of the PLO leadership from Jordan at the end of September 1970. In that month, the PLO in Jordan organized an attempt to dethrone King Hussein and take control of the country, but they were crushed by the Bedouin soldiers of the Jordanian army fiercely loyal to King Hussein. Yasser Arafat, other senior PLO leaders, and large numbers of PLO fighters decamped to Lebanon. Once there, their leftist and secularist politics turned them first against the Maronite Christians, and then against the devout Muslim Shiite in the south of the country. The PLO turned southern Lebanon into a virtual occupation zone, lording it over the local Lebanese, both Christian and Muslim, as they dug in to positions from which they planned to attack Israel.

By the mid-1970s, Lebanon's demographic developments and the polarizing of its political system led to the rise of various militia movements to protect the different ethnic communities. One of the largest was the

Phalange, which founded another group, the Lebanese Forces, in 1977. When a clash between Maronite Christians and Palestinian fighters escalated into citywide skirmishes in Beirut, what had once been "the Paris of the East" quickly turned into the Dodge City of the Mediterranean. For the next 15 years, factions and groups betrayed each other and massacred each other, turning Lebanon in the 1980s into a country in which numerous Americans were taken hostage for years and to which the U.S. State Department denied American passport holders the right to travel.

Major Military "Interventions"

Two major international interventions in Lebanon added to the complexity of the turmoil. The first was when Lebanese president Suleiman Frangieh, in June 1976, invited the Syrian army to intervene in order to prevent what he and many others feared might become a massacre of Lebanon's Christians.

In October 1976, the Arab League provided its blessing for Syria to maintain 40,000 troops of an Arab Deterrent Force in Lebanon in order to tame the errant militias and restore order in the country. Syria was only too happy to accept the invitation because it had long maintained that Lebanon was merely part of the Greater Syria of the Ottoman Empire. In fact, Syria and Lebanon established formal diplomatic relations with each other only as late as 2008. Until then, Syria had maintained that Lebanon was simply a "region" of Syria.

The Syrian troops remained in Lebanon for 29 years, changing sides frequently, but always trying to dominate Lebanon's political life. They were finally forced to leave in April 2005, in the face of Lebanese and global outrage at suspected Syrian complicity in the assassination by bomb blast of Lebanon's prime minister, Rafiq Hariri.

The second major foreign intervention was that of Israel. After sustaining some major PLO terrorist attacks launched from Lebanon, the Israeli army made a major incursion into southern Lebanon in 1978, but then withdrew after leaving a Lebanese Christian army officer, Saad Haddad, controlling a strip of Lebanese territory adjacent to Israel as a "security zone."

In 1982, however, the hawkish Ariel Sharon was Israel's defense minister, and he persuaded then-Prime Minister Menachem Begin to authorize an invasion of Lebanon as far as the outskirts of Beirut in order to suppress the PLO once and for all. After Israeli ambassador to London,

Shlomo Argov, was the target of an assassination attempt, Israel had the excuse it needed. It crossed the Lebanese border in massive force on June 6, 1982, in an operation called "Peace for the Galilee."

At first, the Israeli forces were welcome as liberators in southern Lebanon, where the population had grown tired of the arrogant and corrupt PLO presence. Within days, Israeli tanks were ringing Beirut and kept up a withering fire against targets in the city. Israeli jets bombed Palestinian weapons dumps inside Beirut, and Israeli units operated freely in east Beirut, which was the Christian area of the city. During the war, I recall driving in a rental car from Jerusalem, where I was based as a reporter at the time, across the international border into Lebanon, and then dining in the evening in an east Beirut restaurant with Israeli officers sitting at the next table.

The Israeli military pressure on Beirut was unpopular with both the Lebanese and the rest of the world. After intense negotiating with the Palestinians and various Arab states, the U.S. arranged for Arafat and thousands of his fighters to leave Beirut by sea and move their headquarters from Beirut to Tunis. This they did in August 1982. The Israelis agreed to withdraw from Beirut to a position several miles south. This didn't happen, however, before yet another terrible incident in Lebanon's still-continuing civil war.

On September 14, 1982, Bashir Gemayel, the just-appointed president of Lebanon, was assassinated. The next day, the Israeli army entered West Beirut, the predominantly Muslim part of the city, in force. While in control of the area, they permitted about 150 fighters from the Phalange, a Christian militia group, to enter the Sabra and Shatila refugee camps where the Phalangists began a systematic massacre of the camp's residents. At least 800 Palestinians were killed. When the Israelis conducted an official investigation of who had been responsible, Ariel Sharon was pronounced partially responsible and forced to resign from the defense ministry position a few months later.

The Israelis withdrew to a relatively small perimeter in the south of Lebanon where they tried to ensure that the territory of Lebanon closest to their border would not be controlled by terrorist groups hostile to Israel. They found themselves facing, however, one of the best-trained and best-equipped guerrilla groups in the world, the forces of Hezbollah.

Over an 18-year period, the Israelis took steadily increasing casualties from the relatively small but increasingly effective guerrilla forces that ambushed their patrols or exploded roadside bombs by remote control. As the numbers of deaths mounted to the hundreds, domestic political opposition to the Israel presence in Lebanon overshadowed the strategic arguments of Israeli military chiefs for keeping them there.

In May 2000, in a poorly orchestrated withdrawal that at times resembled a rout, the Israeli army finally and hastily withdrew from Lebanon. One tiny, eight-square-mile piece of land on the Lebanese-Syrian border that remained in Israeli hands was the so-called Shebaa farms, which the Israelis had originally captured when they seized the Golan Heights from Syria in the 1967 Six-Day War. Though Syrian historical maps clearly indicated that the area was Syrian, it was a useful fiction for Syria and Lebanon to argue that the territory was Lebanese, and that the Israelis had therefore not completed their withdrawal from Lebanon. The principal beneficiary of this assertion, of course, was Lebanon's Hezbollah movement, which needed a pretext to continue "resistance" (i.e., terrorist operations) against the Israelis.

The Grim Legacy of Lebanon's Civil War

The Lebanese civil war laid bare the tense ethnic and religious crosscurrents that have made Lebanon a fragile nation. Its most lasting legacy, however, was the emergence of a fanatical Lebanese Shiite organization slavishly loyal to Iran and sycophantically supportive of Syria. Iran provided Hezbollah with weapons, equipment and training, and Syria ensured that trainers and weaponry got through to Hezbollah sources in Lebanon.

The first militant Shiite group to emerge in the Lebanese civil war was Amal, an Arabic acronym for Lebanese Resistance Detachments, associated with a political movement called Movement of the Disinherited. This organization had been founded in 1974 by the unfortunate Musa al-Sadr, the Shiite cleric we have already come across as having authenticated the Sunni Muslim *bona fides* of Syrian dictator Hafez al-Assad, and then having mysteriously disappeared on a trip to Libya and Italy in 1978. Amal, however, bit off more than it could chew by taking on a rival Shiite group called Hezbollah (literally, "Party of God") that arose suddenly in 1982 to confront the invading Israelis. Hezbollah was initially headed by the Ayatollah Khomeini in Iran, and from the beginning its military cadres were trained both in Iran and in camps in Lebanon's Bekaa Valley by Iranian revolutionary guards. As the civil war continued in Lebanon, Hezbollah cemented its hold on the Shiite community both by providing health, educational and welfare services to them, and by taking the lead in attacking Israeli forces in Lebanon.

When U.S. forces entered Lebanon in 1982, to attempt peacekeeping functions under U.N. auspices, Hezbollah showed its murderous hand. In April 1983, the U.S. Embassy in Beirut was demolished by a suicide car bomb that killed 63 embassy employees, soldiers and marines. The following October, a suicide bomber drove a truck into the ground floor of the U.S. marine barracks in Beirut, killing 241 soldiers in the ensuing explosion. Minutes later, another car bomb demolished the French military barracks, killing 58 people.

A pro-Iranian group called Islamic Jihad claimed responsibility for both bombings, but a U.S. court in 2003 made a legal judgment that Hezbollah had organized both embassy and barracks explosions. In 1992, a suicide truck bomber thundered into the Israeli embassy in Buenos Aires, killing 29 people. Once again, Islamic Jihad claimed responsibility, but it was assumed by both the Argentineans and the Israelis that Hezbollah was involved, assisted by the Iranians.

Since the 1990s, Hezbollah has been officially declared a terrorist organization. Hezbollah, on the other hand, and on the instructions of Iran, had almost certainly been responsible for the Lebanese hostage crisis of 1985 to 1991, when some 96 foreign hostages from 21 countries were abducted in Beirut, some held for years, and several of them, including a former Beirut CIA station chief and a U.S. marine colonel, brutally tortured and killed by the kidnappers. The longest-held hostage was AP correspondent Terry Anderson, who was kidnapped in 1985 and finally released in December 1991.[11]

The Lebanese civil war tottered to an end in 1990, following an agreement negotiated at Taif, in Saudi Arabia, in 1989. The negotiators were Lebanese politicians, and they understood the need both to change the National Covenant in a way that allotted equal parliamentary representation between Christians and Muslims, and to acknowledge officially that the Lebanese government accepted the Syrian presence in Lebanon.

The agreement allowed the various militias to cease fighting without losing face, but the country had been devastated by the loss of scores of thousands of lives and property destruction amounting to billions of dollars. As it happened, Rafiq Hariri, a Lebanese billionaire—at one point, reportedly, the fourth richest man in the world—who had started his commercial career teaching math in Arabia, helped bankroll the conference and persuade the Saudis to host it. A Sunni Muslim who had been granted Saudi citizenship in appreciation of his massive construction projects in the kingdom, Hariri spent his own money lavishly attempting to restore Lebanon to its pre-civil war prosperity and harmony. After decades of hyperbolic political promises, Lebanese were happy to have a wealthy man demonstrating his faith in his own country by investing generously in it. In 1992, he was selected by the parliament as prime minister.

But the shadow of Syria loomed ever more darkly over the arena of Lebanese politics. Hariri resigned as prime minister in 1998 after Syria insisted on imposing its own candidate Émile Lahoud, as Lebanon's president. After Hafez al-Assad died in 2000, however, Hariri returned to the prime ministership. He was to discover that the "bemused polar bear" Bashar, the junior al-Assad, was as ruthless as his father had been. In 2004, Syria demanded that Lebanon change its constitution in order to permit the pro-Syrian president to stay in power three more years rather than step down after the specified single term of six years. Hariri—and the U.S. and France in a rare sign of agreement—opposed the change. Hariri was summoned, Soviet-style, to Damascus for a dressing-down by Bashar al-Assad who, according to Robin Wright, threatened to "break Lebanon over [his] head" if he opposed the constitutional change.

The U.N. Security Council sided with the U.S. and France and passed Resolution 1559 calling for presidential elections in Lebanon, as scheduled, "without foreign interference or influence." But the following day, Lebanon's parliament succumbed to Syrian pressure and voted for the change. Hariri even went along as well. Within weeks, however, he resigned, and devoted his time to something called the Future Movement, a grassroots political movement aimed at ending the religious divide in Lebanese politics.

As far as the Syrians were concerned, Rafiq Hariri was still dangerously uncontrollable. Lebanese parliamentary elections were scheduled for May 2005, and Syria evidently let Hariri know he was being carefully watched. What they didn't tell him was that his death sentence had already been approved by Damascus.

As Hariri drove from parliament to his home in downtown Beirut on February 14, 2005, a massive bomb, estimated to contain more than a thousand pounds of high explosive, went off in the road as his armored motorcade passed by. Hariri and 19 others were instantly blown to smithereens, 100 bystanders were injured and buildings in downtown

Beirut were reduced to shells. The sense of outrage—and the widespread and instant suspicion that Syria must have been behind the assassination—galvanized Lebanese into massive street demonstrations that became known as the "Cedar Revolution." The "cedar" reference was to the Lebanese national emblem, and the analogy suggested was that of Ukraine's "Orange Revolution" of 2004, when democratic protest against election fraud by pro-Russian politicians enabled a prominent democrat to win the presidency.

Lebanon, however, had become polarized along pro- and anti-Syrian lines during the 15 years of the nation's civil war. As grassroots citizens groups demanded that the country stand up to Syrian bullying, those elements of Lebanese politics that had benefited from the Syrian presence, notably Hezbollah and its allies, decided to organize counter-demonstrations.

On March 8, 2005, several hundred thousand Hezbollah supporters took to the streets as a sign that many Lebanese benefited from the Syrian overlordship. On March 14, the anti-Syrian forces responded with a demonstration in Beirut of more than 1 million people, one quarter of the entire population of Lebanon. It was, for an Arab state, a political demonstration of unprecedented size. The Syrians, nudged also by U.N. Security Resolution 1559, got the message. Though they maintained a relatively discreet intelligence presence in Lebanon, uniformed Syrian soldiers had left Lebanese soil by the end of April 2005.

Meanwhile, in the parliamentary elections held in May 2005, the "March 14 Coalition," a grouping of parties led by Rafiq Hariri's son Saad Hariri that had come together to build on the momentum of anti-Syrian outrage created by Hariri's assassination, won 72 of the 128 seats in the Lebanese parliament. A pro-Syrian, pro-Hezbollah "Resistance and Development Bloc" won 35 seats. Some people wanted Saad Hariri to become prime minister, but he was aware of his own inexperience, at the age of 35, and Fouad Siniora, a former executive in Rafiq Hariri's administration, took the job.

The U.N., meanwhile, ordered up an investigation of Hariri's assassination. In October 2005, it released the Mehlis Report, a summary of the investigations carried out in Syria and Lebanon by German judge Detlev Mehlis. The report unambiguously concluded that both Syrian and Lebanese officials had been involved in the assassination. The Syrians stolidly refused to acknowledge any culpability and in fact continued to interfere murderously in Lebanese politics. As of December 2008, seven more

Lebanese members of the March 14 Coalition had been murdered in car-bomb explosions in Beirut. For their own safety, the remaining members of the parliamentary group were kept under virtual lock-and-key as residents of the Phoenicia Intercontinental Hotel in downtown Beirut.

But the fault line in Lebanese politics, between the increasingly powerful and well-disciplined Hezbollah movement and the rest of the country, remained. Hezbollah conducted impressive—and frightening—parades of its armed forces in Beirut and other Lebanese cities, operated a TV station, Al-Manar, and displayed mass loyalty to its leader, Hassan Nasrallah, with Hitler-style, raised arm salutes. Though Hezbollah, especially after the 2005 elections, had backed off its original goal of making Lebanon an Islamic state, its ferocious hostility to Israel and to Jews in general remained constant. Nasrallah got his start as a military and political leader as the security officer for Iranian Revolutionary Guards training camps in Lebanon's Beqaa Valley in the 1980s. He subsequently studied at Qom, the center of Shiite studies in Iran, and became the leader of Hezbollah, at the age of 32, after the Israeli assassination of the movement's original leader, Abbas al-Musawi, in 1992.

Hezbollah's virulent opposition to Israel and to the Jews in general was apparent from early on. Speaking of Israel, Nasrallah said, "We recognize no treaty with it, no cease-fire, and no peace agreements."[12] In fact, Hezbollah unequivocally calls for the annihilation of Israel as a state and its replacement by Palestine.[13] Not only that, it regards the destruction of the Israeli state as a religious duty for every Muslim in the entire world Islamic community.[14] Hezbollah hates not only Israel, but all Jews. Amal Saad-Ghorayeb, a scholar from Beirut's Lebanese-American University, puts it this way: "Thus the anti-Judaism of Hizbu'llah is as vituperative against Jews, if not more than [sic], conventional anti-Semitism."[15]

One of Hezbollah's goals, in addition to driving the Israelis out of Lebanon and the contested Lebanese-Syrian border enclave of the Shebaa farms, was to obtain the release of its activists—and PLO terrorists—being held in Israeli prisons. This goal was to be accomplished by holding hostage Israeli soldiers, of at least their remains if they had died in Hezbollah hands, and demanding a prisoner swap. There had been several previous instances of Israel releasing Palestinian prisoners in return for the release of its own prisoners, or international hostages held in Lebanon, or even in return for the remains of dead Israeli soldiers and civilians. But on July 12, 2006, Hezbollah carefully orchestrated a plan to "snatch" Israeli soldiers from within sovereign Israeli territory. Early in the morning, members of Hezbollah ambushed an Israeli border patrol with a rocket-launcher fired at two jeeps, killing three soldiers and abducting back to Lebanon two more.

The Israelis tried to recover the captured soldiers and locate their captors, but Hezbollah had carefully prepared for this response and repulsed the initial Israeli attack, killing more Israeli soldiers. This led to a 33-day all-out war between Israel and Hezbollah during which grave damage was done to Beirut by Israeli aircraft trying to bomb the Hezbollah headquarters in the southern district of the city; and 1 million Lebanese fled their homes in the south of the country. But Hezbollah did not sit on its hands during the conflict; they fired nearly 4,000 rockets against towns and villages in northern Israel, the vast majority of the rockets being 122 mm "Katyusha" Russian-designed rockets with a range of about 19 miles. Many of the rockets had been supplied by Iran and shipped to Hezbollah courtesy of the Syrians. Israel's northern port of Haifa (population: 265,000) was hit by 93 Hezbollah rockets. Eleven Israeli civilians were killed, some while sitting in the living rooms of their own apartments.[16]

Eventually a cease-fire was agreed upon at the U.N. under which the Lebanese army and the U.N. would deploy troops to the south of the country, supposedly to keep an eye on Hezbollah and prevent the reinforcement of their military presence there. But after some U.N. soldiers from Spain were killed by Hezbollah-planted roadside bombs, the U.N. did almost no active patrolling to prevent Hezbollah from returning. Meanwhile, to gain favor with Lebanese whose homes had been damaged or destroyed by Israeli airstrikes, Hezbollah organized a massive financial aid program, distributing $12,000 per family to those whose property had been damaged. The money was supplied by Iran.

Though the Arab world was overwhelmingly supportive of Lebanon, and a significant majority of Lebanese backed Hezbollah against Israel during the war, Arab governments like Egypt and Saudi Arabia criticized Hezbollah's decision to provoke a massive Israeli response, and Hassan Nasrallah himself made an astonishing admission of poor judgment. "We did not think, even 1 percent," he said, "that the capture [of the two kidnapped Israeli soldiers] would lead to war at this time and of this magnitude. You ask me, if I had known on July 12 . . . that the operation would lead to such a war, would I do it? I say no, absolutely not." Too bad that the more than 1,000 Lebanese civilians who died in the conflict had to pay the price for this misjudgment. To add to the suffering of Lebanese, both Arab and foreign reporters noted that Hezbollah often fired its rockets against Israel from positions embedded in civilian communities, which of course suffered when Israeli aircraft bombed the rocket sites.

Lebanese politics shuddered on with months of indecision about who the new president would be after Émile Lahoud (Bashar al-Assad's preferred candidate) completed his second term as president in October 2007. In May 2008, militia from Hezbollah and Amal briefly occupied downtown Beirut in a bid to change the political structure of the country. After intensive negotiations urged on them by the Arab League, the Lebanese government of Siniora agreed late in October 2008 to form a national unity government in which 11 out of 30 cabinet seats would be held by Hezbollah and its allies. The presidency, meanwhile, had been assigned after several months' indecision to Michel Suleiman, a Maronite Christian former general.

In effect, Hezbollah is in a position to veto any Lebanese government decision of which it disapproves, and is capable of mobilizing hundreds of thousands of supporters at very short notice. Hezbollah has long since abandoned its public goal of turning Lebanon into an Islamic state, which was the movement's original platform. Lebanon is thus hostage to the most radical and extreme segment of Lebanese politics and society, an organization whose very rationale for existence is to see the elimination of the Jewish state.

For all that, a visitor to Beirut is struck by the European-style familiarity of the country's lifestyle. Fashionably dressed women sit in outdoor cafes smoking narghils, the traditional Arab water pipe sometimes called a hookah. At the Starbucks on Verdun Street, the server speaks English, French and Arabic, and when the power in the district momentarily causes all the coffee-making machines to whine to a halt, he looks at you, grins and says, "Welcome to Lebanon." The city is filled with nightclubs, restaurants and Internet cafés as well, and you definitely feel as though you are somewhere in, say, southern France.

But on the way to the airport, the freeway passes through Haret Hreik, Beirut's southern district that has traditionally been the stronghold of Lebanese Shiites and Hezbollah's leadership. Signs of Israel's bombing from 2006 are clear, but so is the evidence for a massive program of reconstruction. When I strolled through the area with a Lebanese friend, videoing and photographing, an alert young man quickly caught up with me and asked what I was doing. He'd visited the U.S., he said, "several times," and appeared to be part of Hezbollah's ubiquitous security apparatus. Satisfied that I was not an Israeli spy, he cheerily sent us on our way. But his ultimate boss, Hezbollah chief Hasan Nasrallah, can't afford to take any risks. He has not been seen in public for at least three years, out of fear that if he makes any appearance out of doors, he may be assassinated by the Israelis. It is all a sad confirmation of the truth of the principle that those who live by the sword must face the risk of dying by it.

Lebanon is a beautiful Mediterranean country with gorgeous tourist sites and a charming lifestyle, much of the time. But it seems to sit forever on the edge of a cauldron of ethnic strife and Islamic-based vitriol against the Jews. It is a real shame for the Lebanese.

4

EGYPT AND JORDAN

In many ways Egypt and Jordan might seem like the odd couple in a book about the Middle East. The two countries do not resemble each other in either geographic size or population. Egypt is huge, the size of Texas and California put together, or twice the size of France. Jordan is slightly smaller than the state of Indiana, just slightly smaller than Portugal if a European yardstick is needed.

Egypt's population in 2008 was estimated to be close to 83 million, while Jordan's was just over 6.1 million. Egypt's history is one of the longest on record, in the whole world, stretching back to at least 2700 BC as a united kingdom under a single dynasty. Jordan, by contrast, though traversed for millennia by the armies of various empires, became recognized for the first time as an international entity in its own right in 1922, when it was the British-administered League of Nations mandate territory of Transjordan.

While Egypt is colorful, overcrowded, often chaotic, dirty and with desperate poverty seldom out of view, Jordan is clean, well organized, orderly and polite, and in the category of what the World Bank calls a "lower middle income country." The average visitor is unlikely to see any desperate displays of poverty in Jordan.

Finally, Egypt is a republic, with a president who has ruled it since 1981, and who has overwhelming executive powers that he is more than willing to deploy; whereas Jordan is a constitutional monarchy whose king works hard to ensure that he is seen as working in close contact with his citizens.

For all the important differences between Egypt and Jordan, however, the two countries do hold important things in common. While both are members of the 22-country Arab League, both have full diplomatic relations with Israel and are considered key moderate allies of the U.S. in the Middle East. Each has suffered through wars fought with Israel; and because of sharing a common border with the Jewish state, both can be classified as a "front-line" Arab neighbor. Both countries have suffered relentless pressure from forces within and from the larger Arab world to become more confrontational with Israel and less cooperative in Middle East diplomacy with the U.S.

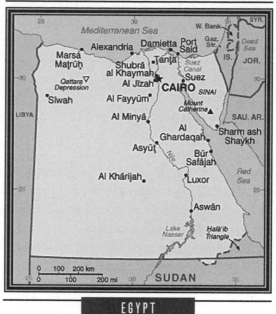

EGYPT

Source: Central Intelligence Agency

Egypt is the 800-pound gorilla of the Arab world. Comprising a quarter of the total population of Arabs in Arab states, it has long been the engine room of Arab culture and ideas. Egyptian movies and TV soap operas are ubiquitous in the Arab world, and Egyptian books, newspapers and magazines are often the starting point for intense discussions wherever Arabic is spoken. The definition of an Arab, incidentally, is purely linguistic: one whose mother tongue is Arabic. There is nothing about hair color, skin pigmentation or physical bulk in this definition. Yet Egyptians, who can easily be the most hospitable and charming people in the entire Middle East, often bristle even at the idea that they are Arab at all. "We are Egyptian," foreigners are often told, as though that ought to settle the question why they may differ in viewpoint from the Syrians, Libyans or Sudanese.

Ancient Egypt

The Egyptian sense of being a unique identity is certainly valid from an historical perspective. More than 5,000 years ago, in about 3200 BC, there arose the first Unified Kingdom in Egypt. The great Pyramids of Giza, which were one of the seven wonders of the ancient world and are forever associated with Egypt in everyone's minds, were built during what is called the Old Kingdom of Egypt, around 2200 BC. It is not until the *New* Kingdom, around 1550-1070 BC, that we come across names forever associated with the great civilization of ancient Egypt: Akhenaten and his wife Nefertiti, Tutankhamun and that villain from the biblical story in Exodus, Ramses II. The ancient Egyptians created a magnificently advanced culture for their era, being able not only to preserve the bodies of their leaders for long periods of time but also to develop the surgical skills to remove cataracts and treat dislocated bones.

Invading Foreigners

Egypt, even during the Old Kingdom period, was occupied for a century by invading foreigners known as the Hyksos; and once we come into the period of classical Greek and Roman civilization, Egypt was repeatedly subjected to foreign conquest.

In 341 BC, the expanding Persians took over; but only 9 years later, in 332 BC, they were dislodged by the all-conquering army of Alexander the Great. As we saw in the story of Syria, Alexander's sons carved up the empire he had conquered, and Egypt was ruled for a few hundred years by the Greek family of one of his generals, Ptolemy.

Although Egypt came under the political control of Rome in 31 BC, with the defeat of Cleopatra, Greek culture centered in Alexandria—whose famous library and lighthouse were among the wonders of the ancient world—continued to flourish well into the era of the Roman Empire of the West (27 BC–AD 476). The Greeks of Alexandria invented the first documented steam-powered device, a windwheel, and a remarkable theatrical show with scenes changing according to ropes and pullies programmed, like computers, to perform certain theatrical functions at certain times.

Islamic Conquests

When the Roman Empire split into Eastern and Western portions, Egypt fell under the control of the Eastern Empire in Byzantium. Egypt gave early Christendom several of its best-known early theologians and historians, such as Origen, Clement of Alexandria, Athenagoras and Didymus. But Egypt's imperial overlords in Byzantium (Constantinople) governed harshly. When the Muslim Arabs poured north out of the Arabian Peninsula in the 630s, some of Egypt's Christians initially welcomed them. The conquest—and coerced conversions to Islam—however, turned Egypt's Christians into a minority community—an estimated 10 percent of the population—within a few hundred years. Most of these today belong to the Coptic church, part of the Eastern Orthodox fold, whose written liturgy is in the original tongue of pre-Arab Egypt.

Egypt became Arabic and Muslim after the Islamic conquests in the seventh century and entered quickly enough into the mainstream of Islamic cultural achievements. Cairo's Al Azhar University, one of the centerpieces of Islamic learning in the Arab world, was founded in AD 972. The dynasty that established it, the Fatimids, actually belonged to the Shia branch of Islam (Egypt today is overwhelmingly Sunni) and constituted the fourth, and final, Arab caliphate.

The Mamluks

During the period of the Crusades (1095-1250), parts of Egypt were conquered briefly by various crusading armies; but it was a new power, the Mamluks, who emerged as the strongmen of the country. Essentially a slave army originally recruited by earlier Arab dynasties to provide a protective corps of loyal shock troops to the regime, the Mamluks were a dedicated military force composed of men who had been taken prisoner as children from Christian domains—generally from Georgia and other domains in the Caucasus—and had spent their adult lives as converts to Islam and brainwashed regime loyalists.

The Mamluks both repelled the French King Louis IX during the Seventh Crusade (1249) and about a decade later became the first Arab power to defeat the Mongols, only two years after the Mongols had in 1258 destroyed the very center of Muslim Arab culture and Empire, the Abbasid dynasty in Baghdad. But the Mamluks had control of Egypt wrested from them in 1517 by the newest big boy on the block, the Ottoman Turks. This powerful new empire, consisting of a Turkic tribal group that had arisen in 1299, had finally conquered Constantinople in 1453, and was set on expanding Muslim power into the Balkans and other parts of Europe.

The Mamluks remained a powerful military force in Egypt until Napoleon Bonaparte invaded the country in 1798 and defeated them that same year in the Battle of the Pyramids. (Napoleon had invaded Egypt because he thought he could use it as a base to cut the British off from their control of India.) Ten days after the Battle of the Pyramids, on July 21, 1798, Britain's Admiral Nelson destroyed the French fleet at anchor in the mouth of the Nile River.[1]

Modern Egypt

It was not until a new ruler came to power in Egypt, Muhammad Ali (1769-1849), that the Mamluks were destroyed as a political force; Ali simply massacred them in a surprise ambush in Cairo, in 1811.

Ali was an Albanian who rose to power in the Ottoman Empire through his administrative skills and would become known as the "founder of modern Egypt." He modernized and enlarged the Egyptian military, founded a navy and weapons arsenals, made cotton the premiere cash crop of the country, and became so powerful that it appeared for a while that he would take over the Ottoman Empire itself in Istanbul (formerly Byzantium and Constantinople). But the powerful European powers of Britain, France and Austria-Hungary did not want to see the Ottoman Empire overthrown, and so they intervened to prevent Muhammad Ali marching with his troops on Istanbul. Ali, however, secured from both the European powers and Istanbul agreement that his family would now be the recognized rulers of Egypt under Ottoman sovereignty. The dynasty lasted until 1952.

Ali's sons and grandsons succeeded him over several decades, drawing Egypt increasingly into the orbit of Europe. One of Ali's descendants, Ismail Pasha (1830-1885), said in 1879, "My country is no longer in Africa, we are now part of Europe."[2] Ismail Pasha, like so many of the Muhammad Ali dynasty, was a spendthrift who brought Egypt to the brink of fiscal ruin, in particular by ordering the construction of the Suez Canal, designed by the French engineer Ferdinand de Lesseps, which was completed in 1869.

The strategic importance of the canal was as obvious to the British as it was to the French, who had dreamed of connecting the Mediterranean and Red Seas even before Napoleon conquered Egypt. But both London and Paris were alarmed by the financial mismanagement of Egypt, so both European powers contrived to acquire seats in Egypt's ruling cabinet. When Ismail Pasha tried to rally Egyptians against this, he was deposed, and his more pliable son Tewfiq was made Khedive, as the ruler of Egypt was now called. Europeans now dominated the officers' corps of the Egyptian army and the higher echelons of the civil service. Their comfortable lifestyle, compared with that of the Egyptians, provoked a nationalist revolt led by Ahmed Urabi, a colonel in the Egyptian army. Urabi has gone down in Egyptian history as one of the country's first modern nationalists, a man who was prepared to resist the control of Egypt by the foreigners (from 1882, entirely by the British). In 1882, Egypt fell fully under British control and became a British protectorate.

Under British Control

During World War I, Egypt was an important strategic asset as the British battled the Turks, and it was from Egypt that British troops invaded Palestine and wrested that territory from the Ottomans. After the war ended, the British found themselves yet again facing Egyptian nationalism. This time, the Egyptian leader Saad Zaghlul organized a massive campaign of civil disobedience, for the most part nonviolent. Initially, the British tried to counter this by arresting Zaghlul and forcibly exiling him to Malta, but the overwhelming display of Egyptian national sentiment forced them to announce unilaterally a provisional independence of Egypt in 1922. Zaghlul was released, and in 1924 became the first popularly elected Egyptian prime minister.

Though the British remained a powerful presence in Egypt and maintained thousands of troops in bases guarding the Suez Canal, in 1936 they signed another treaty with Egypt limiting the number of British troops in the country.

During World War II, as the Germans approached Egypt from Tunisia, many Egyptian officers secretly sought to gain help from them and from the Italians in expelling the British. One of those arrested and imprisoned for several months for involvement in this was Captain Anwar Sadat, later to be president of Egypt.

The resentment of Egyptian nationalists, however, was not limited to the British. In particular they despised the profligate lifestyle of King Farouk, the last in the royal line started by Muhammad Ali. Farouk's fast cars, gallivanting through the fleshpots of Europe and personal thievery (he is popularly believed to have stolen a ceremonial sword from the Shah of Iran and a pocket watch from Winston Churchill) gave him the nickname among ordinary Egyptians of "the thief of Cairo." One of his last, mismanaged efforts was to preside over the Egyptian attempt to overthrow the newly proclaimed Jewish state of Israel. Discontent among senior Egyptian army officers at the debacle in Palestine, in 1948, contributed to a putsch against Farouk in July 1952.

The Rise and Rule of Nasser

The Free Officers' Movement that conducted the putsch arose out of long-simmering discontent at both the mismanagement of Egypt and the fact that the country was still not entirely sovereign because of the British military presence. Its organizing leader was an Egyptian army colonel, Gamal Abdel Nasser, who recruited a general, Muhammad Naguib, to be a figurehead for the coup. Though Farouk fled the country when the coup started and abdicated in favor of his infant son, Nasser emerged as the real nationalist strongman of Egypt, and the monarchy was abolished in 1953.

Nasser was hugely popular in Egypt both because he had overthrown the corrupt monarchy and because he raised expectations of Egypt as the leading standard-bearer of a pan-Arab nationalism that would raise the Arab world to a power status equal to that of the European imperialist and colonialist states.

Nasser was nominally a Muslim, but the regime over which he presided embraced both secularism in the culture and socialism in the economy. His first biggest challenge to Britain was when he demanded that the British withdraw their forces from the Canal Zone in 1954, and then nationalized the canal in its entirety in July 1956. Nasser's nationalization decision was partly in response to the refusal of the West to invest in the massive Aswan Dam project; and in the perpetual linkage of one international event to another, that decision had been prompted both by Nasser's recognition of the People's Republic of China as rulers of China (in contrast with the Republic of China regime based in Taiwan, which the U.S. recognized) and by Egypt's significant arms purchases from the Soviet allies of Czechoslovakia and Bulgaria.

British belief that Nasser was yet another troublesome dictator dedicated to undermining Britain's still considerable interests in the Middle East, and French concern that his pan-Arabist rhetoric was a threat to French control of its North African colonies led to the two countries' deciding to take drastic measures against Nasser. The British, French, and Israelis plotted secretly to coordinate an armed assault upon Egypt with the purpose of taking the Suez Canal back from Nasser.

The military part of the plan went well enough in late October 1956, but London and Paris had reckoned without the Americans, who were in any case preoccupied at that time, as much of the Western world was, by the Hungarian revolt against their Communist rulers. President Eisenhower, worried by threats from Moscow that it might turn the Suez crisis into a major assault upon NATO, threatened the British economy with the withdrawal of American financial support unless the British withdrew. After a week the British did so, leaving the French and Israelis to cope as best they could with the embarrassing international fiasco that their actions, with the British ones, had helped create. The incident pushed Egypt further toward a decisive military and economic realignment with the Soviet Union, which agreed both to fund the Aswan project and to equip the Egyptian military with the latest in modern weaponry.

Nasser's pan-Arabist ambitions prompted him in 1958 to declare a union with Syria and announce that Egypt was now to be called the United Arab Republic. But, as we saw in the preceding chapter, the union fell apart in 1961, after discontent on the part of the Syrians at the high-handed way that Egyptian officials were directing the union. Meanwhile, from 1961 to 1967, Nasser sent 55,000 troops into Yemen to try to support the antiroyalist side in a Yemeni civil war. The troops failed to turn the tide in the civil war.

Nasser's socialistic and nationalistic rhetoric, and his continued close cooperation with the Soviet Union aroused opposition among Egypt's Islamic radicals. In fact, Nasser, though an admirer of socialism, was opposed to Communist theory and cracked down harshly both on domestic Egyptian Communists and Egyptian Islamic radicals who opposed his secularism. There were several attempts on his life, and in 1966, he approved the execution of a prominent Egyptian Islamist, Sayyid Qutb, who was suspected of collaboration with one of the plots. Qutb has acquired the status of an Islamic martyr among Muslim radicals ever since his execution, and his book *Milestones*, secretly written in prison and then smuggled out, has been as galvanizing a document in the cause of Islamic jihadism as *The Communist Manifesto* a century earlier was in fomenting support for Marxist revolution.

In 1967, Nasser's pan-Arabist ambitions were fueled by a false report supplied him by the Soviet Union that Israel was preparing to attack Syria. The misinformation provoked him into closing the Straits of Tiran through which Israel received ship-borne imports into Eilat and to escalating his anti-Israel rhetoric to fever pitch, as we saw in chapter 2. But Egypt's subsequent crushing defeat in the Six-Day War, in June 1967, severely eroded Nasser's credibility. He resigned emotionally on June 9, 1967, arousing tear-filled nationwide street demonstrations by supporters who wanted him to remain in power. Much of the Arab world beyond the borders of Egypt shared in this zeal for Nasser's leadership in the Arab world. When Nasser died in 1970, an estimated 7 million Egyptians turned out for his funeral.

Enter Anwar Sadat

Nasser's successor was his vice president and fellow-plotter in the Free Officers' Movement, Anwar Sadat. The Egypt that Sadat inherited was troubled by economic problems inherited from the Six-Day War and a pervasively low national morale. One of Sadat's first dramatic moves was to expel the thousands of Soviet military advisors who had been attached to the Egyptian military since the 1950s. But he also knew that, to cement his leadership in Egypt, he needed to do something dramatic to erase the humiliation Egypt had suffered from its defeat by Israel in the Six-Day War in 1967.

After carefully concealing his military preparations and lulling the Israeli military into a false sense of security by repeated threats of military action that were never actually implemented, Egypt achieved complete surprise when it launched the October War (in Israel, the Yom Kippur War) on October 6, 1973. By advance agreement, the Syrians simultaneously attacked Israeli positions in the Golan Heights.

Egypt's military thrust was directly across the Suez Canal at the well-entrenched Israeli defensive positions located along the supposedly impregnable "Bar-Lev Line." With the use of fire hoses directed at Israeli sandwalls, and by bringing up mobile antiaircraft missile batteries, the Egyptians were able to penetrate some eight miles beyond the canal into the Sinai in a matter of hours and repel Israeli armored counterattacks.

The Israelis managed to push back, first the Syrians and then the Egyptians, thanks in large part to a decision by President Nixon to deliver by air to Israel vitally needed military replacements and ammunition.[3] Eventually, the Israelis counterattacked Egypt by crossing the Suez Canal at night and surrounding the Egyptian Third Army. In the face of a standoff between the Soviet Union and the U.S. at the U.N. Security Council, a cease-fire was established and the actual fighting came to an end on October 26.

Sadat had certainly accomplished what he wanted in terms of Egyptian national prestige. Even though the Egyptians had not "won" the war they started, their troops had fought bravely and well, and Egyptian honor, many Egyptians felt, had been restored. The subsequent shuttle diplomacy engaged in by U.S. Secretary of State Henry Kissinger led to the first direct Israeli-Egyptian talks since the Israel-Arab armistice of 1949. Even more important, it led to a rapid realignment of Egypt to the West.

In July, President Nixon made a state visit to Egypt, took a train from Alexandria to Cairo with President Sadat and restored the diplomatic relations with Egypt that had been abruptly broken during the Six-Day War in 1967. The sudden new warmth in the U.S. relationship, the promise of generous U.S. aid (more than $50 billion since 1974) and the continuing glow of Egypt's self-styled "victory" energized Sadat to take his most dramatic international gamble yet.

In November 1977, after a flurry of high-profile American TV interviews during which Sadat hinted that he might be willing to talk directly to the Israelis, the Egyptian president flew directly to Tel Aviv, and then to Jerusalem. In the Israeli Knesset, he completely won over his Israeli audience by making a personal commitment to peace with the Jewish state. It was certainly the most dramatic international diplomatic visit by any leader since President Nixon's trip to China in February 1972. (Nixon, whose Egyptian visit in June had done much to boost Sadat's prestige, had long since left the U.S. political scene; he resigned the presidency as a result of the Watergate scandal on August 9, 1974.)

The Sadat visit to Jerusalem was followed up by direct but secret negotiations between Sadat and Israel's Prime Minister Menachem Begin during a tense, 12-day negotiation at the presidential retreat of Camp David in September 1978. The Camp David Accords, signed at the White House on September 17, 1978, led directly to a peace treaty and diplomatic relations between Israel and Egypt in the following year.

The peace treaty was initially very popular in Egypt, where a majority of Egyptians enthusiastically supported it. But Egypt was suspended from the Arab League for 10 years after 1979, for transgressing the Arab states' rule that there must be no relations of any kind between an Arab state and Israel. More ominously, it soon became clear that it was to be a "cold peace." While scores of thousands of Israelis took advantage of peace to plan tourist trips to Egypt, the Egyptian elite, which could have afforded travel to the Jewish state, was markedly more reticent: fewer than 10 percent as many Egyptians returned the tourist favor.

There were other elements spoiling the taste of the relationship. Israel was not as forthcoming on autonomy for the Palestinians living in the West Bank and Gaza as Egyptian negotiators, during and after the Camp David talks, had expected it to be. The Israeli invasion of Lebanon to chase out the PLO in 1982 did not win Israel any friends in Egypt. Old stereotypes of the Israelis as stubborn and aggressive began to appear in the

Egyptian press, and there was even a revival, among some Egyptian intellectuals, of harsh, anti-Semitic opinions.

The Egyptian mood of sourness toward Israel hardened as the Israeli-Palestinian accords seemed to fall apart in the 1990s. One of the most striking outbursts of Egyptian paranoia, however, occurred after the 9/11 terrorist attacks in New York and Washington, DC. Commentaries by Egyptian journalists in establishment newspapers accused Israel of having been behind the September 11, 2001, attacks. Even though 4 of the 19 hijackers were Egyptian, there was a strong reluctance to believe that Mohamed Atta, the leader of the hijacking group, and himself an Egyptian, could possibly have been involved. A rumor that may have started in Egypt, but was certainly fanned by the Egyptian media, held that the Israeli spy agency Mossad had planned the entire 9/11 events in order to embarrass the Arab world. Columnists even maintained with a straight face and without a single piece of evidence, that several thousand New York-based Jews had been warned not to report for work in Manhattan on the morning of September 11, because, supposedly, the Mossad planners of the attacks didn't want them to get killed.

Whether as a reflection of such paranoid rumors, or because of Al Jazeera TV's relentlessly negative portrayal of Israeli treatment of the Palestinians, or because of the continuing standoff between Israel and the Palestinians following the emergence of Hamas, a poll conducted by the Egyptian government in 2006 revealed that 92 percent of Egyptians regarded Israel as "an enemy nation." That sentiment is certainly reinforced by a continuing component of anti-Israeli and even anti-Jewish opinion in the Egyptian media, ranging from Holocaust denial and continuing 9/11 conspiracy theories to ugly cartoon caricatures of Jews as people with hooked noses and devilish expressions on their faces.

The Muslim Brotherhood

That fierce anti-Jewish sentiment was surely built at least partly on Egypt's poor performance in wars with Israel—the exception being the 1973 war—going back to 1949. But it also has its roots in a radical Islamic movement that was founded in Egypt in 1928 and has since spread throughout the Islamic world—the Muslim Brotherhood (MB).

In 1928, an Egyptian schoolteacher, Hassan al-Banna, founded this organization dedicated to restoring global Islam to the purity and power most Muslims associate with the first four caliphs of Islam. The slogan of the Muslim Brotherhood is: "Allah is our objective. The prophet is our leader. Qur'an is our law. Jihad is our way. Dying in the way of Allah is our highest hope."[4] The ultimate goal of the MB is to establish an Islamic caliphate—that is, an Islamic regime ruled by an appointed leader of the community—throughout the world. The caliphate would enforce Islamic law—the *sharia*—universally, and require non-Muslim religions to submit to the caliphate as "dhimmi" (subordinate) communities whose existence is tolerated only by payment of a special *jizya* (tax).

The Muslim Brotherhood officially disavows terrorist violence against civilians, and it has condemned the 9/11 attacks in the U.S. But either it or offshoots of it have been held by many governments as responsible for recruiting Islamists that do subsequently become members of jihadist groups. In Egypt, the Muslim Brotherhood has been technically banned from public life since an attempt on Nasser's life in 1954. Its ideology is aggressively anti-Jewish, and the Egyptian head of the MB, Mohammed Mahdi Akef, has declared the Holocaust to be a "myth." Its Palestine branch, Hamas, even quote in its charter the totally discredited anti-Semitic forgery, *Protocols of the Elders of Zion.*[5]

In the 1980s, a breakaway offshoot of the Egyptian MB, Al-Gama'a al-Islamiya ("The Islamic Group"), began murdering groups of Western tourists visiting Egypt's famous historical sites. But that group's biggest success was in carrying out, or at least organizing, the assassination of President Anwar Sadat on October 6, 1981, the eight-year anniversary of the start of the Yom Kippur War. As Sadat stood up in a reviewing stand to observe army units parading by, an Egyptian army lieutenant, Khalid Islambouli, dismounted from a jeep with three other soldiers and started running toward the reviewing stand with some accomplices. He was shouting, "I have killed the pharaoh!"as he emptied an AK-47 clip at Sadat and other VIPs. In an instant, the man who had made the most courageous diplomatic decision of any leader in the Arab world, paid for it with his life. Two of the assassins were killed on the spot, and the other was arrested on site. Islambouli, and three other fellow conspirators, were executed by firing squad in April the following year.

Mubarak's Iron Grip

Sadat's vice president Hosni Mubarak was himself slightly wounded in the hand during the attack but was officially named as the president to succeed Sadat a few days later.

A former Egyptian air force general who had been trained to fly jet bombers in the Soviet Union, Mubarak was regarded at the time of his becoming president as possibly a transition figure. He was not especially charismatic, was not especially brilliant. But, amazingly, Hosni Mubarak, born in 1928, the same year as the founding of the Muslim Brotherhood, has survived in power 28 years, longer than all but a tiny handful of rulers of Egypt in the country's several-millennia history. He is reported to have survived at least six assassination attempts.

Mubarak's political survival, however, has been more controversial, if less frightening, than his physical one. His position as president was confirmed by majority votes in referenda in Egypt in 1987, 1993 and 1999. The referenda, however, permitted only a "yes" or "no" vote on a continuation of Mubarak, and overwhelmingly pro-government media coverage ensured that any potential arguments for a "no" vote received little attention. But under great pressure from both the Bush administration and international democracy activists to open up Egypt's political system, Mubarak suddenly announced in early 2005 that there would be a referendum to approve a change in the constitution. The presidential election, Mubarak said, would now permit multiple candidates and multiple parties to compete directly with the president. The proposed amendment was passed in May, and elections were held in September 2005.

Not surprisingly, Mubarak won with 88 percent of the vote, and his principal opponent, former member of parliament and founder of the new liberal and democratic El-Ghad ("Tomorrow") Party, Ayman Nour, garnered only 8 percent. Nour founded El-Ghad in 2004 in preparation for the election, and early in 2005 had been arrested by Mubarak's security police. When U.S. Secretary of State Condoleezza Rice cancelled a scheduled visit to Egypt to show her displeasure, Mubarak relented and Nour was released and permitted to take part in the election. He was arrested again, however. On Christmas Eve 2005, he was sentenced to five years' imprisonment for allegedly forging the signature required for the registration of his political party. He was released on February 18, 2009, for health reasons.

Another prominent Egyptian democracy activist, Saad Eddin Ibrahim, might also be in jail if he hadn't seen the writing on the wall in political attitudes toward him and accepted research positions at American think tanks and universities in 2006. Ibrahim, a professor of sociology at the American University in Cairo, had been arrested, in fact, in the year 2000 for allegedly using European Union funds for political purposes. Released in 2003 after multiple appeals and overwhelming foreign pressure on Egypt, Ibrahim continued to work in Cairo at the Ibn Khaldun Center for Development Studies, which he founded in 2008. After a couple of years in the U.S., however, the Egyptian regime slapped a two-year sentence on him in absentia for "defaming Egypt."

But if there is any hope at all for the advent of democracy in the Arab Middle East, it is to be found in many of Ibrahim's ideas. He believes that the autocratic rulers currently in power in most Arab states are able to maintain themselves by warning their own citizens—and the West—that the alternative to them is the rule of Islamists. In most Arab states, most people reluctantly agree that Islamism at the state level would amount to a more severe repression of freedom than continuing autocracy. But Ibrahim argues that though the Islamists—if permitted to run as a political party—would probably gain at least 45 percent of the vote in Egypt in a genuinely free election, "then we democrats have to have confidence that they will discover the world is not black and white, that they too can be pressured, and they too will have to compromise." He adds, "I am not worried about that. I am worried when the West swallows uncritically what the autocrats say."[6]

Ibrahim admits that it would be a gamble if the Islamists were permitted to run for election without restriction. If they won, for example, it might turn out to be a question of "one man, one vote, one time." But Ibrahim says that his conversations with interlocutors in both Hamas in the Palestinian territories and with Hezbollah's leaders give him the impression that the Islamists might be willing to submit to democratic votes even if they thought they would eventually lose. Ibrahim has spoken of the need for a "Magna Carta" meeting in Egypt and other Arab countries in which both secular democrats and Islamists who are opposed to the current autocrats in power would agree definitively to submit to the results of elections.

In fact, Egypt has already sprouted at least one civic consensus association that seeks to open up the country's political system but which does not put forward a specific political platform. It is called the Egyptian Movement for Change. Popularly, however, it is called Kefaya, Arabic for "Enough!" It first appeared at a rally in front of the Egyptian High Court in December 2004. Protesters stood silently with yellow tape over their mouths to protest the difficulty of freely criticizing the government. When they tried a similar protest elsewhere in Cairo the following year, on the occasion of the May referendum to change the constitution about elections, thugs from Egypt's ruling National Democratic Party swept in among them, beating people up and apparently groping some of the female protesters.

Egypt's president Hosni Mubarak was 81 in May 2009. He officially has until 2011 to remain in office because of the 2005 elections. If he should die before then, it is widely believed in Egypt that he will be succeeded in office by his son, Gamal Mubarak (age 46 in 2009), in the same way that Bashar al-Assad acceded to the presidency of Syria when his father died in 2000. Gamal Mubarak has repeatedly denied this and made it clear that he wishes only to remain in his post of deputy secretary general of the ruling National Democratic Party.

Egypt could yet enter another period of social and political turbulence. If it does, then Gamal's prospects of stepping into his father's shoes—whether he wants to or not—will decrease rather than increase. Meanwhile, the Arab world as a whole will continue to look to Egypt for clues as to its future. Egypt—ancient, ramshackle, struggling to stay afloat—is the perpetual wild card of the region. That is why it is always worth watching.

Jordan

No country in the Middle East has more successfully defied dire predictions of its demise or more successfully navigated its way through thickets of war, civil war, assassination and betrayal than Jordan. It has done this, essentially, for the past five and a half decades by dint of the courage, skill, prudence and luck of its long-serving monarch, King Hussein, and his son and successor, Abdullah II. Since King Hussein acceded to the throne of his country in 1953, at the age of 18, he and his son have performed a tour de force of nimble footwork to preserve their state in a singularly unenviable location: between the local regional superpower of Israel on one side, and on three others the conservative Islamist monarchy of Saudi Arabia and the radical, volatile secular states of Syria and Iraq.

An Amazing Story of Survival

The footwork has not been faultless; in June 1967, King Hussein made a nearly fatal error by participating in the Syrian and Egyptian Six-Day War with Israel, losing in the process 6 percent of his kingdom when Israel conquered the West Bank of the Jordan River, which had been Jordanian since 1950.

During the First Gulf War of 1990-1991, he stumbled badly by supporting—though not allying himself with—Iraq's dictator Saddam Hussein. But the king—referred to somewhat cynically by regional foreign correspondents in the 1980s as the PLK ("Plucky Little King"), recovered in both cases from his lurches into radicalism and managed to restore his country to its excellent relations with the U.S. and the West that it had enjoyed throughout most of his reign.

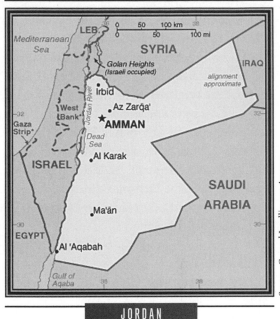

Source: Central Intelligence Agency

JORDAN

The other striking aspect of Jordan's success as an Arab Middle Eastern state has been its ability to maintain strikingly positive—sometimes even warm—relations with Israel at the same time as singing in tune with the predictable chorus of the anti-Zionist Arab fervor of its Arab neighbors. Jordan today remains only the second Arab state to have normal diplomatic relations with Israel. But the truth is that in pragmatic terms, Jordan has consistently cooperated well with Israel during the entire last half-century. Sometimes Israel has acted or spoken in ways that have threatened the stability of Jordan. But at other times, Israel's conduct has saved the day for the Arab monarchy next door.

Like Egypt, Jordan was trampled upon for millennia by the ascendant empires of the Middle East in the era before Christ: Hittites, Akkadians, Persians, Greeks, Romans and, of course, the Egyptians themselves. For hundreds of years it was home to an Arab-speaking civilization aligned with Rome, the Nabateans, whose city carved into solid rock in Petra, in the southern part of Jordan, is one of the most dazzling tourist sites in the entire Middle East.

After the Romans split into Eastern and Western Empires, Jordan fell into the domain of Constantinople, where it remained until waves of expansionist Arab Islamic armies crashed onto its dry domains in the 630s AD. Jordan, like Syria, switched between the Umayyad Dynasty based in Damascus and the newer, more powerful Abbasid Dynasty based in Baghdad throughout 900 years of Arab rule. Then, like the entire region, in 1517 it acquired new rulers, the Ottoman Turks. In Ottoman times what is now the territory of Jordan was carved up into Ottoman regional divisions of vilayets and *sanjaks* that, properly speaking, belonged to the geographical entity of Greater Syria. That all changed during World War I, however, when Britain and France schemed, in what became known as the Sykes-Picot Agreement, to decide what should happen to the Middle Eastern *sanjaks* of the Ottoman Empire once that empire fell, as everyone calculated it would when Germany and the Central Powers had been defeated at the end of the war.

British Influence

By the terms of the Sykes-Picot Agreement of 1916, the area on the east side of the Jordan River, known as Transjordan, fell under the domain of the British. Arab fighters who had sided with the British against the Turks during World War I, however, had played a role in liberating the territory from the Turks. In fact, the Sharif of Mecca, Hussein bin Ali, who claimed to be a direct descendant of Mohammed, had launched the revolt under the impression that the British would reward him after the war by making him the ruler of a large, independent and unified Arab state. Whether the British had ever seriously contemplated that possibility, in the light of the politics of the European powers that surfaced after World War I, they retreated from it.

The great conference to discuss geo-political realities in Europe and the rest of the world after World War I was the 1919 Versailles Peace Conference. King Hussein got nothing from the conference, but his two sons, Emir ("prince") Faisal and Emir Abdullah, were granted by the British, as a sort of consolation prize, two of the large domains they had taken over as conquerors of the Ottomans. Faisal took Iraq and became king of it in 1921. Prince Abdullah became Emir of Transjordan in the same year.

Sovereign Independence Declared

The British were granted a Mandate by the League of Nations for Transjordan, that is, a sort of protective right of supervising the administration of the kingdom. In May 1923, this was turned into a full British recognition of the sovereign independence of Transjordan, with only the state's foreign policy under the control of the British. By the same act of recognition, Transjordan was completely separated from Palestine; Jews could no longer settle on the biblical land of Israel on the East Bank of the Jordan.

In the 1930s the British helped establish Jordan's security force, the Arab Legion, with British officers, and during World War II the Legion played a role in defeating the Vichy French forces—subordinate to the Germans—that controlled Syria. A year after World War II ended, in 1946, Abdullah negotiated an agreement with the British that ended the Mandate and in return assigned certain military base rights to the British. In May of the same year, Abdullah was officially proclaimed king, and his country was renamed the Hashemite Kingdom of Jordan (with "Hashemite" denoting the name of the Hussein family that had ruled Mecca for more than a millennium before being ousted by the Ibn Saud family in 1925).

Left Bank Annexation

Jordan's Arab Legion was one of the five armies that invaded Israel the day after the Jewish state proclaimed independence in May 1948, and Jordanian troops were the only Arab forces that had significant success. During the war they managed to hold on to the Old City of Jerusalem and Arab-inhabited areas on the West Bank of the Jordan. The war ended with a general Israeli victory—the Jewish state had survived—and the Israeli-Jordanian armistice that concluded the end of hostilities between Israel and Jordan was signed in 1949. The following year, Jordan unilaterally annexed the West Bank that it had conquered from Palestine, increasing the size of the Hashemite Kingdom by 2,263 square miles. Jordan now occupied land on both banks of the Jordan River, but only Great Britain and Pakistan recognized the annexation of the West Bank.

Abdullah himself was markedly pro-Western, and his brother, the Emir Faisal who was to become King of Iraq, had conducted in 1919, at the time of the Versailles Conference, a warm exchange of letters with Chaim Weizmann, then head of the Zionist movement, and Felix Frankfurter, Associate Justice of the Supreme Court. To Frankfurter, Faisal wrote in 1919, "We Arabs, especially the educated among us, look with deepest sympathy on the Zionist movement."[7]

He paid for that friendship with his life. During a visit to the El Aqsa Mosque in Jerusalem in July 1951, at Islam's third holiest site, a Palestinian gunman, reportedly connected with the infamous Haji Amin al-Hussayni, stepped up and shot him at point-blank range. He died almost instantly. His 15-year-old grandson, Hussein bin Talal, who was walking beside him, was also hit by a bullet, but it was deflected by a metal medal on his chest.

Hashemite Kingdom Succession

Talal, Abdullah's son, became king but was persuaded to resign within little more than a year because he was suffering from a mental illness described at the time as schizophrenia. Talal's son Hussein had been sent to England for education. He attended the famous British public school (private boarding school) Harrow, Winston Churchill's alma mater, and then briefly went on to the Royal Military Academy Sandhurst, Britain's West Point. In May 1953, still only 17, he was deemed old enough to take the throne, and he began his reign. At the same time, his cousin Faisal II, the son of the emir who had become king of Iraq, was already now king in *his* country. The two were only six months apart in age and had become good friends when Faisal had also attended Harrow.

But the Middle East in the mid-1950s was a region rocked by the volatile combination of Egypt's popular president Gamal Abdel Nasser and a broad upsurge of pan-Arab nationalism in several states of the Arab world. Partly to counter Nasser's pan-Arabism, the British, in 1955, established a treaty organization, modeled on the highly successful NATO, and aimed at mobilizing regional powers alarmed at Nasser's ambitions. It was called CENTO (Central Treaty Organization), or more colloquially, the Baghdad Pact, because its headquarters were in Baghdad. The original members were Iraq, Iran, Pakistan, Turkey and Britain. The U.S. looked on benignly but never formally joined.

The logical idea was that Jordan would join because King Hussein and King Faisal II were cousins and indeed had discussed one day being able to unite their kingdoms. But dangerous rioting broke out in Jordan soon after the Pact was announced, undoubtedly stirred up by Jordanians supportive of what Nasser was trying to accomplish. Hussein wisely decided not to take Jordan into the Pact.

The following year, 1956, he faced a new challenge when Nasserite sentiments brought the National Socialist Party to power in parliamentary elections in Jordan. Meanwhile, the Israeli-British-French attack on Egypt at the end of October 1956—what was to become known as the Suez Crisis—rendered Britain suddenly deeply unpopular throughout the Arab world.

Jordan, in early 1957, felt compelled to end its special relations with the British, losing the large annual subsidy from London but regaining the military bases that it had leased to Britain. Then the new prime minister, the strongly pro-Nasser Sulayman Nabulsi, overplayed his hand. He started planning to establish diplomatic relations with the Soviet Union and acquire Soviet military aid. Nabulsi was suspected by many of wanting to abolish the monarchy and establish a pro-Nasserite republic. This was one challenge too much for Hussein, who exercised his constitutional prerogative and demanded the resignation of the prime minister and his cabinet. In a confusing incident in Amman a few weeks later, rumors spread through the army that Hussein had been killed. Only his appearance at a military base quieted the troops and restored normality to Jordan. The incident demonstrated how fiercely loyal Jordan's largely Bedouin-led army was to the Hashemite monarchy, a relationship that was to prove decisive for the future survival of both the monarchy and Hussein himself.

But the Nasserite threat to the Middle Eastern monarchies was not over, and it was recognized by U.S. Secretary of State John Foster Dulles, who in April 1957 declared that the "independence and integrity of Jordan [was] vital" for the Middle East's stability. Then, in February 1958, Nasser began a sudden new strategic initiative. At the beginning of the month, he proclaimed the formation of the United Arab Republic, the union of Syria and Egypt under one regime. This prompted Hussein and his cousin, Faisal II, to respond on February 14 with the proclamation of the Arab Federation of Iraq and Jordan, an alliance of the two Hashemite monarchies of Jordan and Iraq. Faisal was to be head of state and Hussein deputy head.

Though discussions of what form the federation would take proceeded, other events in the Middle East intervened before plans could be put into effect, as they usually do. Lebanon in the early spring of 1958 was experiencing yet another in its own long string of ethnic tensions when supporters of Nasser's pan-Arabism were demanding that Lebanon align itself with Nasser, not with the West. Lebanon's stability was under great threat. (Those tensions, as we saw in the previous chapter, were to lead to the arrival of U.S. marines to try to stabilize the situation.) But King Hussein, who had experienced serious social disturbances the previous year, was worried that pro-Nasserite demonstrations might lead to strife in Jordan. Accordingly, he appealed to his cousin, King Faisal II, to send a military contingent into Jordan.

That request was an inadvertent signature on Faisal's death warrant. Instead of heading for Jordan, the Iraq military units, commanded by officers sympathetic to Nasser and the Ba'ath Party, staged a coup of their own against Faisal in July 1958. They surrounded the royal palace in Baghdad, accepted the surrender of the king and then ordered him and his family to face the wall of the courtyard of the palace. The coup plotters brutally machine-gunned him, his wife and servants to death and installed a military junta in Baghdad. The young king was just 23 when he died.

Hussein's first response to his cousin's murder was both grief and anger. He was dissuaded by his civilian cabinet from sending troops into Iraq to avenge the murder, but he appealed to both Britain and the U.S. for help because the crisis seemed to threaten the Jordanian monarchy itself. The British sent troops to Amman to help provide a moral and military backing for Hussein, and the U.S. provided an emergency airlift of petroleum. Ironically, to get to Jordan, both the U.S. and Britain had to overfly Jordan's "enemy" Israel, because none of the Arab states would permit over-flights.

King Hussein's government, however, was still far from secure. In August 1960, his pro-Western prime minister Hazza al-Majali was killed by a time bomb concealed in his desk. Four plotters were arrested and hanged, and the evidence of culpability pointed both to Syria and Egypt. Two years after the murder, Hussein secretly sent a special envoy to the chief of intelligence of the Israeli Defense Forces to forewarn him about possible future Jordanian military action against Syria. It was only one of many occasions when senior Jordanian officials—and sometimes the king himself—met secretly with senior Israelis to exchange information and avoid possible misunderstandings.

Jordan's Major Stumble

When the Palestine Liberation Organization was formed on the Mount of Olives in Jerusalem (the part of the city under Jordanian control at the time) in May 1964, its chief sponsor was Nasser's Egypt. It was assumed at the time that Nasser had nurtured the Palestinian organization to be a tool in his own diplomacy of pan-Arabism. But troubles quickly developed for Jordan when PLO guerrilla units began to mount attacks within Israel from bases in the West Bank, without first requesting approval either from Egypt or Jordan.

After the Israelis began responding with military reprisals against West Bank targets—with increasing severity from 1965 onwards—angry West

Bank Palestinians started rioting against the Jordanian government. Syria, meanwhile, which had often planned the PLO assaults, grew increasingly strident against the Jordanian regime.

Whether he felt beleaguered and isolated within the increasingly strident voices of governments in the Arab world, or he simply miscalculated on a grand scale, King Hussein was to make his first major stumble in 1967. President Nasser had mobilized his forces in the Sinai and ordered U.N. observer forces to be withdrawn from Gaza (still in Egyptian hands after the 1948 war), as we saw, on the basis of false Soviet reports that the Israelis were massing troops close to the border with Syria. On May 23, Nasser closed the Straits of Tiran in the Red Sea to Israeli shipping. Israel now mobilized its reserves and the countdown began for a probable major clash.

Egypt, along with Syria, was ratcheting up its anti-Israeli propaganda, and it seemed to many in the Arab world that there would be an Arab military showdown with Israel that the Israelis might lose. In this atmosphere of warlike hysteria, King Hussein flew to Cairo, and on May 30 signed a military alliance with Egypt. The Israelis realized that Jordan might become involved and sent an urgent message to the Jordanians through General Odd Bull, the U.N. Truce Supervision Organization (UNTSO) commander: "This war is between us and the Egyptians. If you don't join in, nothing will happen to you."[8]

But the die had already been cast. The only media reports in the Arab world on what was happening after hostilities began on June 5, 1967, came from Egypt. Radio broadcasts from Cairo were telling Egyptians and the world that 75 percent of the Israeli air force had been destroyed and that Egyptian mechanized columns were heading for Tel Aviv.

Hussein was to ruefully admit later that he had been "misinformed" about the situation. In consequence, on the morning of June 5, the Jordanians began shelling Israeli civilian and military locations around that sector of Jerusalem that was in Israeli hands after the 1948 war. The Israelis immediately counterattacked, destroying most of the small Jordanian air force on its two major airfields. Then they moved to surround Jerusalem and attack Jordanian forces on the West Bank.

By the afternoon of the first day of the war, even Nasser was becoming aware of the military disaster the Arabs were experiencing. In one of the strangest phone conversations in history between two defeated allies—the Arabic conversation was intercepted and recorded by Israeli intelligence—

Nasser called King Hussein very early on June 6, proposing that Jordan and Egypt attribute the crushing defeat of the Egyptian air force to the intervention of Western air forces in the battle. "Shall we say that the United States is fighting on Israel's side?" Nasser asked. "Shall we say the United States and England or only the United States?" "The United States and England," Hussein replied.

Three hours later, Cairo Radio began broadcasting the "news" that carrier-based American and British aircraft had joined the fight against Egypt. As a result, Egypt, Syria, Sudan, Algeria and Yemen promptly severed diplomatic relations with the U.S. There were several attacks against British and American consulates across the region.[9] Interestingly, the king may not have believed Nasser's "explanation" of Egypt's defeat: Jordan coolly maintained full diplomatic ties with both Washington and London. (Of course, neither the U.S. nor Britain had anything to do with the air attacks upon Egypt.)

By June 6, Israeli forces had surrounded Jerusalem, and Israeli paratroopers entered the Old City and captured the Temple Mount and the Western Wall. The young men who fought in this battle were the first Jews to have been able to approach Judaism's most important religious site since Jordan's Arab Legion had captured the Old City in the 1948 war. Meanwhile, Israeli forces swept into the West Bank, captured or destroyed remaining Jordanian units, and advanced as far as the bank of the Jordan River.

None of this had been planned in advance by Israel, which had clearly hoped not to have to fight Jordan at all. The Israeli victory, however, led to another surge of Palestinian refugees eastward, this time to the East Bank of the Jordan and into the remaining portion of Jordan. About 224,000, many of them refugees from the 1948 War, joined the exodus.

The Arab League met in August 1967, in Khartoum, to lick its wounds after the Six-Day War defeat and decide what to do next. It issued a resolution that became famous as "the three noes" declaration: no peace with Israel, no negotiations with Israel, no recognition of Israel. The U.N. Security Council in November unanimously adopted its own diplomatic view of what should now happen. Resolution 242 became one of the most famous of all the Security Council resolutions in the history of the Arab-Israeli conflict. Though most Arab states rejected it outright at first, they have since come to regard certain of its provisions as prerequisites for any peace with Israel. The two main points comprised (a) Israeli withdrawal from "territories occupied in the recent conflict" and (b) "the right [of every state in the area] to live in peace within secure and recognized boundaries free from threats or acts of force" (see appendix A for full text).

The Arabs, naturally, eventually seized upon point (a) to justify their continuing refusal to have any dealings with Israel. For them, Israeli withdrawal from territories captured in the war was a prerequisite of any diplomacy with Israel. By contrast, Israel has repeatedly emphasized that point (b) ("within secure and recognized borders") excuses them from observing point (a) because, they often claim, their withdrawal "from territories occupied" might render their borders "insecure" and "unrecognized." In fact, there is deliberate ambiguity in the text of the Security Council resolution. Lord Caradon, the British representative at the U.N. who crafted it, carefully omitted the word "the" in the phrase "withdrawal from territories occupied in the recent fighting." This meant that the Israelis and everyone else could interpret it as referring to *some* of the captured territories, but not necessarily *all* of them. There is even more ambiguity in the French text—one of the U.N. official languages—because in French *des territoires* means both "from the territories" and "from territories."

In Jordan itself, however, King Hussein had a new headache in the wake of the massive influx of Palestinian refugees from the West Bank: a wave of new attacks against Israel from PLO forces operating out of refugee camps on the East Bank of the Jordan. After one such attack in March 1968, the Israelis mounted a major assault on the village of Karameh on the East Bank, where fighters from Fatah, the largest of the PLO guerrilla forces, were based. As we saw earlier, Fatah put up a surprisingly stiff resistance, and after units of the Jordanian army lent them a hand, the Israelis had to withdraw after sustaining serious losses.

The PLO Moves In

Such morale-boosting accomplishments against the Israelis, however, merely served to embolden the PLO to act as a state-within-a-state inside Jordan. Palestinian guerrillas began setting up checkpoints within Jordan, collecting their own taxes from Palestinian residents of Jordan and refusing to attach Jordanian license plates to their vehicles. They often intimidated and harassed non-Palestinian Jordanians. Some Palestinian groups made unsuccessful attempts to assassinate King Hussein at the very beginning of September 1970. Then, during September 7-9, a PLO group, the Popular Front for the Liberation of Palestine, hijacked five international

airliners (TWA, Swissair, BOAC, El Al and Pan Am) in various locations and
flew four of them to a small airstrip in Jordan. There, the passengers were
deboarded and then the hijackers blew up the airplanes. It was one more
humiliating display of contempt for the Hashemite monarchy of Jordan.

King Hussein reacted vigorously. He declared martial law on September 16, and for the next 10 days his loyal army troops attacked every PLO
military strongpoint in Jordan that they could locate. Two days later, the
Syrians decided to intervene on behalf of the PLO, sending in some 300
tanks, which shelled the outskirts of Amman. Almost panic-stricken by
now, Hussein made a desperate appeal to Washington and London to help.
The U.S. responded by dispatching several ships of the Mediterranean
Sixth Fleet close to the Israeli coast and within easy flying distance of Jordan. But it was actually the Israelis who saved the day. At the urging of the
U.S., the Israeli Air Force made mock bombing over-flights of the Syrian
tank columns, which quickly got the message that they were outgunned
and returned to Syria. Syria, still recovering from the 1967 defeat, was in
no position for an all-out war with Israel.

King Hussein, however, was under heavy pressure from many members of the Arab League to stop attacking the PLO. At a meeting in Cairo,
called by President Nasser, on September 27, the king reluctantly signed an
agreement with the PLO that essentially recognized that organization as
having equal status with the Hashemite Kingdom.

But, as had happened several times previously in his life, Providence
came to Hussein's rescue. The day after Nasser had forced Hussein to accept arbitration, Egypt's president died of a heart attack. Ten days later,
there was a military coup in Syria against the left-wing Ba'ath Party leadership of general Salah Jadid whose decision it had been to send Syrian
tanks into Jordan. Minister of Defense Hafez al-Assad became president of
Syria. He was to become at times a vicious critic and opponent of King
Hussein, but for now he was too busy consolidating his political power in
Damascus to be of any threat to the king. Hussein ordered his military to
resume their assaults on the Palestinian positions.

After the deaths of thousands more civilians in the often intense fighting, there was yet another attempt to negotiate a cease-fire between PLO
forces and the Jordanian army. An agreement at the end of October called
for Arafat to return control of all of Jordan to the king and for PLO fighters to stop walking around in uniform or under arms. There were additional attempts to end the civil war, and Yasser Arafat signed a five-point

agreement in October 1970 to return control of Jordan to the king. But the PFLP (who had planned the plane hijackings) and another PLO group, the DFLP (Democratic Front for the Liberation of Palestine), refused to agree to it. Skirmishes continued and the military position of the PLO began to crumble, though Arafat's propaganda against King Hussein became increasingly shrill.

In June 1971, Arafat actually broadcast a call for the deposition of the king. At this point, the Jordanian army launched a final assault on all PLO military units still holding out in Jordan. Arafat and his lieutenants were forced to relocate their command structure to Lebanon.

"Black September," the PLO terrorist group that took its name from the Jordanian debacle, was quick to attain its own revenge. In Cairo, in November 1971, Black September terrorists gunned down Jordan's fiercely anti-Palestinian prime minister, Wasfi al-Tal. The following year, the group gained its greatest international notoriety by murdering 12 members of the Israeli Olympic team during the summer Olympics in Munich.

A Reclaimed Kingdom

Hussein's resolute and brutal response to the PLO in Jordan saved his monarchy in the civil war and forced the PLO to export its mayhem to yet another Arab state, namely to Lebanon.

By 1973, Jordan had retired from the focus of attention of Arab politics. It was Egypt's turn, under Nasser's successor, Anwar Sadat, to recapture the headlines. This he did in October 1973, with Syrian help, in the devastating surprise attack upon Israel that became known as the Yom Kippur War, or the October War. To his credit, Hussein had learned from his mistake of 1967, and he did not attack Israel directly. He felt pressure to show that he was in "solidarity" with Egypt and Syria, however, and so he sent 3,000 armored troops to Syria to contribute to the Syrian assault on the Golan Heights. Israel was wise enough to understand that a Jordan ruled by King Hussein would be far more palatable than one ruled by any other entity, and so did not counterattack against Jordan once the tide had turned in its favor on the Golan Heights fighting.

The following year, pressure from other Arab states was again directed at Jordan. At the Arab League summit in Rabat, Morocco, in September 1974, there was a unanimous resolution declaring that the PLO was "the sole legitimate representative of the Palestinian people." As a member of the Arab League, Jordan signed the declaration, thereby categorically renouncing any right to speak for Palestinians. With the stroke of a pen, the king also abrogated his 1950 annexation of the West Bank. It was now "totally inconceivable" for Jordan to envisage any kind of associate relationship or confederation with a future Palestinian entity. As recognition of this major concession, King Hussein was assured of an annual support to his kingdom of $300 million in oil subsidies, to come mostly from Saudi Arabia.

Yasser Arafat continued his international comeback after the Black September humiliation by having the PLO officially recognized by the U.N. and by being invited to speak at the U.N. General Assembly in 1975. This he did with characteristic swagger by speaking at the podium with a pistol in a holster on his hip. Back in his own kingdom, however, King Hussein insisted that the Palestinians living in the Hashemite Kingdom must choose between Jordanian and Palestinian citizenship. They already numbered about 900,000 people, by then a majority of Jordan's population.

By the late 1970s, the initiative in the Arab world had returned to Egypt, which was basking in the new warmth of diplomatic relations with the U.S. and significant aid from it. The Camp David Accords of 1978 caught Jordan off balance, and the king expressed annoyance that he had not been included in the negotiations. He nevertheless had expressed interest in the diplomacy being conducted. Thus, when the Arab League convened in Baghdad in November 1978, Egypt was punished by being expelled from the Arab League and by having the Cairo headquarters of the League moved to Tunis. Jordan, by contrast, was wooed with the blandishment of a $9 billion fund, to be paid over several years, to induce it to remain part of the overall Arab solidarity in opposition to what Egypt had done at Camp David.

When the Arab-Israeli peace treaty went ahead anyway, Jordan initially recalled its ambassador from Cairo, and then cut off its behind-the-scenes diplomatic contacts with Israel. It now had a new fear from Israel: senior Likud Party representatives were beginning to discuss in public the notion that "Jordan is Palestine." In March 1979, then Israeli Minister of Agriculture, Ariel Sharon, proposed the idea that the Palestinians take over Jordan and form their state there. This was a crude challenge to the Hashemite Kingdom; King Hussein deeply feared that his own domestic Palestinians might indeed at some point attempt to dismantle his state, as they had back in 1970.

Hussein remained within the Arab consensus against Camp David, but his diplomatic efforts to resolve the Palestinian issue within an alternative framework to Camp David, perhaps through the U.N., were rejected by the other Arab League members.

Meanwhile, Jordan's relations with Syria had grown increasingly acrimonious. The al-Assad regime had been in the throes of an intense struggle against Muslim Brotherhood terrorism since 1978, and there is little doubt that some of the Muslim Brotherhood efforts had been aided by Islamist sympathizers in Jordan. The following year, 1979, was dominated in the Middle East by the overthrow of the Shah of Iran and the coming to power in that country of the Ayatollah Khomeini. When Iraq invaded Iran in September 1980—the war was to last eight years—Jordan drew significantly closer to the Saddam Hussein regime, making its Red Sea port of Aqaba available for Iraq's foreign imports and becoming the most outspoken public supporter of Iraq in the war with Iran.

Once again, developments elsewhere in the Middle East created new opportunities for Jordan. Israel invaded Lebanon in June 1982, and by the autumn forced the PLO to relocate from Beirut to Tunis. In September, when President Reagan introduced a new peace plan under which, as the plan stated, "it was the firm view of the United States that self-government by the Palestinians of the West Bank and Gaza, in association with Jordan, offers the best chance for a durable and lasting peace" between Israel and the Palestinians, Jordan showed interest. So did the PLO, which had been weakened by its setback in Lebanon and needed the help of a moderate Middle Eastern state to regain diplomatic leverage. But despite negotiations between Jordan and the PLO to present a common program in any future peace talks, the idea of partnership didn't come to fruition.

As the 1980s drew to a close, Jordan's relationship with Iraq continued to draw closer as the Iran-Iraq war dragged on and as most of the Arab world was united in backing the Saddam regime against Iran. Jordan's relations with Syria were increasingly strained and the al-Assad regime called openly for the overthrow of King Hussein. Syria itself drew closer to Iran, Iraq's enemy.

Iraq had supplied Jordan with considerable support in revenues and petroleum exports. In effect, Iraq had emerged as the major Arab regional player with which Jordan felt comfortable. This explains why Jordan took—to many Western observers—a nearly incomprehensible position of supporting Iraq when, in the summer of 1990, Iraq invaded and occupied

Kuwait. Jordan not only refused to join the broad Arab consensus, which included Egypt as well as Syria, to condemn Iraq, but also opposed the deployment of U.S.-led coalition forces on Saudi Arabian soil during the second half of 1990, as preparations built up for Operation Desert Storm. King Hussein was under two forms of pressure to remain loyal to Iraq. One was Iraq's continuing petroleum and financial backing of Jordan. The other was the immense popularity of Saddam Hussein in Jordan. When the Coalition airstrikes against Iraqi targets began in January 1991, the Jordanian media blasted them as a brutal onslaught against an Arab and a Muslim people. In February, the Jordanian media lambasted the U.S. for its all-out ferocious war on Iraq.

The U.S. administration of President George H. W. Bush expressed displeasure with the Jordanian position but was willing to reconcile quickly with its old ally once the war had come to an end and Iraqi forces had been withdrawn from Kuwait. But Jordanian relations with Saudi Arabia took awhile to recover, and those with Kuwait took even longer.

The Oslo Accords

Jordan didn't have the luxury of much time to reflect on its blunder in supporting Iraq. By June it was faced with a new diplomatic challenge when the American Secretary of State, hoping to take advantage of the new U.S.-Arab comity in the wake of the successful conclusion of the Gulf War, convened the Middle East Peace Conference in Madrid. This was the first time since the armistice talks of 1949 that Israeli diplomats had sat directly across the table from their Arab opposite numbers.

Though King Hussein had met secretly in London in January 1991 with Israeli Prime Minister Yitzhak Shamir, he had come to accept that Jordan was no longer a principal player in Israeli-Palestinian relations. Thus it was with great shock that the king learned of the success of the Oslo Accords in the summer of 1993, which were the culmination of secret negotiations between Israelis and Palestinians. King Hussein attended the formal White House ceremony of the signing of the Declaration of Principles by Arafat and Rabin, but he remained frustrated that he had been kept out of a process that might ultimately entail a political resolution of the status of the West Bank, former Jordanian territory.

With the encouragement of the U.S., however, Jordan warmed up to Israel as the Oslo Accords initially bore fruit with the withdrawal of Israeli forces from Palestinian towns on the West Bank. The leaders of the PLO, moreover, returned to Palestinian territory from Tunis. Israel had also now abandoned what the Jordanians had termed "the alternative homeland conspiracy" of asserting that Jordan was Palestine. At the time of the Oslo Accords in 1993 Israel's foreign minister Shimon Peres had told the king, "Jordan is Jordan and Palestine is Palestine." This helped induce the king to recognize the momentum of Israeli-Palestinian comity and to establish Jordan's diplomatic relations with Israel in October 1994.

Israel's leaders at the time of the Oslo Accords, of course, had belonged to Israel's Labor Party, with whose prime minister Hussein had long enjoyed cordial, though necessarily secret, relations. Thus when Likud Party politician Binyamin Netanyahu won the Israeli elections in 1996, it was a difficult adjustment for Hussein. Netanyahu reiterated to the king that he didn't support the "Jordan is Palestine" idea, but his sometimes brusque manner and forceful, even opinionated way of expressing himself made the relationship tense at times.

The Continuance of the Monarchy

In February 1999, King Hussein died after years of battle with non-Hodgkin's lymphoma. In the last weeks of his life, aware of his impending demise, he had removed from his brother Hassan the title of crown prince, which Hassan had held since 1965. The king wanted to be sure that his own son Abdullah succeeded him to the throne

Born to Hussein's second wife, the Englishwoman Antoinette Avril Gardner, who became a Muslim and changed her name to Princess Muna, Abdullah was a chip off the old block. Educated at private schools in England and the U.S. (Deerfield Academy), Abdullah had briefly attended Pembroke College, Oxford, and then Sandhurst Military Academy, where his father had been trained.

While King Hussein flew planes, Abdullah parachuted from them, raced fast cars and was a scuba diver. By the time his father died, moreover, Abdullah had received a graduate degree in international relations at Georgetown University in Washington, had been promoted to major general and was in command of Jordan's special forces. He was married (for the second time) to a woman of Palestinian origin, Queen Rania al-Abdullah. He was well placed both to keep Jordan firmly pro-Western and at the same time to pursue domestic policies calculated to retain his popularity at home.

He increased Jordan's direct foreign investment, opened new trade zones and continued strong investment in education. Adult literacy early in the third millennium was 90 percent, one of the highest in the Arab world. Already by the end of the 1980s, Jordan had more students in tertiary education than any country except the U.S. Abdullah II, as he became, broadened access to medical care for Jordanian citizens in rural areas, but also devoted much of his energy to attempting to broker Middle East peace in general.

During 2006, he tried to arrange a cease-fire between Israel and Hezbollah, and the previous year he had met with Pope Benedict XVI to attempt to bridge the gap between Muslims and Christians.

By 2009, the king was demonstrating as deft a hand at the tiller of Jordan's ship of state as his father had (with two exceptions) demonstrated during a 46-year reign. The country continues to be, in many ways, a model of a country that pays attention to the views of its inhabitants and seeks to avoid all political extremes.

THE PERSIAN (BUT REALLY ARABIAN) GULF

Like the term "Middle East," "Persian Gulf" is itself a challenge to seman-tic peaceful coexistence among nations. The correct geographic term for this vast, gangling-arm, inland sea extension of the Indian Ocean is Persian Gulf. The United Nations, normally reluctant to offend multiple differ-ent countries, has dug its heels in and insisted that the term "Persian Gulf" be applied to all official references to the region.

The alternative, of course, would be "Arabian Gulf," which the states of the Arab Middle East insist on using as their preferred term. Historians and geographers might point out that history and logic is on the side of "Persian Gulf." This is so not only because Iran's southern border takes up the entire length of the Gulf's northern coast and because Iran's pop-ulation of 75 million outnumbers all the Arabs together living in the dif-ferent states along the shore facing Iran. It is also true because, for several hundred years, Iran was the dominant regional power, exercising its influ-ence and control over chunks of the Arab world opposite its own Gulf coast borders. Without a doubt the Arab states facing Iran are so reluc-tant to use the word "Persian" in reference to the Gulf because modern Iran seems bent on reasserting its influence in the Middle East.

The tension between Iran and the Arab Gulf states is real, just as is the tension of many Arab Shia communities in the overwhelmingly Sunni Is-lamic states in which they live. If the mini-states that dot the Arabian side of the Persian Gulf continue to thrive and prosper, however, it will be in large measure due to a legacy they neither sought nor initially wanted. This was the historical fact that, in the nineteenth century, it was ex-tremely important to Britain that the Persian Gulf be an orderly place. It was from Britain that the Gulf's mini-states acquired their independence, and it was British common sense and good order that enabled their economies, societies and politics to be launched fully upright into a turbulent part of the world.

Britain's lengthy role as the major power-player in the Persian Gulf began about the time when the Gulf became an important way station on the trade route to British India. It is true that there had been rivalry among European powers operating from the sixteenth century onward in the Gulf: the Portuguese, the Dutch and the British. The Portuguese were the first of the European powers to enter the Gulf forcefully, not least because Portuguese navigators had pioneered the Atlantic route around the Cape of Good Hope to India and places in Asia beyond. The Portuguese and all subsequent foreign powers to explore the Gulf routinely referred to the Arab side of the Gulf as "the pirate coast." The small islands and nooks and crannies of the Arabian peninsula coast were thick with shipborne merchants and corsairs—the terms were sometimes interchangeable—who made passage through the area hazardous for outsiders. In many instances, the pirates added to their zeal for plunder a serious religious component: they had been infected with the zeal for Islamic jihad (literally "struggle") by the puritanical zeal of the Wahabbis who took over Saudi Arabia in the eighteenth century.

It wasn't until Britain's Royal Navy started entering the Gulf in force (partly to suppress the slave trade) that the inland sea began to quiet down.[1] Eager to establish the *pax Britannica* in an area dangerously close to the trade routes to India, the British began to negotiate with the sheikhdoms along the coast to suppress piracy. In 1820, the British signed their first official treaty with some of the sheikhdoms. Their Arab interlocutors said they would agree to keep piracy down in return for British naval protection of their domains against any outside powers. The treaties were described as being with the "Trucial Coast," by which the small sheikhdoms were recognized. By the end of the nineteenth century, Great Britain had become the undisputed hegemon of affairs within the Persian Gulf, its political agents and advisors to the individual sheikhs helping provide judgment in domestic administration and international recognition in the world beyond.

At the northernmost end of the Gulf are the two most populous states in the Gulf, Iraq and Iran (which will be discussed in detail in a later chapter). For eight years, from 1980 until 1988, these two large and powerful countries slogged it out in an ultimately inconclusive war whose infantry casualty rates rivaled those of Europe during World War I. In many respects, the war represented a conflict between two completely different views of how the Middle East should develop. On the one hand was the leftist, pro-Soviet, secular Arab nationalism of Iraq, a Stalinist dictatorship. On the other was a resurgent Shia Muslim revolutionism that had taken over Iran in 1979. But the conflict in a larger sense evoked more ancient animosities between Persia and the Arab world, animosities that preceded the rise of Islam.

The Gulf States

The Gulf states represent something of an anomaly in the Arab world: small, well-governed kingdoms uniformly committed to the continuation of hereditary monarchical rule, but in some respects less conservative, more outward-looking, better integrated into the business and cultural affairs of the modern world than republics like those of Egypt or Syria that have existed far longer. This chapter will consider them all, from Kuwait at the northernmost end of the Gulf down to Oman at the southern entrance to the Indian Ocean. It will also discuss Yemen, not a Gulf state but possibly the most ancient, and certainly the poorest, state on the Arabian peninsula.

Kuwait

Most people above the age of 30 are familiar with Kuwait for at least one reason: in the first two months of 1991, the U.S. led a 34-nation military coalition to liberate the country from the Iraqis, who had invaded, occupied and annexed it in August 1990. With an overwhelming demonstration of high-tech pyrotechnics and military precision, the U.S. and its allies overwhelmed the Iraqi occupiers and drove them back across the border into Iraq, but not before the defeated and retreating Iraqis engaged in a massive act of environmental vandalism by setting fire to nearly 700 oil well heads. The oil fires took several months to extinguish completely.

Source: Central Intelligence Agency

KUWAIT

Some 12 years later, in 2003, Kuwait repaid the courtesy of the earlier rescue by the U.S. when it provided the staging and launching ground for Operation Iraqi Freedom, the U.S.-led invasion of Iraq. Since the first Gulf War, American troops had enjoyed massive support facilities and training areas in the vast desert areas of Kuwait, having complete liberty in as much as 60 percent of Kuwait's total land area of 6,880 square miles, or a space approximately the size of Connecticut (or Israel). Imagine 60 percent of New Jersey being made available to a foreign power. Kuwait has provided the entry and exit route for personnel, equipment and supplies moving into Iraq ever since the war began in 2003. The country can easily handle 100,000 American troops in the country at any one time with ordinary Kuwaitis hardly noticing.

Not surprisingly, because it is still grateful for liberation from the brutal Iraqi troops of Saddam Hussein, Kuwait is probably the most pro-American of any Arab state, with 54 percent of Kuwaitis saying that the U.S. was a "dependable" ally (a figure which compares favorably with the 48 percent of Saudis who think this). Kuwaitis are also exceptionally wealthy, with the eleventh highest per capita GDP in the world (at $39,849). They enjoy high ranking among countries in the category of Quality of Living index. Mercer's annual global Quality of Living Survey placed Kuwait City, within whose surrounding 77.2 square miles some 88 percent of all Kuwaitis live, in 125th place out of a total of 215 global cities reported on. The survey asks executives of multinational corporations to rate cities by an evaluation of 39 criteria, ranging from political and personal safety factors to health, education and public transport. Not surprisingly, Baghdad was at the absolute bottom of the list (215), while Vienna and Zurich were at the top (1 and 2). In the Middle East, Tel Aviv was 103 and Tehran—not counting Baghdad—was at 178.[2]

Kuwait's wealth, of course, derives from its oil. Its national petroleum reserves amount to approximately 10 percent of the global total, and it produces approximately 2.7 million barrels of oil per day. Some 90 percent of Kuwait's citizens work in the public sector, and the government provides a generous social welfare network of education, medical and other services. Kuwait's population of approximately 3.4 million, however, includes only 1.05 million Kuwaiti citizens, a ratio of foreign workers to Kuwaitis of more than 3:1. Though 85 percent of all the residents of Kuwait are Muslim, the enormous community of foreign workers includes large numbers of South Asians, many of whom are Hindu, Buddhist or Christian. Of the native-born Kuwaitis, 70 percent are Sunni Muslim and 30 percent Shia Muslim, an indication of the influence upon Kuwait of the proximity of Iran just across the top of the Gulf.

A location for pearl fishers and shipbuilders in the ancient world, the modern community of Kuwait was not founded until tribes from what is now Saudi Arabia moved north and settled there. The ancestor of today's Kuwait royal family, Sabah Ibn Jabar, established his tribal presence in Kuwait in the middle of the eighteenth century. Kuwait then became a flourishing commercial community dealing in the trade of pearls, spices, dates, horses and wood from India. Technically, it fell within the Ottoman Empire province on Basra, but in 1899, the then emir of Kuwait, Sheikh Mubarak Al-Sabah—"the Great"—signed a treaty with Great Britain pledging himself, in return for British protection, neither to cede territory nor deal with any foreign power without British consent.

When Mubarak died in 1915, Kuwait's population was around 35,000 and its chief commercial activity was shipbuilding, using Indian wood. All of Kuwait's subsequent rulers have descended directly from the sons of Mubarak, notably the long-reigning Ahmed Jabir Al Sabah, who ruled Kuwait from 1921 to 1950 and whose reign coincided with the discovery of oil. At the end of World War I, with the defeat of the Ottoman Empire, Kuwait's status as a British protectorate quite separate from Iraq seemed to be confirmed.

That proved to be a mixed blessing. After Kuwait became independent of Great Britain in 1961, its oil resources attracted the covetous attention of Iraq. The conglomeration of provinces of the Ottoman Empire that included Iraq had been controlled by the British from 1918 until Britain granted independence in 1932, and then again, after Iraq threatened to ally itself with Nazi Germany, from 1941 until 1947.

When the Iraq monarchy was reinstated, it lasted until a military coup overthrew it and installed a left-wing military regime in 1958. At this point, the Iraqis began to dispute Kuwait's right to be independent of them, and seemed to threaten invasion. The speedy arrival of British troops in 1961 deterred Iraq from moving on Kuwait—at least for another three decades or so.

Meanwhile, when Iraq decided to try to overthrow the newly formed Islamic Republic of Iran under Ayatollah Khomeini by invading in 1980, it received substantial financial support from Kuwait, building up a total debt of $65 billion by 1988 when the war ended. Resentment at what it owed Kuwait was a huge factor in the action. In addition, the Iraqis' complaint that Kuwait had forced down oil prices by flooding the market with crude and was conducting "slant drilling" into Iraq's Rumaila oil field deteriorated into a war of words between the two countries. Finally, in August 1990, Iraq decided it would deal with Kuwait by force. It invaded the country wholesale, occupied it, then annexed it and declared that the country was Iraq's nineteenth province.

The occupation was brutal; around 1,000 Kuwaiti civilians lost their lives after the takeover, and there are still 600 Kuwaitis unaccounted for since the beginning of the occupation in August 1990. These Kuwaitis were never heard from again after the liberation of the country from the Iraqis on February 26, 1991.

The U.N. responded to the invasion with a series of Security Council resolutions condemning it, then issued a final ultimatum that demanded Iraq quit Kuwait by January 15, 1991, failing which U.N. Security Council members would employ "all necessary measures" (military force) to compel it to withdraw.

The war started on January 17, 1991, with a sustained aerial bombing campaign against Iraqi positions in Kuwait and strategic targets within Iraq itself. Hundreds of aircraft from several countries in the 34-nation coalition—but principally from the U.S. and Great Britain—flew sorties around the clock for days, pounding the Iraqi troops into dazed submission. Some Iraqi ground units actually surrendered to American helicopters. The ground offensive that followed on February 22 was an invasion of Kuwait from Saudi Arabia and lasted only four days; President George H. W. Bush ordered a cease-fire after it was obvious the Iraqis had left Kuwait and were beaten, and before Coalition ground troops had a chance to extend their conquest deep inside of Iraq itself.

When the war was over, it took Kuwait two years and $50 billion to restore its economy to the production level it had reached before the Iraqi invasion. Much of that time was spent repairing the damage to oil installations set on fire by retreating Iraqi troops. Not surprisingly, many Kuwaitis still nurture a deep resentment of Iraq, unmollified by the 5 percent of Iraqi oil production assigned to Kuwait to compensate for the damage inflicted on Kuwait during the Iraqi occupation.

Though Kuwait is a hereditary monarchy—Kuwaitis say "emir" rather than "king"—Kuwait has a thriving parliament. There are 50 elected representatives; and approximately 33 belong to opposition groupings, including 21 members who are Islamist in their thinking. They cannot vote the ruling family out of office, but members of parliament are permitted to question government ministers, which means they can delay legislation the government wants to pass. The Kuwaiti media is substantially free, though they need to exercise caution in reporting on the ruling emir's family. In August 2007, a Kuwaiti journalist was arrested for insulting the emir in an online posting. He was quickly released after Kuwait-wide protests.

Kuwait, in some respects, is a model—at least in the Arab world—of moderation in interreligious affairs and in Islamist v. secular coexistence. The Islamists in parliament have not pushed for imposing *sharia* on Kuwait, and there is no contingent of *mutawwa* (morals police), as in Saudi Arabia, ready to swipe long canes at the ankles of women who are considered to be insufficiently covered up. Unlike the situation in Saudi Arabia, women in Kuwait are allowed to drive; and since 2005, they have been permitted to vote in parliamentary elections. Still, there is a broad national respect for Islamic traditional practices. During the annual Muslim fasting month of Ramadan all restaurants close during the daytime hours, and even in luxury hotels it is difficult to encounter either gambling or mixed dancing. That said, when the government recently switched the official weekend from Thursday and Friday to Friday and Saturday, in order to align more closely to the weekly timetable of most of the modern world, there was little vocal objection.

The main problem of governance in Kuwait is not a lack of free speech or other civic liberties, but the foot-dragging of the more traditionalist and Islamist Kuwaitis in parliament in agreeing to approve major new national infrastructure projects. The Kuwaiti government since 1982 has deposited 10 percent of its income into a reserve fund designed to provide a soft landing for the economy when the country's oil reserves eventually run out. It is called the Fund for Future Generations. The problem is that parliament has been slow to authorize needed infrastructure improvements or the licensing of tracts of potential gas fields in the north of the country for exploration by foreign corporations. This reluctance by parliament to approve new projects flies in the face of Kuwaiti public opinion that, by larger than two-thirds majority (68 percent), says it approves of "large foreign companies."[3] In April 2007, Prime Minister Nasser al-Mohammed al-Sabah said that he would present Project Kuwait, the long-anticipated Kuwaiti national infrastructure project, to parliament in the next two months. It's been a long two months since then.

Kuwait has nothing to fear from Iraq as long as the Americans are present there in significant numbers. Yet Kuwaiti officials worry whether the eventual departure of American troops from Iraq (by 2011, according to President Obama's latest timetable) will lead to a new eruption of Iraqi domestic unrest that will, willy-nilly, spill over into their own country. Kuwait's desert border with Iraq is very porous.

A bigger worry, however, is Iran. Though Kuwait has publicly maintained cordial relations with Tehran—bearing in mind its significant Shia minority—it knows that a militant and expanding Iran could quickly threaten both Kuwait's domestic security and its relations with the U.S.

Iran's nuclear reactor at Bushehr is only about 194 miles from Kuwait. If the U.S., Israel or any other foreign power decided to attack Iran's nuclear facilities, U.S. forces bases would be vulnerable to Iranian regional retaliation in Kuwait, and Kuwait's own infrastructure would be at serious risk. Particularly worrisome for Kuwaitis is the difficulty of protecting from Iranian missile attack their water desalination plants, which are crucial to the physical needs of its people.

By a convenient coincidence, Kuwait's current Prime Minister Nasser al-Mohammed al-Sabah knows Iran better than most senior Gulf Arabs, having served as ambassador there at the beginning of the Khomeini revolution in 1979. He speaks fluent Farsi and may have a better feel for Iranian future actions than Kuwaitis without that experience. Kuwait, says one recent study of the country's domestic and external situation, "like other Arab Gulf states, will discreetly advocate sustaining a very robust U.S. military presence in its vicinity, including a continuing commitment to Iraq sufficient to keep that country from disintegrating or falling into the hands of Iran."[4]

Bahrain

Some two miles south of the southernmost border of Kuwait is a flyspeck of an island among an archipelago of small islands in the Persian Gulf called Bahrain. Only 257 square miles in area—about five-sixths the size of New York City—and with a population of about three-quarters of a million people, Bahrain has the distinction of having the freest economy in the entire Middle East (Israel is in second place) and the sixteenth freest economy in the world. The Washington, DC-based Heritage Foundation, which annually surveys global economic conditions from the perspective of economic freedom, gives Bahrain a score of 74.8 percent. The survey ap-

praises such items as trade freedom, property rights, labor freedom and taxation issues.[5] In 2008,
moreover, London's Global Financial Centres' Index named Bahrain
as the region's fastest-growing
financial center. Bahrain is also a
prolific source of publishing in
the Arab world, with far more titles
per head of population that exists
for other parts of the Arab world.

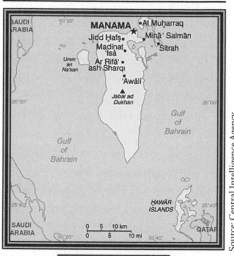

BAHRAIN

Source: Central Intelligence Agency

Bahrain was one of the Trucial States that benefited by being
protected by Great Britain when
the British were still the dominant power not just in the Per-
sian Gulf but the entire Middle East. A constitutional monarchy ruled
by a king, with a prime minister who is also a member of the royal family (as are about 80 percent of the cabinet), Bahrain prior to the arrival
of the British had come under varieties of Arab rule, the Portuguese (for
80 years, from 1521 to 1602), and then the Persians when that country's
Safavid dynasty broadly expanded Persian power during the seventeenth
century.

Bahrain's miniscule population of 708,573 includes about 235,000
non-Kuwaitis and is by reputation more tolerant and socially liberal than
both Kuwait and Bahrain's neighbor to the south, Qatar. As many as 10
percent of residents say they are Christian. In the early nineteenth century,
Bahrain briefly came under the control of both the Wahabbis, who were expanding their control beyond the borders of Arabia and the Omanis. But
the current ruling Al Khalifa family was already in political control of
Bahrain at the time of the 1820 Trucial States' treaty with the British, and
the British strongly influenced the governance of Bahrain until it became
independent in 1971. By then, petroleum had been discovered, and though
Bahrain today has one of the fastest-growing and rapidly diversifying
economies in the world, petroleum exports even today account for about
60 percent of the country's export receipts. Bahrain was the first Gulf state
to sign a free trade agreement with the U.S., a commercial agreement that
was later imitated by Oman.

Bahrain, though an island, is connected to Saudi Arabia by a causeway constructed in 1986, and is thus frequently visited by Saudis wishing to spread their social wings a little outside the heavy social controls of their own society. Women are allowed to drive, as in Kuwait, and were also accorded the right to vote in 2002. But the links to Arabia have been historically turbulent.

In the year 899, two-and-three-quarter centuries into the emergence of Islam, a utopian, millenarian Islamic sect called the Qarmatians, a Shia group opposing the Sunni caliph in Baghdad, seized power in eastern Arabia and instituted a brief reign of terror over what is now Bahrain and eastern Arabia. They massacred thousands of Muslim travelers en route to Mecca to perform the Muslim pilgrimage, raided Mecca in the year 930 and then removed the Muslim sacred black stone that is part of the Ka'aba, the focus of Islamic devotion in Mecca. They held the stone for about 22 years until the Abbasid dynasty in Baghdad recovered it by paying a huge ransom. When it was returned by the Qarmations, it was delivered in a sack and hurled into a mosque in Kufa, about 100 miles south of Baghdad. Some Islamic scholars believe that the black stone's broken condition—about seven separate pieces cemented together with a silver frame—dates from this period. Under plans for eventual construction is a gigantic bridge—which, when completed, will be the longest in the world at 25 miles—connecting Bahrain with its nearest non-Saudi Gulf State neighbor, Qatar.

Qatar

Yet another hereditary monarchy, which for several decades nestled under the protecting wings of the British, is Qatar (pronounced, approximately, *cut-tar*). It extends as a peninsula 100 miles north into the Gulf from the coast of Saudi Arabia. Though much larger than Bahrain and about the size of Connecticut, Qatar used to be controlled by Bahrain. In fact, when the Qataris revolted against Bahrain's ruling Al Khalifa clan and the clan once again conquered Qatar, the British, supervising the external affairs of all the Trucial States, slapped Bahrain on the wrist and arranged for the separation of Qatar from Bahraini control. That was in 1867. It wasn't until 1916, however, that Qatar acquired the official status of a British protectorate.

Britain had granted independence to Kuwait in 1961, and by the late 1960s was announcing plans to quit the Gulf completely. This prompted

Qatar and Bahrain to join seven of the Trucial States in attempting to form a new federation in the Gulf. Before an agreement
could be crystallized, however, both Bahrain
and Qatar decided to go their own way and
the United Arab Emirates came into existence at the end of 1971 without them.

Qatar, according to the International
Monetary Fund, has (after Luxembourg
and Norway) the third highest per capita
income of any country in the world at
$93,204.[6] It has an important connection
with the U.S. because United States Central Command, a theater-level command
of the U.S. military, has its forward headquarters in Qatar. CENTCOM is responsible
for U.S. military efforts in Iraq and Afghanistan, and there are actually military units
based in Kuwait and Bahrain, as well as
Qatar. The commander of Centcom is General David Petraeus, who achieved wide

Source: Central Intelligence Agency

QATAR

recognition for the success of the "surge" operation against insurgents
in Iraq.

Another of Qatar's claims to prominence: Its capital, Doha, is the
headquarters of Al Jazeera, the news and current affairs satellite channel
that is broadly popular throughout the Arab world. Al Jazeera, which literally means "the island" (as Qatar is sometimes known), is watched by
satellite in the Arabic language by 40 million to 50 million people, and in
English by approximately 100 million.

Al Jazeera got its start in 1996 with a grant of $150 million from the
Emir of Qatar, Sheikh Hamad bin Khalifa. The Sheikh, who had himself
come to power by conducting a bloodless coup against his father in 1995,
during the latter's vacation in Switzerland, clearly felt secure enough to
provide seed money for what was to become a satellite TV news service of
wide influence. Early reporting staffers included BBC World Service Arabic-
language TV journalists who had faced difficulties operating a Saudi-
owned TV station in Saudi Arabia. In fact, because there was almost no
independent Arabic-language news service throughout the Arab world,

there was a great hunger in most Arab countries for TV reporting that was not completely controlled by one or other of the Arab governments.

Al Jazeera sprang into global prominence after the 9/11 attacks, when its reporters were able to obtain and air the first statements being issued by the Al-Qaeda chief Osama bin Laden. Later, Al Jazeera reporters encountered difficulties after the U.S.-led invasion of Iraq in March 2003, when both American military authorities and officials of the post-Saddam Iraqi government suspected them of showing sympathy for Iraqi insurgent actions against both the Americans and Iraqi security forces. Both Vice President Dick Cheney and Secretary of Defense Donald Rumsfeld accused Al Jazeera of being "irresponsible" and "misleading."[7]

In 2007, an Iraqi official, Ayad Allawi, accused Al Jazeera of reporting unfairly on the internal situation in Iraq because, when U.S. forces were battling to capture from insurgents the Iraq town of Fallujah, an Al Jazeera reporter based inside the town "relentlessly focused his camera on the civilian casualties and the destruction that was being visited on the town."[8] The Al Jazeera office in Baghdad was actually closed for a while in 2004. American military press officials have also made it clear at times that Al Jazeera reporters were not welcome in Iraq. Israelis have also complained that, during the 2006 war with Hezbollah forces in Lebanon and the 2009 Israeli incursion into Gaza, Al Jazeera coverage lopsidedly favored Palestinians.

In fact, during the Israeli Gaza incursion, it was the Egyptian government, not Israel, that prevented two senior Al Jazeera journalists from entering Gaza. Egyptian officials gave no explanation for the entry denial, but Al Jazeera was critical of Egypt's opposition to Hamas. One of the two Al Jazeera representatives, Ghassan Ben Jido, head of the Al Jazeera office in Lebanon, had produced a TV special in 2008 and given a reception honoring a Palestinian terrorist who had just been released from an Israeli prison and returned to Lebanon as part of a prisoner exchange between Lebanon and Israel. The terrorist, Samir Kuntar, had murdered Israeli civilians in cold blood during a PLO operation in northern Israel in 1979. The director general of Al Jazeera later admitted that parts of that program had "violated" Al Jazeera's Code of Ethics.[9]

Al Jazeera, however, is careful to avoid offending the emir of Qatar or his relatives. Even TV journalists with an agenda, it seems, are reluctant to bite the hand that feeds them.

Though many Americans—and certainly Israelis—find the viewpoint of Al Jazeera distasteful because it seems to relentlessly promote the Palestinian perspective in the Arab-Israeli dispute, and because it often voices the views of conservative, and even radical Islamist clerics, the TV network has done several positive things. One was to air an interview with an American-based Iraqi woman, Wafa Sultan, who had abandoned the Islamic faith into which she was born and was now openly—and many thought elo-quently—criticizing Islam in areas where she thought it was reactionary and intolerant.[10] However, it is an unspoken rule of Al Jazeera's coverage of Qatar that the hand of its chief sponsor, the emir Sheikh Hamad bin Khalifa, will not be bitten by critical coverage of him or his government.

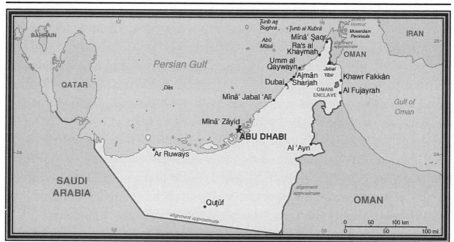

UNITED ARAB EMIRATES

Source: Central Intelligence Agency

United Arab Emirates

Qatar shares a common border with the largest of the Trucial States that became independent from the British, the United Arab Emirates (UAE). Slightly smaller than Maine, the UAE came into existence in 1971 when seven of the Trucial States—Abu Dhabi, Ajman, Dubai, Fujairah, Ras al-Khaimah, Sharjah and Umm al-Quwain—came together as a federation to combine their assets. The discovery of oil in the UAE accelerated the need for a government structure to coordinate the actions of the states. After initially being invited by the other states to join, Bahrain and Qatar each decided to go its own way, and the UAE became the largest Arab Gulf state to emerge from British dependency.

The UAE has a much larger population than Kuwait, Bahrain or Qatar, at about 4.6 million, but it still has the third highest per capita GDP in the Middle East. Only about 19 percent of the UAE's population, however, is originally from the Emirates; some 23 percent are of other Arab or Iranian origin, and 74 percent are noncitizens. Of these, 1.4 million are from India alone. Hundreds of thousands of European and North American expatriates reside in Kuwait, and approximately 120,000 of these are British. Because of the presence of so many nationals from non-Arab societies, the UAE has the reputation of being the most "tolerant" and "liberal" of the Arab states in the Gulf. There are clear limits to that tolerance, however. Though Emiratis are used to the presence of thousands of foreigners in their midst, they are not always comfortable with European lifestyles. In 2008, a British couple was arrested and deported under suspicion of having had sex on a public beach. Homosexual relations are considered a crime and in theory could be punished by the death penalty.

The UAE, meanwhile, has major problems of human rights abuses of the 95 percent of its work force who are migrant workers, usually from third-world countries. Labor laws are frequently not enforced, passports are often confiscated from workers and wages are not paid.

Actually, the UAE is not the worst of the Arab Gulf states found seriously wanting in efforts to combat labor and sexual trafficking. *The Trafficking in Persons Report, 2008*, is a country-by-country examination by the U.S. Department of State of sexual and labor trafficking problems throughout the world. The report assigns three "tiers," or categories, of compliance with efforts to combat trafficking. "Tier One" is the label applied to countries that try, in a significant way, to locate and liberate sex workers who are in involuntary servitude, and to enforce labor regulations to eliminate abusive labor conditions. Countries such as France, the U.K., Sweden and Switzerland belong in Tier One. Tier Two is more problematic, and applies to those countries with persistent complaints of labor abuse or sexual servitude. The United Arab Emirates falls in this category. Tier Three is much worse, and includes Kuwait, Qatar and Oman.[11] Many of the women being trafficked for prostitution come from Eastern Europe and Russia, or from India and Ethiopia.

The UAE's special demographic problem is one of the most serious gender imbalances of any country in the world, with the ratio of men to women in the age group 15-65, actually 2.74. The imbalance in the UAE is duplicated in Kuwait, Bahrain, Oman, Qatar and Saudi Arabia. It is very likely that the sexual trafficking problem in the Gulf states derives at least in part from the shortage of women. Though prostitution is banned in both the UAE and other Gulf states, it clearly exists. The need to import hundreds of thousands of foreigners into the Arab Gulf states to perform jobs for which there are not enough local hires is bound to distort working relationships, and it does. The best thing that can be said is that the governments of most of the Arab Gulf states are making efforts, if belatedly, to deal with the problem.

Oman

The borders of the UAE with Saudi Arabia are still not demarcated in some parts of the "empty quarter" of Saudi Arabia. But as the coast of the UAE sweeps toward the strategic Straits of Hormuz, at the mouth of the Persian Gulf, it is abruptly interrupted by a tip of land, the Musandam Peninsula, which belongs to Oman. The coast of this projection into the Gulf of Oman, the final opening of the Gulf to the Indian Ocean, lies only 50 miles from Iran on the opposite side of the Strait of Hormuz, and is thus a strategic outpost of the Arab states of the Gulf, taken as a whole.

Oman is certainly one of the most historically exotic outposts of Arab power in the Gulf. It was mentioned by the Roman historian Pliny the Elder (AD 23-79) and thereafter was controlled by all the major imperial powers of the region: the Parthians, the Sassanian Persians, the Arab Umayyad and Abbasid dynasties, the Qarmatians (who briefly dominated Bahrain), the Seljuq Turks. In 1508, the Portuguese arrived, barely a decade after Vasco da Gama pioneered the sailing route to India, and did not leave until pushed out by tribes from the interior of Oman in 1648.

In the 1690s, the Omani ruling family, led by Saif bin Sultan, sent an expedition down the east coast of Africa and ousted the Portuguese from their powerful fort in Mombasa (today on the coast of Kenya). The real objective of the Omanis, however, was the prosperous

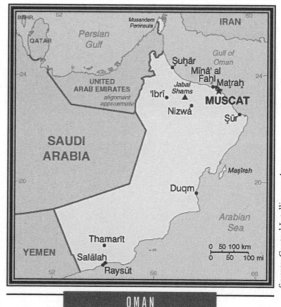

OMAN

Source: Central Intelligence Agency

slave-trading port of Zanzibar, which a nineteenth-century Omani Sultan, Sa'id ibn Sultan, turned into his official place of residence. The British, ever diplomatic, persuaded him to participate with them in ending the East African slave trade and, on his death in 1856, resolved a dispute between his two sons by persuading one to stay in Zanzibar and the other to limit his holdings to Muscat and Oman, as the territory was then called.

With its key strategic location at the mouth of the Persian Gulf and the Indian Ocean, Oman was important to the British, who signed a series of friendship treaties with the Sultans. In 1951, Great Britain recognized the formal independence of Oman, but continued to maintain a tight control of political and economic life in the country through British advisors who essentially ran the country. In 1970, however, the Sultan's British advisors connived to have him peacefully removed from power while on a trip to the U.K., and his son, Sultan Qaboos took over. The resulting change was like an overnight time warp from the Middle Ages to the modern world. Prior to the coup, Oman had only three formal schools with a total of fewer than 1,000 students in the entire country. Today, after an uninterrupted series of social, economic and political reforms, there are more than 1,000 state-sponsored schools and more than 650,000 students. Oman is about the size of New Mexico and has a total population of about 3.3 million, of whom fewer than 600,000 are non-nationals.

Oman is a hereditary monarchy whose head of state and head of government is Sultan Qaboos bin Said al-Said. The monarch picks the cabinet, but under a constitution he promulgated in the 1990s, there are two legislative chambers, though neither of them has authority to override the decisions of the sultan. Women have the right to vote, and three are currently members of the elected lower chamber.

Although Oman's GDP per capita income, at approximately $13,845 per person, is far lower than that of its wealthier cousins to the north, its strategic significance is clear to everyone on the Arab side of the Gulf, because 90 percent of petroleum extracted in the Gulf passes through the Straits of Hormuz.

Oman experienced a 13-year rebellion in a province called Dhofar during 1962-1975, when Communist and leftist forces in South Yemen tried to foment a rebellion that would eventually embrace all Arab states in the Gulf. The revolt was put down with significant involvement by the British military, but relations with neighboring Yemen have sometimes been tense since the end of the revolt.

Oman, like the other Arab states in the Gulf, has benefited from the high global price of petroleum, but its own reserves, unlike those of Kuwait, for example, are rapidly dwindling. The government has an economic program, cleverly called Vision 2020, to reduce the percentage of the national income from oil to 9 percent by the year 2020.

Oman is a member of the six-country Gulf Cooperation Council, which was created in 1981 to create a unified economic zone for the Arab side of the Gulf. The six countries are: Bahrain, Qatar, Kuwait, UAE, Oman and Saudi Arabia. A common market in products was initiated in January 2008, and other cooperative ventures include finance, trade, customs, tourism and scientific research. The GCC had hoped to launch a common currency by the year 2010, but Oman has already said that it will not be ready by that date.

Yemen

The last and largest nation on the Arabia peninsula is also the most potentially unstable. It is Yemen, the only republic on the peninsula. Yemen is about the size of New Mexico, with both the largest Arab population in the Gulf, about 23 million, and easily the lowest per capita GDP (estimated currently to be $978).

Yemen also has had a very troubled recent past. Americans are likely to recall that it was in the port of Aden, Yemen, in October 2000, that Islamist terrorists steered an explosive-laden rubber dinghy into the anchored U.S. navy destroyer *USS Cole*. In that attack, which was less than a year before the 9/11 attacks on New York and Washington, DC, 17 Americans died and 37 were wounded. Even more disturbing than the attack itself is the fact that the 10 apprehended suspects in the Cole attack escaped from jail in April 2003. But the following year, seven had been recaptured, and two of the Al-Qaeda operatives at the center of the attack were

Source: Central Intelligence Agency

YEMEN

sentenced to death. The dinghy had been purchased by sympathizers in Saudi Arabia.

To the Romans, Yemen was known as *Arabia Felix*, "Happy Arabia," because it was such a rich source of the spice trade, particularly of myrrh and frankincense, in the Arab world. The Roman Emperor Augustus (63 BC-AD 14) even tried to annex it to the Roman Empire, but the expedition he sent out in 26 BC was a failure. Yemen had diplomatic relations with Rome, but it never became part of the empire. It fell briefly to the Persians in pre-Islamic times and became Muslim in 628. After the death of Mohammed in 632, it belonged to various Arab dynasties until the conquest of the Arab world by the Ottomans in 1517 and later.

The British were the first modern power to see the strategic value of Aden for their administration of India, and in 1839, they simply annexed the port of Aden and designated the territory to be administered by British India. In 1937, Aden was declared a crown colony with land on either side of it defined as east and west protectorates of Aden. By 1965, the British had persuaded most of the tribal states within these protectorates to be part of what they called the Federation of South Arabia. But a terrorist anti-British movement had been forming, and increasingly violent attacks on British forces forced Great Britain to leave.

In November 1967, south Yemen became the People's Republic of Yemen. Both the Soviet and, to a lesser extent, the Chinese embassy were a major source of influence; and in the manner of many revolutionary movements, the original National Liberation Front leaders were ousted from power in 1969 by a more radical faction. In December 1970, south Yemen became the People's Democratic Republic of Yemen, the first Arab state anywhere to be avowedly Marxist. All political parties except the Yemeni Socialist Party were banned. The country was turned into a Marxist-Leninist totalitarian state.

The situation in northern Yemen was different. In 1962, Imam al-Badr, the last in a line of ruling emirs, was overthrown in a coup led by Nasserite pan-Arab military officers. The officers seemed to be emulating the seizure of power in Egypt a decade earlier by the Free Officers' Movement who seized power and turned Egypt into a secular republic.

The plotters even changed the country's name to Yemen Arab Republic, an echo of the Egyptian regime change. Saudi Arabia did not recognize the overthrow of the emir and supported royalist forces against the new government. For its part, Egypt dispatched ground troops and units of its air force to suppress the rebels. Egyptian pilots, flying jets provided by the Soviet Union, not only fought against royalist forces in Yemen, but bombed Saudi towns close to the Saudi-Yemeni border. Nasser was forced to withdraw in 1967 after Egypt's humiliation by Israel in the Six-Day War. By the end of the decade the republican forces had prevailed and Saudi Arabia recognized the new government.

The consolidation of Marxist-Leninist political power in the south and the formation of a totalitarian police state led to the flight of thousands of southern Yemenis to the north. There were intermittent talks between the two Yemens on forming a political union, but these were inevitably undermined by sharp political tensions and mutual suspicions. A more moderate leader, Ali Nasir Muhammad, replaced Abdul Fattah Ismail as president in 1980, and the PDRY backed off supporting insurgency both in the YAR and neighboring Oman. But when Ismail returned from exile with followers in an attempt to seize power in 1986, a violent struggle broke out in which thousands of Soviet advisors and their families had to be rescued by Soviet military units. Thousands of southern Yemeni civilians were killed in the clashes and there was another huge refugee exodus to the north. Finally, the president of the YAR, Ali Abdullah Saleh and the president of the PDRY in 1989 signed an agreement for a national union, and the Republic of Yemen—a union of north and south—was proclaimed in 1990. The new country's capital was proclaimed to be Sana'a, which had been the capital of the YAR.

The south tried one more time to secede, and a brief new civil war broke out in 1994. No foreign state recognized the secession, however, and the more powerful military forces of the north overwhelmed those of the south. In October 1999, Saleh was elected convincingly in the first direct presidential elections for the whole country. In September 2006, he was reelected to a second, seven-year term as president in what were generally acknowledged by international observers to be free and fair elections.

Aside from the presidency, Yemen has a bicameral legislature with an elected 301-member House of Representatives and an upper house of an appointed Shura Council of 111 seats. The current ruling party is the General People's Congress, the party that was the power base for Saleh in the north of the country before unification.

Oil resources, until recently, accounted for 90 percent of the country's export revenue, but the World Bank predicted that these will decline severely during 2009 and 2010 and fall to near zero by 2017. The country is so poor that it is vulnerable to violent economic fluctuations. One of these fluctuations occurred when several countries in the Arab world and beyond suspended their air programs over Yemen's decision in 1980 not to support a U.N. Security Council resolution threatening violence against Iraq for its occupation of Kuwait. About 850,000 Yemeni workers were forced in 1990 to return to Yemen from well-paying jobs in the Gulf.

Yemen has a poor human rights record, with the government vulnerable to rampant corruption and the security forces reported to have acted with frequent brutality, especially in the south. There have been reports of arbitrary arrests, torture, and even extrajudicial executions. Though tourism began to grow in the 1990s, several tourists were kidnapped to extort concessions from the government or simply for the purposes of commercial extortion. The known presence in Yemen of Islamist terrorist groups, the country's poverty and the fragility of its democracy has many Arab states in the Gulf and beyond concerned that if a new bout of instability afflicts Yemen, this time it might spread far abroad.

Yemen has applied for membership in the Gulf Cooperation Council but may have to wait until the other member-states consider that it has attained sufficient economic power and sophistication to be admitted. That could be a few years yet. Meanwhile, the Persian Gulf states are all, in a sense, waiting upon the actions of their principal rival and possible future adversary in the region, Iran. The Persian Gulf could yet become Persian.

6

IRAQ

For more than six years—longer than American involvement in World War I or World War II, though not yet as long as the Vietnam experience—the U.S. has been fighting a war in Iraq. The first three weeks of the war were a lightning-fast conventional assault that started on March 20, 2003, and had overcome resistance in Baghdad by April 9. Most observers were astonished by the speed and thoroughness of the initial attack, and the decisive defeat of the Iraqi army. The years that have elapsed since that day in April 2003, when a tall concrete statue of Iraq's dictator Saddam Hussein was pulled down by a chain tied to an American armored vehicle, have been long, weary and often painful ones.

By comparison with previous American wars of the same duration, the war in Iraq has led to surprisingly few deaths: 4,242 (as of May 6, 2008) over a period of six years. That is fewer than two deaths per day, on average, over the entire period. By comparison, in the U.S. there were only slightly fewer traffic fatalities in the state of California for the whole year 2008—3,974—which itself was the lowest number of deaths on California's roads since 1975.[1]

But every death of every soldier—and every traffic fatality—is its own tragedy. The challenge for Americans is that since the Vietnam War, they have grown used to conflicts that have been short and sharp, and almost casualty-free.

The American invasion of Grenada in 1983, the first major U.S. conflict since the Vietnam War, lasted just a few days and resulted in 19 American combat deaths and 119 wounded. The American intervention in Lebanon during 1982-1983 was much worse, for it was dominated by the blowing up of the U.S. marine barracks in Beirut, resulting in the death of 241 marines.

IRAQ

The first Gulf War, or Operation Desert Storm in 1991, involving nearly 20 major belligerent nations and nearly a million troops, in its ground action lasted four days. Fewer than 200 Americans were killed in combat-related action. The Pentagon-supplied videos of smart bombs crashing precisely into ventilator shafts of targeted buildings suggested that war had now become—well, a video game. You never saw bodies or blood, just the astonishing precision of electronically guided weaponry. War seemed to have become . . . "virtual." Thus, even though the total number of Americans and allied Coalition personnel killed in Iraq has been, by comparisons with previous wars, surprisingly small, the steady drip-drip of combat deaths, often from vehicles being blown up by roadside bombs, was a shocking reminder that war is still war; and people caught up in war are killed, severely wounded or permanently maimed.

The war in Iraq, however, officially called Operation Iraqi Freedom, was controversial from almost the outset. It is true that the vast majority of Americans supported the contention of President Bush that Iraq was somehow linked to the terrorist threat to America that had been unleashed on September 11, 2001. But very quickly it became apparent that the citizens of many of America's traditional allies opposed the war. In France and Germany, opposition to what the U.S. initiated in Iraq was especially strong and scarcely lessened in intensity as the war ground on. Three circumstances, however, turned Operation Iraqi Freedom into one of the most controversial American foreign policy initiatives of the beginning years of the twenty-first century.

The first circumstance was the collapse of one of the major premises upon which the attack on Iraq had originally been based. It had been repeatedly claimed by the U.S.—and largely believed even by those who opposed American intervention—that Iraq was in possession of weapons of mass destruction (WMD) that posed a serious strategic threat to both the U.S. and to Iraq's neighbors. Several months after the invasion of Iraq had begun, however, no evidence of any stockpile of WMD were found. The allegation was then made by some in the U.S. that the Bush administration had "lied" about the WMD allegations from the outset.

The second circumstance that rendered the Iraq war especially controversial was the revelation, beginning in 2004, that Iraqi prisoners of the U.S., held in Baghdad's Abu Ghraib prison, had been subjected to abuse, torture and even murder at the hands of American military units tasked with supervising the prison. The revelations disgusted much of world public opinion and confirmed many people in their conviction that the American-led invasion had been profoundly misconceived from the outset. In the U.S., Abu Ghraib made it much harder for supporters of the invasion to make the case that the American intervention in Iraq, on balance, was a positive development for the Iraqi people.

The third circumstance was the realization that though the execution of the initial military assault upon Iraq had proceeded almost flawlessly, the U.S. military had vastly underestimated the challenge of occupying and administering Iraq after defeating the regime of Saddam Hussein. Almost no one argued that the fall of the Saddam Hussein regime had not been a good thing; almost everyone, however, was dismayed at the lack of preparation that seemed to characterize American plans to govern Iraq once the country was under American control.

The initial signs of that lack of preparedness, though symbolically powerful, were of little strategic significance: the wholesale looting of the Iraqi National Museum in the first few days after the American conquest of Baghdad and the painfully long period of time it took the U.S. to restore basic Iraqi infrastructure facilities, such as electricity and water supplies. Far more important was the realization that the American military had not reckoned on having to fight a determined insurgency even as it struggled to construct the institutions necessary for Iraqi self-government.

In a matter of months, the Coalition Forces were facing increasingly sophisticated attacks from insurgents employing everything from sniper rifles to the notorious Improvised Explosive Devices (IEDs), or roadside bombs that became a major threat to the Coalition's ability to move freely throughout Iraq and to keep forces already in Iraq resupplied by road from Kuwait.[2]

The intensity of fighting in 2006 revealed that whatever the military strategy had been to deal with both anti-U.S. insurgency and ethnic factional bloodletting, it was not working. At the beginning of 2007, therefore, President Bush announced a new approach of greatly strengthening U.S. forces in Baghdad and Al-Anbar Province that became known as the "surge" strategy. By the middle of 2008, the "surge" had greatly reduced the level of violence as well as the number of U.S. combat deaths. In July 2008, the fewest number of Americans were killed in combat in Iraq since the war began in April 2003, just 13. Even the *New York Times*, consistently critical of President Bush and Operation Iraqi Freedom in general, stated on August 21, 2008, that "the surge, clearly, has worked, at least for now. . . . The result, now visible in the streets, is a calm unlike any the country has seen since the American invasion."[3]

Whether the "surge" really worked, however, won't be clear until Iraq demonstrates that it can ensure security within its borders without the presence of U.S. troops. U.S. troops had been asked by the Iraqi government to be out of all Iraqi cities by the end of June 2009. It may also become apparent, at that point, whether the U.S. invasion of Iraq, for all of its blunders and the falsehood of the premise that legitimized it, has for the foreseeable future made the lives of Iraqi people far more bearable than they would have been if Saddam Hussein had still been in power.

Iraq's History

Iraq would be a major player on the Middle East scene regardless of who ruled it. Its size, slightly larger than the state of California, and its population, 27.5 million, fourth largest in the Arab world, would make it significant even if nothing else did. Its oil reserves are by some estimates the third largest in the world and thus of immense potential importance. But Iraq's real significance cannot be disconnected from its phenomenally rich history.

Iraq was, quite literally, "the cradle of civilization." A geographical area historically and even recently referred to as Mesopotamia (literally, "between the rivers," i.e., the Tigris and Euphrates rivers), Iraq was the location of one of the oldest cultures and writing systems known to the human race, that of the Sumerians. Dating from the end of the sixth millennium BC through the fourth, Sumerian cities were among the first in the world to practice year-round agriculture. The Sumerians were also among the first civilizations (scholars argue whether they preceded ancient Egypt or not) to develop a writing system, around 3500 BC. Hundreds of thousands of texts in Sumerian have survived, the majority of them inscribed by a pointed reed on clay tablets that were later hardened by being baked. The system of writing that evolved in this way is known as cuneiform, because the impression of the triangular tip of the stylus upon wet clay is wedge-shaped (*cuneus* means "wedge" in Latin).

The Sumerians were replaced in power and influence by Semitic-speaking groups historically associated with the city of Babylon. One of the first kings of the Babylonian Empire was Hammurabi (c. 1795-1750 BC), whose famous "Code of Hammurabi" consisting of 282 laws, with harsh proscribed punishments for infringement of them, is one of the oldest known set of laws in the ancient world.

The greatest empire associated with Babylon, however, was that of the Assyrians, who in general occupied the land on the West side of the Tigris river.

The empires and cultures of the Mesopotamian region were highly developed in mathematics and astronomy, and contributed to the modern world the notion of 60 as the base unit of counting (still used in the division of hours and minutes). Babylon was the capital of the empire of the Chaldeans, whose monarch Nebuchadnezzar II famously conquered Jerusalem in the year 586 BC and took into exile in Babylon the leading families of the Jewish kingdom of Judah. But the empire of Babylon was itself overthrown by a much more powerful new empire, that of the Medes and Persians, whose founder Cyrus II, or Cyrus the Great, is revered in Iran today as a wise administrator and a tolerant ruler. Indeed, after his conquest of Babylon in 539 BC, Cyrus enters Jewish history as the Persian ruler who in 537 BC permitted the Jews to return to Jerusalem from the exile in Babylon. According to biblical accounts, about 40,000 Jews did so.

The Persian Empire was overthrown by the Greek warrior Alexander the Great in 331 BC, and for two centuries most of what is now Iraq was ruled by a successor dynasty called the Seleucids. This Greek empire eventually gave way to a determined enemy of Rome, the Parthians, and then to the Sassanid Persians. A powerful and ruthless military empire, the Sassanids were in almost constant warfare first with the Roman Empire in the West, and then with the Byzantine Empire based in Constantinople. The only occasion when a Roman emperor of the West was captured by an enemy power was when the emperor Valerian (ruled AD 253-260) was captured by the Sassanid Persian emperor Shapur I. The dividing line between the two empires for most of the period of intense rivalry was the Euphrates River.

When Arab armies burst out of the Arabian Peninsula in AD 633, the Byzantine provinces of Egypt, Judea and Syria quickly fell to the Muslims; and in 633 Mesopotamia was conquered by the Arabs. Though Persia itself was not brought under Muslim Arab rule until 656, Mesopotamia fell into the hands of the Umayyad Dynasty based in Damascus (AD 661-750) and then of the Abbasid Dynasty (AD 750-1258), whose capital was Baghdad.

Baghdad under Muslim Arab rule for five centuries was one of the most prosperous and cultivated cities in the medieval world. It was both one of the largest cities in the medieval world, with a population of more than a million, and the center of Muslim Arab civilization at its very height. In fact, for the first two centuries of the Abbasid dynasty, Muslim-Arab culture in Baghdad became a fertile intellectual center for medicine, philosophy and science. Baghdad itself had a "House of Wisdom" where scholars of all backgrounds were encouraged to translate the world's knowledge and wisdom into Arabic. It was Arabic translation that helped introduce the Greek philosopher Aristotle to Europe in the middle ages.

But in 1258, the great Islamic civilization, weakened by internal strife and the corruption of its own wealth, came crashing down when the Mongolian leader Hulegu, the grandson of the great Mongolian conqueror Genghis Khan, attacked Baghdad with a massive army of some 200,000 warriors, and sacked the city. Hundreds of thousands of its citizens were slaughtered. Hulegu had Baghdad governed by the Mongolian rulers the Il-Khans, who had conquered Persia a few decades earlier.

Over a period of several years, the Il-Khan Mongol dynasty split into several small states, making each of them unable to resist the next great conqueror to storm out of the steppes of Central Asia—Timur, or Tamerlane (1336-1405). Timur decimated every city that opposed him, from Damascus to Delhi. When his armies fell upon Baghdad in 1401, they slaughtered at least 20,000 of the inhabitants of the city and piled up the decapitated heads of the dead in pyramids outside the city walls.

Although Timur defeated the rising power of the Ottoman Turks in a battle in 1402 when he actually captured the Ottoman Sultan, Bayezid, his own death as he was embarking on a campaign to conquer China brought an end to his campaign to conquer the entire Middle East.

The Ottoman Turks, meanwhile, had recouped their losses sufficiently to capture Constantinople, or Byzantium, the capital of the Byzantine Empire, in 1453. The Persians, under a powerful new monarch of a new dynasty, the Safavids, took over Mesopotamia in 1508, but by this time the Ottomans were moving forcefully into the Arab world. In 1517 they had conquered Jerusalem and were starting to move into Egypt and the Arab world beyond. In Mesopotamia they turned against the Persians and captured Baghdad from the Safavids in 1535. It was the beginning of nearly three centuries of Ottoman Turkish control of the Arab world. Though the Persians briefly retook Baghdad in 1632, what is now Iraq owed allegiance to Istanbul until the end of World War I.

As we saw in the preceding chapter, Britain had long experience in the Arab world through its forays into the Persian Gulf. It was only natural, therefore, that when Turkey entered World War I as an ally of the Central Powers, Britain should have tried hard to shake loose its control of the Arab world.

The first British military encounters with the Turks were disastrous. At Gallipoli in 1915 and 1916, the British were unable to dislodge Turkish forces that were guarding the shores of the Hellespont and the naval route to Istanbul. In 1916, a large British force surrendered to the Turks at Kut, about 100 miles south of Baghdad on the Tigris river in Iraq. But destiny was flowing in the direction of the British, and by 1917, they had not only captured Jerusalem but also regained the initiative in the struggle for Mesopotamia. In March 1917, the British captured Baghdad from the Turks, and by early 1918, they had extended their control of Iraq as far as Mosul.

A Monarchy Under British Control

The British and French mutual agreement on how to divide up the spoils of the conquered Ottoman Empire resulted in French control of Syria and Lebanon, as we saw in chapter 3. The Sykes-Picot Agreement of 1916 had specified that the British would have control of former Ottoman territories to the south of the geographical line designated in the agreement. In practice, this meant Iraq and Palestine. In 1920, the League of Nations confirmed the reality of British control of Iraq by designating Iraq a League of Nations Class A Mandate.

Faisal bin al Hussein, the son of Hussein bin Ali, Sharif of Mecca, who had led the Arab revolt against the Turks in alliance with T. E. Lawrence ("Lawrence of Arabia"), had originally been promised an Arab state by the British as a reward for his anti-Turkish activities. When the French in control of Damascus expelled him in July 1920, however, the British needed a new location for him.

At the Cairo Conference in July 1921, the British decided to make a new Arab state of the Ottoman provinces of Baghdad and Basra, and they appointed Faisal the new monarch of this entity. Five years later, Mosul, the capital of the Kurdish-dominated region of northern Iraq, was added. Thus, fatefully, Iraq, whose population is about 55 percent Shia Arab, began its history as a state cobbled together from three ethnic groups—Shia Arab, Sunni Arab, and Kurd—ruled by a leader who was of Sunni Arab origin.

The British had the best of intentions. When British troops first entered Baghdad in 1917, posters were plastered over the city signed by the British commanding general, Sir Stanley Maude. The general asserted that the British forces "do not come into your cities and lands as conquerors or enemies, but as liberators." "You, the people of Baghdad," Maude's poster continued, "are not to understand that it is the wish of the British Government to impose upon you alien institutions. It is the hope of the British Government that the aspirations of your philosophers and writers shall be realized once again, that the people of Baghdad shall flourish, and shall enjoy their wealth and substance under institutions which are in consonance with their sacred laws and with their racial ideals."[4]

Many Iraqi Arabs, not surprisingly, mistrusted the intentions as a cloak for the continuation of European imperial control over the heartland of the Middle East. By 1920, the British were already facing a series of dangerous uprisings by both Shia and Sunni Arabs. Winston Churchill, who had been given the impossible task as Colonial Secretary at the beginning of 1921 of both preserving Britain's power in the Middle East after the defeat of the Ottoman Turks and drastically reducing British military expenses, was exasperated by the conflicting challenges of the task. With T. E. Lawrence as newly appointed advisor to the Colonial Office, he hoped that the emplacement of a Sunni Arab monarch as titular ruler of Iraq, Faisal I, son of Hussein, Sharif of Mecca, would placate things. They scarcely did. Though Faisal did not openly oppose the British presence, many prominent Iraqis did, forcing the British to negotiate repeatedly with Hussein to preserve their influence over Iraq.

In 1930, the Iraqi parliament ratified a new Anglo-Iraqi agreement that set a date for the eventual termination of the British mandate in Iraq. In 1932, Iraq became formally independent of Great Britain and joined the League of Nations. Though the British presence in the country was still powerful—Britain had military bases outside Baghdad and Basra—it was not enough to protect Iraq's Christian community of Assyrians from a pogrom in the north of the country that resulted in the death of 300 and the emigration to Syria of many others. The Iraqi government of the day supported the pogrom, as did many Iraqis.

As World War II developed, Iraqi politics became increasingly dominated by pro-German nationalists who opposed the British. In April 1941, four pan-Arabist generals seized power in a putsch and forced the regent, Nuri al-Said, the uncle of the future king, Faisal II, born in 1935, to flee the country. The new prime minister was Rashid Ali al-Gailani, a pro-Axis politician who believed and hoped that Germany would win the war. When he requested help from Hitler to remove the British, London responded forcefully and used both the Royal Air Force and ground troops to oust al-Gailani. The British restored the regent, al-Said, and remained in occupation in Iraq until 1947.

In 1948, the Iraqi government signed yet another treaty with Britain that would in theory permit the British military to continue to have bases in Iraq until 1973. But the Iraqi army for several decades had been influenced by the secular modernism that characterized Turkey under its founder Kemal Atatürk. Pan-Arabism, socialism and, above all, anti-Western nationalism were powerfully attractive ideas to many Iraqis hostile to continued control from outside their borders.

When King Faisal II, who had come to power in 1953, at the age of 18, joined together with his cousin, King Hussein of Jordan, to form the Arab Federation of Iraq and Jordan in February 1958, angry officers in the army took action. An Iraqi officer, Brigadier-General Abdul Karim Kassem, was in charge of Iraqi units ordered by King Faisal to move into Jordan to assist King Hussein against unrest in that country. Kassem, who had formed an Iraqi version of the Free Officers' Movement that had brought Nasser to power in Egypt, took his troops instead, as we saw, to the Royal Rihab Palace in Baghdad where Faisal and his family lived and murdered them all. Faisal II died of his wounds on the way to the hospital after the attack. Kassem then appointed himself both prime minister and commander of the armed forces.

A Revolving Door of Power

Kassem's supporters included the Communists, and he lifted the ban that had been imposed on the Communists under the monarchy. He quickly took Iraq out of CENTO, the Baghdad Pact, provoked a confrontation with the Kurds and was the first Iraqi leader to begin making claims on Kuwait. But Kassem's emerging rival was Colonel Abdul Salam Arif, who had participated in the 1958 coup. The colonel's loyalties were with Iraqis who supported the Ba'ath Party and the pan-Arabism of Egyptian president Nasser.

In 1963, after fighting for several days in the streets of Baghdad, Arif came to power. A pan-Arabist and Ba'athist who had advocated the union of Egypt, Syria and Iraq before Syria opted out of the United Arab Republic in 1961, Arif quickly tried to persuade Nasser to resume his Arab unity efforts. But Nasser was losing patience with the Ba'ath Party in Syria, and Arif could not gain any traction with the notion. After Arif's death in a helicopter crash in 1966, his brother took his place. Abdul Rahman Arif eagerly carried on his brother's pan-Arabist plans and committed Iraqi troops to Syria's help during the Six-Day War. But he was himself purged from power in a bloodless coup in 1968 and sent into exile.

Iraq had by now become an almost comic-book parody of revolving-door military coups and dictatorship. This time, the Ba'ath Party was firmly back in power, and in July 1968, Ahmad Hassan al-Bakr, who had helped oust the second Arif brother, became president. He was to hold the post, at least in ceremonial terms, for an unprecedented 11 years. In the first period of his presidency, he nationalized the Iraq Petroleum Company and signed a friendship treaty with the Soviet Union. In retrospect, however, al-Bakr's most important move may have been the formal elevation of the man who was to dominate Iraq for the next 27 years, Saddam Hussein.

Saddam's Early Political Years

Unlike all of the previous Iraqi leaders who had come to power since the murder of Faisal II in 1958, Saddam was not from the military. In fact, he was the consummate party apparatchik who had built his political career entirely by allying himself with powerful factions in the Ba'ath Party. After being named first vice president to al-Bakr, Saddam came to dominate the Iraqi national scene.

Saddam (1937-2006) was both a populist by political instinct and a student of the methodology of totalitarian control whose skills at it have probably rarely been rivaled anywhere in the world, let alone in the Arab world. After attempting to assassinate Kassem in 1958, in a Bonnie-and-Clyde machine-gunning of Kassem's car, Saddam escaped to Syria and then to Egypt, where he studied for a time at Cairo University.

In 1963, he returned to Iraq after the coup that ousted Kassem. His rise to power in the Ba'ath Party was given a big impetus in 1964 by none other than Ba'ath Party founder, the Syrian-born Michel Aflaq, who recommended that Saddam be promoted to the Regional Command, the highest policy-making body of the Ba'ath Party; in effect, its politburo.[5] Though his promotion did not take place then, Saddam spent the years from 1966 to 1968 as Assistant Secretary-General of the Ba'ath Party. Thus he was well placed when al-Bakr took power in 1968.

When oil revenues began pouring into Iraq after the global oil price rise of 1973, Saddam took the initiative in ensuring that the funds were used for ambitious education and infrastructure projects. It is an undeniable fact that under Saddam in the 1970s Iraq had medical and other social services that were the envy of the Arab world. Saddam led an ambitious literacy program that enabled thousands of hitherto illiterate Iraqis to read. He expanded university education. Above all, he imposed on Iraq an intense secularism. In many respects, this may have been his most lasting—and ultimately beneficial—legacy. He introduced a legal system based on Western style, entirely lacking in the *sharia*-based laws and penalties then current in the other Arab countries of the Gulf.

He also maneuvered relentlessly for political power to rival that of his nominal boss al-Bakr. In July 1979, he forced the President to resign over al-Bakr's secret communications with Syria to institute an Iraqi union with Syria. Six days later, in a chilling display of Stalin-like power and control, Saddam convened an assembly of Ba'ath Party leaders and read out loud the names of 68 members who were accused of being spies and fifth columnists. Those named left the hall and were later summarily shot.

Saddam Hussein ruled by terror, with an interlocking system of intelligence and security agencies whose personal loyalties to him were additionally ensured by the placement in many of the security organizations of relatives and clan members from his hometown of Tikrit. One of Saddam's first chiefs of Internal State Security was a man called Nadhim Kzar. His reputation for sadism and cruelty struck terror even within the Ba'ath Party itself. Reportedly, he liked to extinguish his cigarette in the eyeballs of prisoners who were being interrogated. Many of his victims were Communists and Kurds. The Iraqi Communist Party in 1971 issued a list of 410 people who had perished in one of Saddam's many torture houses in Baghdad. This one was called, apparently without irony, Palace of the End.[6] Kzar, like Stalin's last secret police chief Beria, got a little too big for his boots, and after trying to stage his own coup against al-Bakr, was caught and executed in 1973.

Saddam had to walk a narrow political tightrope in ruling Iraq. While the Sunni dominated the country politically, the Kurds in the north were perennially in rebellion. In particular, they opposed the pan-Arabism of Saddam's Iraq and the Ba'ath Party in general. The other ethnic group, the Shia, who actually formed a majority of Iraqis, were opposed to Saddam's enforced secularism.

Had Saddam been faced with merely domestic threats to his rule, he would probably not have embarked on any of the foreign adventures that were eventually to lead to his downfall. But when the Ayatollah Khomeini came to power in neighboring and Shia Iran in 1979, Saddam became seriously worried about the loyalties of his own Shia subjects. In September 1980, accusing Iran of trying to topple his regime, he launched a military invasion of the country. The initial ostensible objective was the recovery of the Shatt al Arab, a 120-mile waterway from the conjunction of the Tigris and Euphrates Rivers to the mouth of the Persian Gulf whose sovereignty, divided between Iraq and Iran, had been settled at a treaty signed in Algiers in 1975. (Actually, Saddam himself had been the Iraqi signatory of that treaty.)

The war was a brutal slogging match between numerically superior and more fanatical numbers of Iranian troops and Iraqi forces who were willing, when pressed, to use mustard gas. It was to be the longest conventional war of the entire twentieth century. A landmark event relatively early in the war, in June 1981, was the destruction by the Israeli air force of an Iraqi nuclear reactor, named Osiraq by the French engineers who designed it, outside Baghdad. The Israelis feared that Iraq might be planning to develop nuclear weapons.

Though the Iraqis had the military initiative at the outset and made significant advances into Iran in the first two years of the war, by 1982 the Iranians had recovered all of their lost territory. From 1982 to 1984, the Iraqis fought off efforts by the Iranians to penetrate Iraqi territory around Basra, in the south. From 1984 to 1986 both sides were bombing each other's major cities, and the Iraqis did their best to disrupt Iranian oil exports at the Kharg oil terminal on the Persian Gulf. For the next two years, when the Iranians responded by targeting ships headed for Iraqi destinations, the U.S. and major Western powers intervened by guarding the ships with U.S. navy warships.

Meanwhile, as the Iranians mounted repeated human-wave assaults on Iraqi positions (sometimes using children equipped with plastic "keys" to enter Allah's paradise as martyrs), the Iraqis responded by widespread use of mustard gas. In northern Iraq, when the Iranians captured Halabja in Kurdistan in 1988, the Iraqis unleashed a mustard gas attack that killed an estimated 5,000 civilians. Gas was used by the Iraqis in the remaining two years of the war, and Iraq gained the strategic advantage by being able to launch surface-to-surface missiles against Tehran. Both sides used conventional aircraft to bomb each other's capital.

Finally, like punch-drunk boxers, the two combatants accepted U.N. Security Council Resolution 598, calling for an end to hostilities. After eight years of brutal infantry fighting, neither side had any territorial advantage. The Iraqis even reluctantly acknowledged the validity of the 1975 Shatt al Arab treaty whose rejection by them had been one of the proximate causes of the war in the first place. Total deaths on both sides, civilian and military, may have exceeded a million.

As we saw in chapter 5, the Iraqis had depended heavily on Gulf Arab financial support during the conflict, and had built up an indebtedness of $65 billion by the time the war ended. Frustration over deflated oil prices because of Kuwait's allegedly excessive oil production was another factor, as well as resentment that Kuwait would not forgive Iraq's debt.

Invasion of Kuwait

In the summer of 1990, Saddam felt confident enough to amass 100,000 Iraqi troops on the Kuwaiti border. With a possible war looming, last-minute talks between representatives of Iraq and Kuwait were held in Saudi Arabia. The Kuwaitis refused to yield to Iraqi demands both on finances and on yielding part of their territory to Iraq. Early in the morning of August 2, 1990, Iraqi troops crossed the border and occupied Kuwait. The Middle East crisis that was to become Operation Desert Storm, or the First Gulf War, was about to begin.

Quite possibly, Saddam had calculated that the U.S. would not respond forcefully to his invasion. After all, the U.S. had provided considerable assistance to Iraq during the Gulf War, including, by many accounts, substantial intelligence information about Iranian targets. In addition, the U.S. ambassador to Iraq at the time of the invasion, April Glaspie, had held meetings with both Iraqi president Saddam Hussein and Iraqi foreign minister Tariq Aziz a few days before Iraq forces crossed the Kuwaiti border. In transcripts of the conversation released by Iraq to the *New York Times* and other Western news agencies—but never confirmed as accurate by the State Department—Glaspie reportedly said, "We have no opinion on the Arab-Arab conflicts, like your border disagreement with Kuwait" and "the Iraq issue is not associated with America."[7] Responding to questions shouted at her by British journalists in Baghdad in September 1990 (after the invasion, but before Operation Desert Storm began), Glaspie reportedly said, "Obviously, I didn't think, and nobody else did, that the Iraqis were going to take all of Kuwait."[8]

Until and unless the State Department ever declassifies Glaspie's cables from Baghdad, no one will know for sure what the exact contents of her exchanges with both Saddam and Tariq Aziz were. Only one thing is clear: Saddam did not calculate that the U.S. would respond so forcefully as to mount a 34-nation military expeditionary force to expel him militarily from Kuwait.

On August 6, 1990, the U.N. Security Council passed Resolution 661 imposing sanctions on Iraq. But it was not until November 29 that the Security Council passed Resolution 678, allowing "all necessary means" to be used to expel Iraq from Kuwait. The U.N. resolution gave the green light to President George H. W. Bush, who had gradually been building up a massive air and ground military force in Saudi Arabia, to attack Iraq militarily. The U.N. ultimatum required Iraq to withdraw from Kuwait by January 15, 1991.

The allied air bombardment of Iraqi positions in Kuwait as well as Iraqi strategic targets inside Iraq began at 2:30 A.M. local time, January 17, 1991, and continued uninterruptedly until the end of hostilities on February 28, totaling an incredible 86,000 sorties against Iraq.[9] The ground war started on February 24 and ended within 100 hours, by which time all of Kuwait had been liberated and Iraqi forces were retreating pell-mell into their own country. As they retreated, they set fire to as many Kuwaiti well heads as they could.

A complicating factor in the war was Iraq's firing of Scud missiles at targets in Tel Aviv and Haifa the day after the Coalition (the name for the collective anti-Iraqi, but U.S.-led alliance) air attacks began. Altogether, 39 Scuds were fired, but Israeli casualties, miraculously, were limited to just two deaths (one from a heart attack) and extensive property damage. Saddam's intention in targeting Israel, which his foreign minister Tariq Aziz had made clear was what Iraq would do in the event of a war, was to provoke Israel to retaliate. If that had happened, the Coalition delicately assembled against Saddam might have fallen apart. The Arab countries that had joined the Coalition would have been unwilling to be associated with an Israeli attack upon a fellow-Arab state.

After angry demands within Israel to retaliate directly against Iraq, the Israeli government held its fire. There had been intense personal diplomacy by the administration of President George H. W. Bush and cajoling and arm-twisting as well. The Israeli government grudgingly acknowledged that the quick defeat of the Iraqi regime as a whole outweighed Israel's emotional need to be seen to respond to the Scud attacks. The U.S. hastily deployed Patriot anti-ballistic missile batteries to Israel to reassure the Israeli public of its commitment to Israel's safety. The Patriots, however, worked only some of the time. When they were used in Saudi Arabia, they failed to prevent a Scud attack on a U.S. military base in Dahran, Saudi Arabia, which resulted in the deaths of 28 U.S. service personnel. It was the largest single-action loss of life on the Coalition side in the war. Despite intense aerial surveillance of the whole of Iraq in an attempt to locate and destroy the Scud launchers while the war was still proceeding, it was only when the Iraqis surrendered that the Scud danger was eliminated.

The ground attack on Iraqi forces occupying Kuwait started February 24. The Coalition was aiming not just at Kuwait and the Iraqi military who occupied it, but also at any Iraqi units inside Iraq itself that threatened to block the Coalition's liberation of Kuwait. When Iraqi troops on February 26 began moving out of Kuwait, their long retreating columns were hammered by Coalition warplanes, leading to massive losses of life and equipment among Iraqi troops. It has been speculated that the extensive bloodletting in the last hours of the war persuaded President Bush to call for a suspension of hostilities. Iraq's military leadership signed a cease-fire agreement February 28, by which time the only Iraqi troops in Kuwait were those who had been taken prisoner. The total number of combat-related deaths among U.S. troops was 148, with a further 145 dying in accidents of various kinds. For a total American force of around 600,000 men and women, the casualty figures were almost miraculously low.

By a tragic miscalculation, however, the Coalition forces allowed the Iraqis after the cease-fire to continue to use military helicopters, which Iraq claimed it needed because of damage done to civilian transportation. But when rebellions broke out against Saddam's regime in the north of Iraq among the Kurds and in the south of the country among the Shia, Saddam used the helicopters to ruthlessly suppress the rebellions. The violent internal suppression of the uprisings stunned and shocked both the U.N. and the Coalition. Thus were created the "no-fly zones" over the north and south of Iraq, areas where patrolling U.S. and British aircraft not only excluded flights by Iraqi aircraft, but often attacked Iraqi ground installations in the course of their patrols.

Scrutinizing Iraq's Intentions

The 12 years that elapsed between the end of the Gulf War and the beginning of Operation Iraqi Freedom, the invasion of Iraq by the U.S. and Great Britain, was a period when it was never clear whether the Iraqis had genuinely abandoned their Weapons of Mass Destruction (WMD) program, as required by the U.N., or whether they were holding out on international inspections and actually bent on developing an operational WMD program. There were no fewer than 16 U.N. resolutions passed during the decade of the 1990s relating to Iraq, all of them referring to U.N. dissatisfaction with Iraq's compliance with demands for disclosure of WMD-related activities.

In September 1998, when Bill Clinton was president, the U.S. House of Representatives passed the Iraq Liberation Act, which called for regime change in Iraq and designated U.S. government funding of political groups outside of Iraq that were opposed to Saddam Hussein. The U.N.-created agency to monitor Iraqi compliance with the WMD resolutions was called the United Nations Special Commission (UNSCOM) and was led by a feisty Australian diplomat, Richard Butler. In 1998, Butler complained that the Iraqis were obstructing UNSCOM's operations, and he and his team left the country. By the end of October, President Clinton had signed H.R. 4655 (the Iraq Liberation Act) and the U.S. military was arguing for military action against Iraq that would not only "degrade" Iraqi capacity for WMD production, but would weaken Saddam's hold on power.

The result was a massive four-day bombing raid on Iraq in December 1998 by U.S. and British aircraft and U.S. cruise missiles during which not only Iraqi defense facilities were targeted, but even one of Saddam's palaces. There was a sharp negative reaction at the U.N. Security Council not only by Russia and China (as expected) but by France, a foretaste of the U.N. combination that would oppose the American initiation of Operation Iraqi Freedom in 2003.

Civilian Iraqis, meanwhile, were clearly suffering from the effects of the U.N.-imposed sanctions, finding great difficulty in obtaining adequate food supplies and medicine. There were repeated charges from human rights organizations that as many as half a million Iraqi children had died from starvation. Even though some groups estimated that figure to be much lower—170,000—a United Nation Children's Fund (UNICEF) study conducted in 1999 concluded that the infant mortality rate for Iraqi children under the age of five had doubled in the years following the imposition of sanctions (1991).[10]

It was President Clinton who signed the congressional bill mandating regime change in Iraq, but it was the administration of his successor, George W. Bush, that would implement it. Indications that Iraq was high on the foreign policy agenda of the incoming Bush administration were apparent at the first meeting of Bush's new National Security Council, under the leadership of National Security Advisor Condoleezza Rice, on January 30, 2001. The topic of Iraq was the main item on the agenda, and Rice bluntly told the assembled NSC members, "We have a regime change policy that isn't really working."[11] Bush, who presided, asked the various participants at the meeting to examine different options relating to their cabinet departments—Secretary of Defense Rumsfeld, for example, was asked to look at military options—and to attend a follow-up session one week later, a meeting chaired by Rice, and not by Bush, who was absent.

Meanwhile, a holdover official from the Clinton administration, Richard Clarke, the NSC's counter-terrorism chief, was trying to get Rice's attention. Clarke was deeply concerned about Al-Qaeda, and he presented Rice early on with a detailed memo warning that Al-Qaeda had a network of terrorist groups in the U.S. Clarke suggested a detailed program of American response to Al-Qaeda, including aid to the Northern Alliance, the principal opposition group to the Taliban regime then ruling Afghanistan, raids on the Afghan camps where Al-Qaeda operatives were being trained and use of the Predator unmanned surveillance aircraft over Afghanistan. Rice told Clarke she would study his memorandum. She was, however, determined to come up with the administration's own counter-terrorism program, one that would not be based on ideas developed within the previous administration. After 9/11, and the search for scapegoats for the intelligence failures that had led to it was underway, Rice came under attack for allegedly not paying due regard to Clarke's concerns.[12]

During the first half of 2001, Iraq remained high on the list of administration concerns for the Middle East; but in late June, Richard Clarke once again raised alarm signals. Something "very, very, very big" was going to happen, he told Rice.[13] At the time, most of the intelligence "chatter"—intercepts of electronic communications gathered by the U.S.—suggested actions by Al-Qaeda overseas; but with the American holiday of July 4 approaching, the CIA was also hearing about possible direct threats to the U.S. On July 10, 2001, CIA director George Tenet was given a briefing by the CIA's own counter-terrorism expert who informed him that Al-Qaeda was preparing an imminent attack on American interests, possibly within the U.S. itself.

September 11, 2001

Tenet was genuinely alarmed by the briefing and asked for a meeting at the White House with Rice to cause the administration to focus seriously on the threat. Rice duly convened it, and Tenet and others who attended it appeared to share the view that the administration was responding vigorously. Unfortunately, two key pieces of information in the possession of the U.S. government were not being given attention at all. The CIA had learned that two known Al-Qaeda terrorists, Khalid al-Mihdhar and Nawaf al-Hazmi, were in the U.S. at this time. For some reason, they were not put on an FBI watch-list. Second, FBI headquarters in New York had ignored a warning from an FBI agent in Phoenix that Arabs suspected of terrorist connections were attending flight schools in order to learn how to handle Boeing 747 airliners. On September 4, a frantic Clarke sent Rice an emotional note warning that the day might soon come when "hundreds of Americans lay dead in several countries, including the U.S."

One week later, his dire prediction came true as four American airliners were hijacked from Logan Airport in Boston and Dulles International Airport in Washington, DC, and brutally taken over in mid-flight by 19 hijackers, 15 of them from Saudi Arabia. Two of the airliners were crashed into the twin towers of the World Trade Center in New York City; one was crashed into the Pentagon; a fourth crashed to earth in a field in Pennsylvania. It was believed to be heading for either the White House or the Capitol in Washington, DC, when passengers stormed the cockpit in an attempt to take back control of the aircraft. Instead, it flew out of control and crashed.

The vast majority of the 2,974 civilians who died in the 9/11 attacks—excluding the 19 terrorist hijackers who perished—were in the twin towers of the World Trade Center or its vicinity. They represented more than 90 different nations and were symbols of the fact that the Al-Qaeda assault upon the U.S. was also an assault upon global civilization. The terrorist organization Al-Qaeda that had been established by Saudi millionaire Osama bin Laden in the 1990s had essentially set itself up against the entirety of global culture.

For the U.S., however, the national shock caused by the attack quickly turned into a national determination to strike back at Al-Qaeda's base of operations, Taliban-controlled Afghanistan. A U.S. and British aerial assault upon military and political targets in Afghanistan began on October 7, 2001. U.S. Special Forces worked closely with leaders of the Northern Alliance (Afghan ethnic groups under warlords who had stood aside from the Taliban) and, in a combination of precise airstrikes and well-planned ground advances, the Northern Alliance forces were able to enter Kabul, the Afghan capital, on November 13. Soon afterwards, the Taliban lost complete control of Afghanistan, and the way was open to a new regime completely sympathetic to—as well as dependent on—Western military and political support.

Even as Afghanistan was entering the bull's-eye of U.S. planning, however, so was Iraq. At an administration war council meeting at Camp David on September 15, 2001, just four days after the 9/11 attacks, the Defense Department produced a document that mentioned Iraq as a possible priority target in fighting back against terror. Deputy Secretary of Defense Paul Wolfowitz said at the Camp David meeting that he thought there was a strong probability that Iraq might have had a connection to the 9/11 terrorist attacks, though no details were presented to show this. Meanwhile, U.S. military officials were sent to various countries to brief officials there on what the U.S. was planning. When General Greg Newbold, the deputy chief of operations for the Joint Chiefs of Staff returned from one such trip to London, he assured a Pentagon official, Doug Feith, that everyone was working hard on how to conduct the assault upon Afghanistan. "Why are you working on Afghanistan?" Feith reportedly countered. "You ought to be working on Iraq."[14]

Iraq was clearly uppermost in the mind of President Bush when he delivered his State of the Union speech to Congress in late January 2002. Bush said that it was an American goal to prevent terrorist threats to the U.S. sponsored by regimes that he said were seeking to develop WMD, regimes like those of Iran, North Korea and Iraq, which collectively, he said, constituted an "axis of evil." The phrase immediately captured attention in the U.S. and generated considerable criticism overseas, not least because many European countries thought the U.S. was "warmongering."[15]

Needless to say, Iran, Iraq and North Korea responded with furious de-nunciations of the phrase.

By the spring of 2002, Secretary of Defense Rumsfeld had ordered up detailed Pentagon planning for a possible attack on Iraq. The officer in charge of United States Central Command (CENTCOM), General Tommy Franks, was tasked with developing the plans. There were disputes among top American military commanders over how many troops would be needed to conduct an invasion when it was set in motion, with Secretary of Defense Rumsfeld continually trying to keep the number of troops down.

By August 2002, planning by CENTCOM for an invasion of Iraq was far advanced. Even more importantly, Bush already seemed clearly in-clined to go forward with the invasion. The administration realized that it faced a skeptical global community at the U.N. and even among Amer-ica's traditional allies. The White House also had to persuade the U.S. Congress that it should be given the authority to hit Iraq militarily, if it needed to do so. The Congress, by large bipartisan majorities, obliged. On October 11, 2002, Congress voted a Joint Resolution to authorize the use of force against Iraq. Though the resolution said it "supported" diplo-matic efforts to resolve the situation, it reiterated points made in the Iraq Liberation Act of 1998 that it should be U.S. policy to remove Saddam Hussein from power.

Conspicuously among high administration officials, Secretary of State Colin Powell argued strongly that the U.S. ought to bring the U.N. on board before initiating any military action against Iraq. Bush and NSC members agreed. Powell went back to the U.N. and tried to persuade fel-low Security Council members that Iraq really needed to be pressured to demonstrate compliance with previous U.N. resolutions ordering it to abandon WMD programs. In November 2002, the Security Council voted 15-0 on a resolution ordering Iraq to submit to weapons inspections again or face "serious consequences," a euphemism for war. But after a U.N. weapons inspection team arrived in Baghdad in December, the Iraqis of-fered confusing information about past weapons programs and what they currently had on hand. The U.N. didn't seem to be willing to be categori-cal that Iraq either had WMD or was impeding inspections by UNSCOM.

At the White House, Bush was impatient. What on earth did the CIA think was the actual situation in Iraq? On December 21, 2002, CIA direc-tor George Tenet arrived at the White House for a briefing with President Bush on evidence of Iraq's alleged WMD program. Bush seemed dubious about the quality of the evidence Tenet was producing and expressed his skepticism. At that point, Tenet made a remark that was to haunt him later, "It's a slam dunk!"[16] He was referring to what he claimed was an open-and-shut case that Iraq did indeed have WMD.

Despite the momentum of the entire administration in the direction of war, according to Rice's recollection, Bush had not made any final decision as late as Christmas 2002. At a meeting in the Oval Office just before Christmas, the President directly asked Rice, "Do you think we should do this?"

"Yes," Rice replied.[17]

But Powell insisted that the U.N. should be approached one more time. On February 3, 2003, Powell delivered an impressively researched presentation before the U.N. Security Council during which he made a vivid case that Iraq had all kinds of WMD programs, some of them successfully concealed in mobile labs that could be transported by road.

Later, after it became clear that Iraq did not have any discernible stockpile of WMD, or even an ongoing program to develop them, he expressed disappointment that none of the "evidence" turned out to be factual. The fact was, a widespread consensus existed both at the U.N. and among U.S. allies that Iraq *did* have WMD. True, many and perhaps most of them did not want the U.S. to initiate an attack upon Iraq. But even France, one of America's most vigorous opponents and critics in the Iraq invasion, was convinced that Iraq had stockpiles of anthrax and botulism toxin, a deadly chemical agent of which a single drop on the skin could kill a person.

As it became apparent that the U.S. was intent on invading Iraq, global opposition to such a step increased markedly. Between January and April, by which time the invasion of Iraq had started, there were mass demonstrations in several countries and several American cities, with millions of participants.

By this time, March 2002, the die had been cast: the U.S. had moved into place in Middle East locations—principally Kuwait and Qatar—the forces it needed for the initial air and ground assault on Iraq. U.N. weapons inspectors in Baghdad, who made it clear they did not believe Iraq had WMD, were asked by the U.S. to withdraw from Baghdad. The U.S. did not have any U.N. Security Council resolution to support the military action it was planning to unleash, but it did have the strong support of one important ally, Great Britain. The British agreed to join the invasion and be responsible for capturing and occupying Iraq's important southern city of

Basra. American officials began to refer to America's allies in the invasion (initially including Australia) as "the Coalition of the Willing."

Operation Iraqi Freedom

On March 20, 2003, the invasion of Iraq began. At first the plan was dubbed with the code-name Operation Iraqi Liberation, but later the preferred term was Operation Iraqi Freedom. In the first few hours of the invasion there was a spectacular bombing campaign of Baghdad and other Iraqi cities in an attempt—unsuccessful, it turned out—to kill Saddam Hussein and the top Iraqi leadership at one stroke.

The U.S. employed B-2 stealth bombers and F-117 stealth fighters, as well as cruise missiles fired from U.S. Navy ships in the Persian Gulf. But the main thrust of the invasion was a conventional land assault by the Army's Third Infantry Division and the Marine Expeditionary Force. In a brilliantly planned operation, and starting off at the Kuwaiti border on March 20, 2003, the Marines and the Third Infantry Division reached Baghdad and pulled down a 20-foot high statue of Saddam Hussein on April 9.

The U.S. forces covered 500 miles in 10 days, often facing fierce dust storms as well as strong opposition. Though the vaunted Republican Guard, the supposed elite of Saddam's armed forces, didn't put up an effective resistance, there were some fierce firefights with the Saddam *fedayeen*, an irregular force of regime supporters trained to operate as a guerrilla force, to attack invading enemies in the rears, to dress as civilians and to melt into the civilian population.

Some 140,000 U.S. military troops were deployed in the initial assault—the total number of U.S. military personnel involved was closer to 248,000—and were clearly sufficient to overwhelm Saddam's military resistance to the invasion. They were clearly insufficient, however, to secure Baghdad and other major Iraqi cities after Saddam's regime fell. The day after the pulling down of Saddam's statue, there were scenes of bacchanalian looting of several government buildings in Baghdad, with Iraqi civilians hauling away computers, TV sets, and pillaging any valuable infrastructure material they could rip away from the walls. It was at this time that the Iraqi National Museum was robbed of priceless artifacts. Questioned about the civilian disorder in Baghdad, Secretary of Defense Donald Rumsfeld responded at a briefing on April 11, 2003, with apparent flippancy. "Stuff happens," he said, a remark that was regarded by some as callously indifferent to the lives of ordinary Iraqis caught up in the destruction of their tyrannical government.

In fact, the Pentagon had been charged with overseeing the administration of Iraq after the invasion. Rumsfeld had recruited a retired army general, Jay Garner, to run something called the Office of Reconstruction and Humanitarian Assistance, in order to help establish an eventual Iraqi government to run Iraq after the invasion. But Garner lost precious time—through no fault of his own—waiting impatiently in Kuwait for safe transportation into Baghdad. Meanwhile, the impression grew around Washington that real incompetence was being displayed by the Americans in occupying Iraq after the fall of the Saddam regime.

A Difficult and Dangerous Transition

In May 2003, Bush responded to the need for decisive action by sending over, in effect, an American "viceroy" to Iraq, a senior former career foreign service officer, Reagan administration ambassador to the Netherlands, L. Paul Bremer. Bremer had been chief of staff to Henry Kissinger in the 1970s. He was both a professional diplomat and savvy at handling himself in the rough world of Washington bureaucratic politics. His job was to run the Coalition Provisional Authority, which would handle the transition of Iraq from just-conquered nation to sovereign new regime.

Bremer dressed crisply in a suit and Timberland hiking boots and brought to the job both dignity and diplomatic skills. That did not prevent him, however, from making serious mistakes in two of his first major policy moves in Iraq. Both of these had been discussed and decided on in principle in the Defense Department before the invasion, and Bremer lost no time in implementing them. Bremer's Order No. 1, issued May 16, 2003, less than a week after his arrival in Iraq, ordered the firing from all government posts in Iraq of the top 30,000 officials of the Ba'ath Party. The decision eliminated from decision-making an entire layer of Iraqis with experience of hands-on governance.

The next decision, Order No. 2, was even more drastic. This ordered the dissolution of the entire Iraqi army, numbering between 300,000 and 500,000 men. The effect was to release onto the street large numbers of angry Iraqis with weapons experience.

General David Petraeus, who at the time was a two-star general commanding the 101st Airborne Division, soon after the decision told Walter Slocombe, one of Bremer's senior staffers, that the decision would put at risk the lives of American soldiers because many of the demobilized Iraqi soldiers would join the ranks of the insurgents.[18] It did, as a new wave of insurgent recruits joined the fighting against the Americans.

For the first three years of the American invasion and occupation of Iraq, U.S. and British forces were hard at work trying to eliminate pockets of insurgency in Baghdad and other parts of the country. One of the most dangerous areas of the insurgency was the so-called "Sunni Triangle," a heavily populated area to the northwest of Baghdad with mostly Sunni Arabs as residents. It was here, in fact, that the most intensive search got underway for the elusive Saddam Hussein and his two sons, Uday and Qusay, who had slipped out of Baghdad within days of the entry of U.S. troops into southern Iraq. On July 22, 2003, the two sons were gunned down, not in the Sunni Triangle, but in Mosul, in the far north of Iraq. The Americans had been tipped off by an Iraqi informant about the location of the sons in a certain house in Mosul. Overwhelming U.S. force, including airpower was used to attack, and the two sons were found killed inside the house.

After an intensive search and some skillful intelligence work by the U.S., Saddam was located hiding in a tiny underground spider-hole beneath a farm near Tikrit, Saddam's ancestral home and a key center of his support. He gave up to U.S. soldiers without resistance on December 13, 2003. TV footage, repeatedly shown around the world, showed a heavily bearded and unkempt Saddam being given a medical examination by an American military doctor wearing surgical gloves.

The Fact-finding Report

But what about the weapons of mass destruction, whose existence in Iraq had been the ostensible reason for the American invasion of Iraq in the first place? Shortly after the invasion, the Multi-National Force-Iraq, the official name of the U.S.-led Coalition running Iraq, created an organization called the Iraq Survey Group (ISG). This was a 1,400-member fact-finding team, mostly American, but including Australians, Britons and other nationalities, asked to investigate once and for all whether Iraq still had stockpiles of WMD, at least at the time of the invasion in March 2003.

The ISG released an Interim Progress Report in October 2003. Its conclusion: it had discovered evidence of recent WMD program activities, but not actual chemical, biological or nuclear weapons. In January

2004, the head of the ISG, former weapons inspector David Kay, resigned. He had come to the conclusion, he said, that no stockpiles of WMD would be found in Iraq in the future. Charles Duelfer, who replaced Kay as head of the ISG, concluded in October 2004 that Iraq had essentially destroyed all its WMD in 1991 after the conclusion of the Gulf War.[19] The U.S. had been mistaken about WMD in Iraq, but so had most of the world.

Atrocities in Anbar Province

Meanwhile, the de-Ba'athification problem and the dissolution of the Iraqi army were creating problems for U.S. forces operating in the heavily Sunni areas around Tikrit. One of the most troublesome areas in the Sunni-dominated Anbar Province was the town of Fallujah. Four American civilian contractors from the Blackwater Company (a private security corporation) were dragged from their cars and beaten to death in Fallujah, their burned bodies then strung up on city overpasses.

An early attempt to flush insurgents out of the city was inconclusive, and the Second Battle of Fallujah, one of the most intense U.S. ground battles in an urban area since the Battle of Hue during the Vietnam War, was fought in Fallujah in November and December 2004. The U.S., in overwhelming numbers, prevailed and regained control of the city. What they found, however, shocked them. There were fewer "foreign fighters," Muslim extremists from other Arab countries and even from non-Arab parts of the Muslim world, than they had expected to find. But they discovered "beheading chambers" where insurgents tortured and murdered civilians they thought opposed their presence in Fallujah.

One of the many gruesome beheadings by foreign fighters in Iraq was carried out by Abu Musab al-Zarqawi, a Jordanian leader of Al-Qaeda, in May 2004. Nicholas Berg, an American businessman in Iraq who had been kidnapped by al-Zarqawi's gang, was beheaded by five black-clad masked men standing behind him. The beheading was captured in a gruesome video that recorded Berg's screaming before his death. Al-Zarqawi was believed responsible for the deaths by bombing, shooting and beheading of perhaps thousands of people in Iraq after the American invasion—Americans and others—including the bombing of the U.N. headquarters in Baghdad in August 2003.

Al-Zarqawi was one of the most loathsome fanatics ever to emerge from the Middle East, a region that has been top-heavy in loathsome fanatics, and was involved in bombings from Casablanca in Morocco to

Jordan, as well as Iraq, where he preyed on members of the Shiite community. He was finally killed by bombs dropped by American fighters on a safe house where he was attending a meeting. He had been betrayed by an associate.

Al-Zarqawi's alleged reason for beheading Nick Berg was the Abu Ghraib scandal, the American mistreatment of Iraqi prisoners at Abu Ghraib prison in Baghdad. The story came to light in April 2004 in a *60 Minutes II* episode on CBS television. Essentially, it showed that Iraqi detainees had been mistreated in the prison by soldiers, male and female, of the 372nd Military Police Company of the U.S. Army, a reserve unit. The detainees had been subjected to humiliating sexual actions, grotesque physical positions while naked and intimidation by German Shepherd dogs, among other actions. There had even been homicides. What made the matter worse was the instant availability of photographs of the abuse on the Internet.

After an army investigation, seven soldiers were court-martialed and two (a man and a woman who featured prominently in photographs of the abuse) sentenced to 10 years and 3 years in prison respectively. The damage to U.S. prestige internationally from the scandal was incalculable. It was certainly the worst scandal involving the U.S. military since the My Lai Massacre in 1968 during the Vietnam War, and several U.S. senators called for Defense Secretary Donald Rumsfeld to resign. Rumsfeld apologized publicly for the abuses, describing them as "wrong" and "inconsistent with the values of our nation." He also told National Security Advisor Condoleezza Rice that he had offered his resignation to President Bush, who had declined it.[20] Rice told her biographer Elisabeth Bumiller later that she thought at the time that the U.S. would never recover from Abu Ghraib.[21]

Balancing the New Iraqi Government

Bremer and other American officials, however, were too deeply involved in trying to run Iraq to be distracted by Abu Ghraib. They were trying to smooth the transition from direct American occupation and administration of Iraq to something the Iraqis could call their own. Initially, Bremer appointed a 25-member Iraqi Governing Council, composed of 13 Shia Iraqis, 5 Sunni, and 5 Kurds, an ethnic Turk and an Assyrian (the original ethnic inhabitants of Iraq before the Arab invasion. The Assyrians were overwhelmingly Christian). On June 28, 2004, however, Bremer officially handed over Iraqi sovereignty to Iraq in a low-key ceremony that had been deliberately brought forward two days ahead of schedule to forestall possible demonstrations or violence.

The new Iraqi body was called the Iraqi Interim Government, which was charged with organizing a referendum on the constitution and then scheduling national elections. These took place as scheduled in January 2005, and they offered the first chance for other Arabs to see what democracy was going to look like in Iraq. After negotiations among parties that emerged from the elections, the Iraqi Transitional Government was formed in May 2005. This body held power until May 2006, when the first permanent Iraqi government was formed.

According to the Iraqi constitution approved by Iraq's voters in a referendum in October 2005, both the president of the country, the prime minister and the cabinet must be approved by two-thirds of the 275 total membership of the Iraqi National Assembly. The current president of the country is a Kurd, Jalal Talabani, and the prime minister a Shia politician, Nouri al-Maliki, a man who fled Iraq in 1979 when he heard that Saddam was planning his execution. He returned to Iraq in 1990. Al-Maliki is a Shiite and a member of the Dawa Party, a conservative Shia political group.

One of al-Maliki's first decisions was what to do with the arrested Saddam Hussein. He had been tried initially in 2005 before a special tribunal of five Iraqi judges called the Iraqi Special Tribunal. He and seven other defendants were charged with crimes against humanity, primarily for reprisals against Iraqi civilians after a failed assassination attempt on Saddam in 1982. When the Iraqi judge first asked his name, Saddam replied, "I am president of Iraq" and continued to speak in a defiant and truculent manner. The trial was marred by kidnappings and assassinations of defense attorneys for Saddam and his codefendants, and was ended without conclusion in 2005. A second trial began in August 2006 and culminated in Saddam's conviction and his sentencing to death. The Iraqi president Talabani rejected appeals for clemency.

Saddam was executed by hanging on December 30, 2006, but the execution itself was an almost grotesque affair that reflected badly on the newly sovereign, democratic state. Some of the guards of Saddam were supporters of Iraqi Shia militant Muqtada al-Sadr, who had vociferously opposed the American presence and whose private militia, the Mahdi Army, had fought against the Coalition by Iraq's own security forces. (In 2008 in Basra, Iraqi forces eventually took over positions the Mahdi Army had held throughout the city.)

An unauthorized video of the Saddam hanging, complete with the shouts of the taunting guards, was captured on a videophone and quickly transmitted on the Internet. It drew strong disapproval from around the world, as well as from the Bush administration.

Growing Pains

The first six months of al-Maliki's administration were very difficult for Iraq. The insurgency against U.S. and Coalition troops had intensified throughout 2005. But another problem was growing sectarian violence between the majority Shia community and the embattled Sunni minority. There were claims of "ethnic cleansing" on both sides. In December 2006, a suspected Sunni suicide car bomber exploded his vehicle in the overwhelmingly Shia sector of Baghdad known as Sadr City. At least 215 people were killed; it was the single worst car bomb explosion in Iraq of the entire war.

The year 2006 was a landmark for the Americans in Iraq as well. In December came the release in Washington, DC, of the official report of the Iraq Study Group (another ISG), a 10-person bipartisan commission asked to look into the entire Iraq war situation by the U.S. Congress. This ISG was co-chaired by former Secretary of State (under President George H. W. Bush) James Baker and former U.S. Representative (Democrat) Lee Hamilton. The impressive members of the assembled panel included former Supreme Court Justice Sandra Day O'Connor and another former Secretary of State (also under George H. W. Bush), Lawrence Eagleburger.

The Survey Group's final report recommended a phased withdrawal of U.S. troops from Iraq and diplomatic dialogue with Iran and Syria, two neighbors of Iraq whose assistance in helping Iraq settle down was considered essential by the group. The fact that Iran was directly involved in supplying dangerous roadside projectiles to insurgents for use against Coalition forces in-country may not have received the attention it deserved.

President Bush was clearly put on the defensive by the report. It added to the pressure he felt from Democrats in the Congress, who had secured significant victories in elections in November 2006 to the House and Senate. He admitted that the situation in Iraq was "bad" and that a "new approach" was needed. While there was wide support for the ISG's recommendations within the Congress and elsewhere, not everyone supported them. The American Enterprise Institute, on December 14, 2006, eight days after the release of the ISG report, held an event to discuss the war. A scholar at the Institute, Frederick Kagan, came up with the idea of a "surge" of U.S. troops in Iraq as the means to securing U.S. victory. Not much was said about U.S. withdrawal from the country.

After the U.S. Troop Surge

In January 2007, President Bush announced a new military strategy for Iraq that was to become known as "the surge." The U.S. would deploy an additional 20,000 troops to Iraq to take up station in Baghdad and other areas of the country where the insurgency was intense. As Bush indicated in his State of the Union message in January 2007, the purpose of the troop increase would be to suppress violence wherever it was found and to secure neighborhoods that had been cleared of enemy fighters.

Opponents of the new strategy were quick to raise their voices in the Senate. Democratic Senators Joe Biden and Barack Obama were among them, but Republican Senator Sam Brownback added his voice.

The initial results of the heightened U.S. troop presence, which took several months to reach full strength, were conflicting. During April, May and June 2007, American combat deaths in Iraq were at their highest level of the entire war, reaching 126 in May. Campaigning in New Hampshire in July 2007, then Democratic candidate Senator Barack Obama made clear his disapproval of the surge. "Here's what we know," he said. "The surge has not worked."[22]

But he was already behind the curve of actual events in Iraq. The casualty figures even by the middle of 2007 were already showing a significant decline. Ethnic and sectarian violence in Iraq's cities was also plunging by November 2007, to the lowest level since the American invasion of Iraq itself. In December 2007, a report by the Brookings Institution, a liberal Washington think tank, reported that "Iraq's security environment is considerably improved, with security at its best levels since early 2004."[23] A CNN report at the end of December 2007 reported that the death toll in combat for U.S. troops had been the second lowest of the war.[24]

By the time that Obama had emerged as the Democratic presidential nominee for the party, he had changed his tune completely. Speaking in a one-on-one interview with Bill O'Reilly of Fox News, in September 2008, Obama said, "I think that the surge has succeeded in ways that nobody anticipated."[25] Well, not quite "nobody." Presumably Frederick Kagan, the author of the American Enterprise Institute report suggesting the surge, the U.S. military commanders who approved of it and President George W. Bush who ordered its execution, anticipated it.

Some commentators have argued that the decline in civilian violence in Iraq was less the result of the success of the "surge" than of the success of ethnic cleansing; in other words, Shia or Sunni militia attacks on each other's communities had systematically altered the demographic geography of Baghdad so that, with areas now almost totally dominated by one group or the other, there were no longer minority communities to kill or terrorize.

Others have argued that U.S. forces simply got more effective at identifying and targeting insurgents. Though there were contradictory views of how the surge was being perceived in the U.S., the situation on the ground in Iraq was viewed by both Iraqis and Americans in that country as significantly improved by late winter of 2008-2009. In a March 2009 ABC News TV report, correspondent Terry McCarthy was almost euphoric about what he had just seen during a recent visit to the country. "In the last six months everything has turned around," he said. "That cloud of fear that has been hanging over Iraq for the last 3 to 4 years just seems to have lifted." He also quoted an Iraqi poll that showed 84 percent of Iraqis said they now felt safe in their own neighborhoods, and 64 percent of Iraqis said they now felt that democracy was the best system for their country.[26]

By the spring of 2009, the most important event on the horizon in Iraq was the planned withdrawal of American troops from all Iraqi cities by the end of June 2009. This had been agreed to in a Status of Forces Agreement (SOFA) signed by both Iraq and the U.S. at the end of 2008. When President Bush made a final visit to Iraq in December 2008 to sign a new security agreement, however, his visit was marred by an incident at a joint press conference with Prime Minister al-Maliki. An Iraqi journalist threw two shoes at Bush (he missed), shouting, "This is a good-bye kiss from the Iraqi people, dog." Throwing shoes at someone is a great insult in Arab society. Though the shoe thrower, an Iraqi TV journalist for a Cairo-based station, was later sentenced from one to three years in prison for insulting a foreign head of state during a state visit, Bush dismissed the incident with a joke. "If you want the facts," he said afterwards, "it's a size 10 shoe that he threw."

Will President Obama be able to display such light-heartedness once the Americans are fully out of Iraq, as they are scheduled to be by the end of 2011? That depends on many yet unknown factors. An opponent of the U.S. intervention in Iraq from the start, Obama has consistently favored

American withdrawal at the earliest opportunity. Whether or not that actually happens in the year 2011, however, the success or failure of the entire American presence in Iraq will accrue to the presidency of George W. Bush. If Iraq survives and prospers as a democratic state—if, in effect, it becomes "normal"—then its success should go almost entirely to President Bush, who took the enormous risk of launching an invasion of it in the first place. It Iraq fails, if it succumbs to a new bout of internal strife, or somehow reverts to a status for its people even more deadly than under dictator Saddam Hussein, then the failure for that will also lie at the door of President Bush.

The overthrow of Saddam Hussein was certainly a blessing for the Iraqi people, and it is doubtful whether any nation other than the Americans could have achieved it so swiftly and efficiently. The real historical question, however, is whether America can be equally successful in launching Iraq down the slipway of political democracy. The answer to that question may take years to arrive.

7

IRAN

To many people in North America and Europe, the mention of Iran brings a frown. Europeans are likely to be offended by the fact that Iran's current president, Mahmoud Ahmadinejad, has repeatedly denied the magnitude of the European Holocaust against the Jews during World War II and has threatened to wipe out the state of Israel from the global map. More diplomatically sophisticated Europeans will recall that Iran has constantly defied European diplomatic efforts to ensure that the country's nuclear program is not utilized for the production of nuclear weapons. Americans beyond the age of 40, especially, will frown at the memory of the 1979-1981 hostage crisis when 52 American diplomats were held prisoner in Tehran for 444 days after militant students invaded the grounds of the embassy. That event is also probably associated with photographic images of the leader of Iran's Islamic Revolution, Ayatollah Ruhollah Khomeini, glowering at the world with his characteristic angry frown.

As recently as 2002, Iran was declared by President George W. Bush to be part of the "axis of evil," three countries (Iraq, Iran and North Korea) that either possessed or were deemed to seek nuclear weapons and had at various times been associated with promoting international terrorism.

Finally, there are probably few literate Americans unaware that Iran has for nearly three decades reciprocated the American ill will by consistently referring to the United States as "the Great Satan." Whether the American-Iranian mutual bad feeling is a consequence of American actions against Iran, or Iranian actions against the U.S., depends on which country you belong to. In some respects, the Iranian resentment of the U.S. is only the latest of a series of resentments against foreign powers—Britain, Russia, Turkey, the Arabs—that have over the centuries imposed their will on Iran through force of arms or economic power. Americans in general

don't think of themselves
as having done anything
harmful to Iran, but this
country, more than most,
has a memory for slights,
both perceived and real.

Iran obviously deserves
its own chapter in any
book on the Middle East
because it is such a major
presence within the region.
With a land area larger
than the largest American
state of Alaska (or in European terms, Britain, France,
Germany and Spain all
bundled together), a population of 75 million, with

IRAN

Source: Central Intelligence Agency

the largest reserves of natural gas and the second or third largest reserves
of oil in the world, and sharing borders with Turkey, Iraq, Pakistan,
Afghanistan and the republics of the former Soviet Union, not to mention
sharing the waters of the Persian Gulf with much of the Arab world, Iran
could never be ignored. But even if Iran did not play a major geo-strategic
role in the world, it would deserve a separate chapter because of the impressive role it has played in world culture and history.

Background History

Iran, in fact, is the location of one of the oldest and continuous major
civilizations in the world. Though there are archaeological traces of culture on the Iranian plateau dating back 7,000 years, the earliest civilization definitively identified with Persia is that of the Elamites, whose
culture is traceable to 2800 BC. The history of Persia, however, takes its
origins from the migration of tribes speaking an Indo-European language
(Indo-European is the language group that includes Sanskrit, Latin,
Greek and most of the modern European languages that descended from
them) onto the central Iranian plateau around 1000 BC. The Persians,
however, entered Middle Eastern history with a big splash when they conquered the empire of Babylonia.

The Hebrew Bible, or Old Testament, records the Persian emperor Cyrus (600 BC or 576-530 BC) permitting the Jews to return to their homeland after languishing for 70 years in exile in Babylon (see Ezra 6:3-5). In fact, Cyrus is the only Gentile king in the Bible to be described as "anointed one" (see Isa. 45:1). Cyrus founded a great empire and dynasty (the Achaemenids) that dominated the Middle East for 200 years and formed the basis of successive Persian imperial dynasties that dominated the region until the arrival of the Arabs. Cyrus is justly celebrated by the Iranians not only as a wise ruler but also as a man of great moral wisdom, permitting freedom of religious worship in all the areas he conquered and prohibiting slavery in the royal Persian domains.

Under the successors of Cyrus, Persian rule continued to grow, until the Persians invaded Greece. The Greek wars with the Persians are part of the rich classical legacy of the West, with such dramatic incidents as the attempts of the Spartans to halt the Persian invasion at Thermopylae in 480 BC. The Spartans were overwhelmingly defeated by superior Persian numbers; and in the same year, the Persians managed to raze Athens. But they were defeated by the Greeks at sea, and in 479 were decisively defeated on land at the battle of Plataea in modern-day Greece east of the Peloponnese. That put an end to Persia's attempts to conquer Greece.

The Achaemenid Persian empire continued for another 150 years until Alexander the Great (356-323 BC), a Greek of Macedonian origin, overthrew them at the Battle of Issus in 333 BC. Alexander burned to the ground the splendid Achaemenid capital of Persepolis and left Persia in the hands of generals who divided up his conquests after his death.

Persia fell to a dynasty called the Seleucids, whose domain embraced both Persia, what is now Syria and much of the Levant. But the Persian sector of the Seleucid empire was defeated by a new Persian empire of the Parthians (238 BC-AD 226), a fiercely warlike group whose fighting skills were deployed incessantly against both the Romans and invaders of Iran from the east. The Parthians were famous for a military tactic of mounted archers firing arrows behind them while at full gallop (the famous "Parthian shot") and for inflicting serious defeats on famous Roman generals (notably Mark Anthony in 36 BC). The Parthians themselves were then defeated by another Iranian dynasty, the Sassanids, who were as troublesome to the later Roman Empire—the Byzantines—as the Parthians had been to the Roman Republic and early Empire. That Roman emperor we met earlier who was captured by the Persians—Valerian—may have received his just deserts: in A.D. 258, he had conducted a merciless persecution of Christians.

The Sassanids followed the ancient Iranian faith of Zoroastrianism, which held that a universal and transcendent god, Ahura Mazda, created the world. Under this deity, order and truth were the natural order, but were constantly under threat from chaos, falsehood and disorder. At the end of time, Zoroastrians believe, Ahura Mazda will prevail over his evil opponent, Angra Mainyu, and a savior-figure will bring about a final renovation of the world. The religion, which clearly has had influences upon Judaism and then Christianity, religions that also originated in the Middle East, was tolerant of other faiths and did not engage in proselytizing. But because it was monotheistic, when the warlike Arab tribes of Islam poured out of the Arabian peninsula in the 630s, Zoroastrianism was easier to absorb into the new, expanding faith of Islam. Still, the Persians resisted the Arabs as fiercely as they could. Although the Sassanid Persians were decisively defeated by the Arabs at the battle of al-Qadisiya in AD 636, the Sassanids tried to rebound and were not finally overcome until about 653.

Iran was decisively under Arab rule from that year onward. But Persian culture, like Chinese, has had a habit over the centuries of affecting its conquerors more than the other way around. Arabization never really succeeded, even though the Persians adopted the Arabic alphabet as the written script of their own language.

During the golden age of the Arab Abbasid Dynasty (750-1258), the Abbasid caliphs were often served by Persian viziers. Many of the greatest geniuses of the Abbasid dynasty were Persian, even though they adopted Arabic names and wrote in Arabic. The physician and polymath (mathematics, poetry, astronomy, chemistry, psychology) Avicenna, or Ibn Sina (980-1037), was a Persian whose medical discoveries had a profound influence on Europe for several centuries. His contemporary, Hakim Abu'l Qasim Ferdowsi (935-1020), was a Persian poet whose masterpiece, the *Shahnameh* (Story of Kings), with some 50,000 rhyming couplets—four times longer than Homer's *Iliad*—is the national epic of Persia.

Although Shia Islam was the actual faith of Ferdowsi, what is unique about the *Shahnameh* is Ferdowsi's successful renewal of the Persian language and his purging of Arabic vocabulary from the Persian languages. The story of the *Shahnameh* focuses on Iran's historical achievements in the pre-Islamic period, and the Arabs themselves are given short shrift. Literate Iranians are all supposed to be able to quote Ferdowsi's couplet:

> Damn on this world, damn on this time, damn on fate,
> The Uncivilized Arabs have come to force me to be a Muslim.[1]

Sandra Mackey, author of a well-informed book on Iran, writes, "Ferdowsi, in essence, separates Islam from the Arabs, whom he holds responsible for the diminution of what he judges a superior Persian culture."[2] Ferdowsi's resurrection of the Persian language in its pre-Islamic form has had a profound impact ever since not only on Persian literature but, right up until today, on Iranian perceptions of their national identity. Even today, many Iranians speak slightingly of the Arabs, even if they do not question where their Islamic faith originated.

The Abbasid dynasty came to an end in 1258, when Hulegu, the grandson of the great Mongolian conqueror Ghengis Khan, sacked the Abbasid capital of Baghdad and brought an end to the Arab empire. But Persia itself had experienced the brutal ferocity of the Mongols decades earlier than that, when Genghis himself descended upon the Persian heartland and decimated the population. After conquering Herat in 1219, the Mongols massacred 1.6 million people, piling skulls by the hundreds in neat pyramids around the city, next to the cadavers of slain dogs and cats. It has been estimated that Persia did not recover their population losses brought on by the Mongols until the nineteenth century.

The murderous onslaught from Central Asia did not end with the departure of the Mongols. In the last quarter of the fourteenth century, Timur, a Central Asian Turk descended from the Mongols, set out to establish a new version of the Mongol empire. With his capital city in Samarkand, where captive artisans built magnificent architectural monuments, he surged through the Middle East and even India (where he ordered the beheading of 100,000 captives). After capturing Baghdad, he moved on to Persia, depopulating entire areas as he conquered them in 1405.

Persians were culturally disdainful of Arabs, but they had already in large numbers adopted the second most important variant of Islam, the Shia variant. Shia Islam constitutes about 15 percent of all the world's Muslims. "Shia" in Arabic means "partisan," as in "partisans of Ali." Ali was one of Mohammed's earliest converts, and was his cousin as well as the husband of Fatimah, Mohammed's daughter. When Mohammed died in

632, Ali was passed over for Caliph (ruler of the Muslims) in favor of Abu Bakr, the first of the celebrated "four righteous caliphs," also known in Arabic as the *Rashidun*. Ali finally was selected as Caliph in the year 656, but was assassinated in AD 661. It was after Ali's death that the real story of the Shia begins.

The Damascus-based ruler Muawiyya, who had played an active rule in wresting control of Syria away from the Byzantines during the first years of the Arab conquest, had refused to accept Ali's position as Caliph because, he claimed, Ali had been unwilling to apprehend the murderers of Othman, who had been the third Rashidun Caliph and was Ali's predecessor. Muawiyya had been a Meccan opponent of Mohammed but converted to Islam after Mohammed's conquest of Mecca in 632. He resented Ali's supporters because they insisted that the Muslim Caliph must be related to a descendant of the prophet. This hostility caused him to attempt to stamp out Ali's own children and supporters. In a compromise between the two camps in 661, Ali's younger son, Hussein, agreed to allow Muawiyya to be the Caliph who would succeed his father until his own death, whereupon he, Hussein, would become Caliph. But when Muawiyya died in 680, his son Yazid grabbed the Caliphate.

Hussein attempted to wrest it back, but at Karbala, in modern-day Iraq, he and his miniscule band of 72 were massacred outright by Yazid's forces. Yazid became founder of the Umayyad Dynasty (661-750) based in Damascus. Hussein became the founding martyr of Shia Islam, the man whose murder in 680 is the focus of the holiest period of the year for all Shia Muslims, the Day of Ashura. Actually, Ashura is the climax to 10 days of grief known as Muharram, during which faithful Shia commemorate the 10-day siege of Hussein leading up to his death.

After the death of Hussein, the Shia elaborated a scheme of perfect imams (Muslim leaders) extending back to Ali. Thus Hasan, Ali's eldest son and, hence (through Fatimah), the grandson of Mohammed, became the second imam, and Hussein the third. There were nine more imams in this tradition, most of them living and dying in Shia Arab areas of what is today Iraq.

Shia Islam is sometimes called "Twelver Shiism" because the twelfth imam, Muhammad ibn al-Hasan, who allegedly began his imamate in the year 868, disappeared sometime after that. (No one quite knows in which year.) Devout Shia say that he "went into occultation" (i.e,. hid himself in a spiritual way) but will come back as the Mahdi, a messianic figure who will return to earth at the end of the age with Jesus to restore justice and peace. Many Sunni Muslims, influenced by Sufi mystical Islam, also believe in the Mahdi, but in their version this person will be a descendant of Mohammed, not someone necessarily connected with Jesus.

Shia Muslims often have a passionate belief in the ability of Hussein and the other 12 imams to answer prayer. Sandra Mackey quotes a female theology student from the Iranian city of Qom as saying, "All the imams are infallible. They can hear us, see us, and answer us. Whatever we ask for they give to us with God's permission."[3] The devotion to the memory of the martyred Hussein is linked also to Iranians' sense that they have been martyred as a nation through repeated foreign conquest and despotic and corrupt rulers of Persia.

Pious grief in Shia Islam, however, should not be confused with quiescence. Sunni and Shia Muslims coexisted in Persia until the reign of the last shah or monarch. But there is little that is passive about Shia Islam, especially within the context of Persian history. It was not until Shah Ismail I (1487-1524) that Shia Islam became the dominant Islam variant in Persia. Ismail came to the throne in 1501 and founded the powerful Safavid Dynasty, based at first in Tabriz. As he was establishing control over the country, he forced Shiism on all his subjects. Ismail had started his conquests in Azerbaijan, where his followers bore the name Qizilbash ("Redheads") from red turbans they wore. Though Ismail was defeated by the Ottoman Turks in 1514, he extended the boundaries of Persia to what they are today. Ismail was a poet (he wrote more in Turkish than in Persian) and a mystic who believed not only in his direct descent from Ali but also in a quasi-divine status. His title in Turkish meant, "I am God's mystery,"[4] and he proclaimed his own divinity: "I am very God, very God, very God!"[5]

The greatest of the Safavid shahs was Shah Abbas I (1587-1629). Abbas recruited two Englishmen, the brothers Robert and Anthony Sherley, to reorganize his army into a properly led and trained force that could use against the Ottoman Turks the resources of disciplined training and gunpowder the Ottomans had adopted from the West.

Abbas pushed the Portuguese out of Bahrain in 1602, and the English out of Hormuz, though he permitted the British East India Company, Britain's mercantile monopoly for trade with the East, to establish trading entrepots on the Gulf coast of Iran and even permitted European Catholic monastic orders to establish monasteries within his kingdom. He turned the Safavid capital of Isfahan into a magnificent repository of art and architecture, which today has earned it UNESCO recognition as a World Heritage Site. Despite his diplomatic skills and his cultural taste, however, Abbas became almost paranoid toward the end of his life over fear that he would be assassinated. He executed one of his own sons and blinded two others. When he died in 1629, there was no son capable of succeeding him.

The Safavids faltered badly when rebellious Afghans defeated the Persians in 1722 and besieged Isfahan. But a brilliant military tactician, Nadir Shah (1698-1747), arose in the vacuum left by the Safavid's weakness to create a brief but powerful Persian domain throughout Central Asia. Described by some historians as the Napoleon of Persia, Nadir Shah repulsed the Russians and Ottomans who had invaded Persia and for a short time presided over a Persian-ruled domain that encompassed Persia, Afghanistan, Pakistan and parts of the Caucasus and Central Asia.

The zenith of his power was when he conquered Delhi in India in 1739 and brought back to Persia the famous Peacock Throne, which was to serve thereafter as the symbol of Persian imperial power. Like Abbas, Nadir Shah became paranoid and cruel in his later years, blinding his own son, Reza, and executing dozens of suspected enemies. He emulated Timur by making pyramids of decapitated heads whenever he found it necessary to conquer rebellious parts of his conquered kingdom. He paid for his paranoia with his own life, being assassinated by his own officers who feared he was about to execute them.

Persia in the later eighteenth century experienced brutal civil wars until yet another shah-tyrant, Agha Mohammed Khan, fought his way to power in 1794 and founded a new dynasty, the Qajars, which lasted until 1925. The new shah moved the Persian capital to Tehran, where it has remained until today.

One of the Qajar shahs, Nasir ed-Din, traveled several times to Europe with wives and concubines. He shocked English society by offering an absolute fortune to an attractive English upper-class beauty to join his harem. (She declined.)

Persia was repeatedly at war with Russia in the nineteenth century, and her southern portions were at times under the control of the British, though she was never directly colonized by either Britain or Russia. At one point, Nasir ed-Din sought to pay for his excesses by granting a 60-year tobacco concession to the British Imperial Tobacco Company for 15,000 pounds a year. There was widespread popular protest, and the shah, like so many of his predecessors, was felled by an assassin's bullet in 1896.

The Qajars had so worn out their welcome in Iran that the country went through a dramatic popular and constitutional revolt between 1905 and 1911. Discontent with the monarchy, however, took two varying forms. European-trained and European-oriented intellectuals sought a secular and constitutional system that essentially disavowed Iran's pious Shia past. At the other end of the spectrum, high-ranking Shia mullahs led a popular movement against the corrupt Qajar dynasty and argued strenuously for Islam-based reform. They rejected the wholesale adoption of Western institutions and habits that the secular, European-educated constitutionalists were demanding. This dichotomy was to foreshadow protests against another shah more than 70 years later.

In 1906, massive popular unrest against the monarchy culminated in thousands of Persian merchants taking refuge within the British embassy out of fear that, if they failed to open the stores they had gone on strike to close, their property would be expropriated. The protest then spread from merchants to teachers, and the shah was finally forced to consent to a constitution and the creation of a parliament or national assembly, the Majlis. The parliament met for the first time in October 1906, and the constitution that emerged several months later from its deliberations was essentially modeled on the 1831 constitution of Belgium. Though the constitution restricted the powers of the monarch, there remained a great divide between Western-oriented, secular republicans and the deeply conservative clergy traditionalists determined to continue implementing Shia Islam in its fullest dimension. In essence, the Shia senior clergy, the *ulama*, wanted to have a veto decision over any constitutional reforms that were being debated in the Majlis, the newly formed national assembly.

But Britain and Russia had managed to resolve their mutual suspicions over how much power each nation was wielding in Iran by signing an Anglo-Russian Agreement of 1907. In effect, both empires now agreed that they did not want the Majlis to prevail in the struggle for power with the monarchy. In 1908 Russian troops ringed the Majlis building and exchanged fire with the defenders of the constitution. After several hours, the Majlis seemed to have conceded. But its supporters continued the fight in other Persian cities until 1911, when the shah, backed up once again by Russian troops, decided to quell his political opponents once and for all.

In 1911, the Majlis called on an American, W. Morgan Shuster, to try and bring order and integrity into Iran's corrupt and notoriously inefficient fiscal system. When Shuster ordered his tax collectors to take possession of the residence in Tehran of a Persian prince living in exile in Russia, Russian soldiers tried to deny the American and the Persian officials entry. Shuster and his excise officials barged in anyway. This, however, precipitated a full-scale assault upon Tehran by Russian troops. On December 24, 1911, the Russians shelled Tehran's parliament building and brought an end to Iran's experiment with constitutionalism.

World War I temporarily distracted both the Russians and the British from paying much attention to Persia, but the long-term British interest in the country was rooted in profound geopolitical reality. Britain's Royal Navy had converted from coal-powered propulsion to oil. As the war clouds of Europe gathered, it was becoming vitally important for Britain to locate and control a rich source of petroleum.

Persia provided the answer. Oil had been discovered by British petroleum prospectors in Iran (in the so-called "neutral sector" of the country between the Russian and the British zones). The Anglo-Persian Oil Company was formed in 1908 (later to be renamed the Anglo-Iranian Oil Company), and in June 1914, just weeks before World War I broke out, First Lord of the Admiralty Winston Churchill persuaded the British House of Commons to take a controlling interest in the company (for 2.2 million pounds). With the savings made by the conversion from coal to oil, the British were able to pay for a major naval expansion just when they needed it.

Russian pressure on Persia was relieved after the Germans began defeating the Russians in World War I and, later, when the Bolshevik Revolution of November 1917 threw everything in Russia into chaos. During the war, Turkey trampled upon Persian territory to attack Russia and for a time threatened the Anglo-Persian oil fields. In February 1917, there began the series of tumultuous events in Russia that led first to the downfall of the tsar, and then in October to the triumph of the Bolsheviks in a coup d'état. The Bolshevik Revolution had a major impact on Iran when the new Russian revolutionary regime of Lenin unilaterally renounced "the tyrannical policy" of tsarist Russia and abandoned extraterritorial privileges for Russian citizens in Persia. Persia and Russia signed a treaty in 1921 that codified these concessions by the Bolsheviks. It was hugely popular in Persia and quickly ratified by the Majlis.

As for the British, after the war ended, Britain in 1919 proposed an Anglo-Persian agreement, which would have permitted London to appoint advisors to the Persian government in both its civilian and military branches. The notion that the ancient nation of Persia might become a

distant satrapy of the British empire was profoundly offensive to both
the Majlis and many ordinary Persians. The Majlis refused to ratify the
agreement and the British advisors who had arrived in anticipation of the
agreement's implementation were sent home.

Yet the years of chaos, corruption, incompetence and humiliation by
foreigners had created a hot-house of resentment against both the totter-
ing Persian monarchy of the Qajar dynasty formed in 1794 and the foreign powers—notably Britain—that continued to attempt to manipulate
Persian politics. This led to the appearance of a dynamic military commander who had been trained in the shah's Cossack brigade and had been
persuaded by reformers to march on Tehran and seize power. His name
was Colonel Reza Khan. He entered Tehran February 21, 1921, had himself named first Minister of War, and then Prime Minister.

Reza Khan quickly formed a regular, and regularly paid army and put
down various local disturbances around the country. The last Qajar
monarch, the seriously obese Sultan Ahmed Shah, had left Persia for medical treatment in 1923. Reza Khan became prime minister that same year,
quelled rebellions in various parts of the country, and convinced the
British that Persia under his control would be stable enough to leave to
its own devices.

The prime minister was greatly attracted to the example being set in
neighboring Turkey, where Mustafa Kemal, also known as Atatürk, had
transitioned from a successful general in the Ottoman armies of World
War I to the president of a new nationalist and emphatically secularist
Turkey. Reza Khan began to wonder if Persia might not also become a republic under his own leadership. As rumors spread that this was his thinking, the Shia religious leaders of Qom rose in revolt. They were alarmed
that, in a republic that was overtly secular, there might be little room for
political power yielded by the Shia clergy.

A deal was struck: Reza Khan would not push for a republic, and in return the clerics would consent to his becoming monarch at the head of a
new Persian dynasty. In April 1926, Reza Khan became the first shah of
the new Pahlavi dynasty.

The Modernization of Persia

Reza Khan quickly made his mark on life in Persia. He was obsessed with
modernizing the country and pushed hard and fast for the development
of a railroad system linking Tehran with other cities across the country. He

mandated Western-style dress for both men and women, and shocked the Shia clerics by decreeing abolition of the veil for women. He ripped down whole sections of Tehran and constructed in their place grandiose public buildings designed architecturally to evoke the splendor and glory of ancient Persia. He ordered people to adopt family names in order to facilitate administration of the country, and made it clear that he preferred traditional Persian names to Islamic ones. In a move calculated to undermine the power of the Shia clerics, the *ulama*, Reza Khan introduced a Western-style civil code to overlap, and in places replace, the *sharia* traditions.

In 1935, he undertook three of his most radical policy changes. He officially changed the name of Persia to Iran. He established the University of Tehran with Western academic standards and several imported European faculty members. Third, and most radically, he declared that the wearing in public of the *chador*, the all-encompassing black dress that completely concealed women from sight, was henceforth illegal. He decreed that the university belonged to the state, and that it be secular. The least controversial of these moves was probably changing the name of the country. The name Iran was closer to the ancient notion that Persia was the place where the Aryans lived.

Reza Khan was a nationalist in sympathy with the nationalistic aspirations being pursued in Germany and Italy in the 1920s and 1930s. He was, in a way, Persia's fascist leader, determined to crush political and cultural opposition to his innovations from any source. He repeatedly humiliated Iran's clergy with his innovations, particularly his laws that Iranian women were not allowed to attend movie theaters or ride in public transport or in taxis while wearing a *chador*. But he never succeeded in undermining the power of the Shia *ulama*.

Reza Khan, however, was to find that the changing dynamics of international geo-politics threatened Iran in the mid-twentieth century no less than those same dynamics had repeatedly threatened Persia in the nineteenth century. Though nationalist memories of humiliation at the hands of the Russians and the British led many Iranians to favor Nazi Germany in its struggle with Great Britain, when Germany invaded the Soviet Union in June 1941, a new element came into play. German advances deep into the Soviet Union toward the oil resources of Baku threatened, unless turned back, to envelop Iran itself. The U.S. had pledged military assistance to Great Britain in the 1941 Lend-Lease agreement. After Germany invaded the Soviet Union in 1941, the U.S. strongly encouraged the provision of

Lend-Lease supplies to the Soviet Union through Iran. When Reza Khan officially rejected a joint British and Soviet request to send arms overland across Iran to the Soviet border, both Moscow and London took military action. On August 25, 1941, a simultaneous Soviet and British invasion of Iran ensured that the arms were delivered.

On September 16, Reza Khan was forced to resign. He was replaced by his 23-year-old son Mohammed Reza Pahlavi, a convenient British-Soviet puppet. After the U.S. entry into World War II in December 1941, the Americans added their weight to the military assistance of Moscow. Iran obligingly declared war on Germany, and in December 1943, Stalin, Roosevelt and Churchill conducted a key wartime summit in Tehran. The Soviets, however, retained a hold on three northern provinces of Iran, Azerbaijan, Gilan and Mazandaran. That presence was to mark the beginning of the emergence of a major new force in Iranian politics, the Tudeh Party, the new and increasingly formidable Iranian Communist movement.

British and American military forces withdrew from Iran at the end of World War II; but in the case of the Soviets, the Russians had to be prized out of Azerbaijan by American pressure. Moscow had intended to annex the northern Iranian territory to the Soviet Union.

Resentment of Foreign Interests

Despite Moscow's dilatoriness in respecting Iranian sovereignty, the next chapter in Iran's long and angry history of resisting foreign intervention involved the British, not the Russians.

The Anglo-Iranian Oil Company (AIOC) had vastly increased its oil production in the decades since the British government obtained a majority share in the company. British employees of AIOC, especially in refinery towns like Abadan, lived a life safely separated from the sometimes squalid realities of Iran. Their neat houses were policed by company policemen, and there were signs on company drinking fountains: "NOT FOR IRANIANS." The Iranian national humiliation of extraterritorial privileges for foreigners (British employees of AIOC could not be tried in an Iranian court) and the more serious issue of AIOC's squeezing out what Iranians felt were excessive profits provoked a nationalist movement that turned into a major international crisis. (During 1944-1949, AIOC profits increased tenfold, whereas Iran's revenues from the production had risen by a factor of only four.) "To Iranians," Iranian observer Sandra Mackey has written, "British control of Iran's petroleum resources represented the

same impotence inflicted by the Mongols, the Turks, and the Russians."[6]
While Mohammed Pahlavi, the shah, was willing to compromise in negotiations with AIOC, the Nationalist Coalition in the Majlis, led by Mohammed Mossadegh, wanted to nationalize AIOC altogether.

A Popular Prime Minister Gets Ousted

Mossadegh rode a wave of popularity into the Prime Ministership in
April 1951. His selection by the Majlis as the nation's political leader had
been supported by waves of strikes and protest by the Tudeh Party, who
favored nationalization. This took place, under Mossadegh's leadership,
at the beginning of May. The reaction of AIOC and allied international
oil companies was swift. The AIOC withdrew all its foreign technical experts, bringing production within months to a virtual standstill.

At the same time, sister oil companies of the AIOC agreed to join a
boycott against the purchase of Iranian oil now that it was in the hands
of the Iranian government. The economic crisis caused by the sudden de-
pletion in national revenues gave rise to great uncertainty in the country.
Mossadegh requested, and received, emergency powers from the Majlis
for a six-month period from July 1952. He took advantage of his increased political authority to begin to replace constitutional restrictions
on the power of the shah.

When Mossadegh requested an extension of emergency powers in
January 1953, Iran's domestic economic situation had deteriorated even
more. By now, the Tudeh Party was a major source behind social unrest
and presented itself to some observers as a force no longer automatically
aligned with Mossadegh.

In the U.S., President Eisenhower had just been inaugurated and was
amenable to arguments by the British government that Mossadegh,
egged on by the Tudeh Party, might be on the point of allowing Iran to
join the Soviet bloc in the Cold War. In March 1953, the American Central Intelligence Agency (CIA) agreed to join with the British MI6 (a secret intelligence service) in a plot called Operation Ajax to remove
Mossadegh from power.

By dispensing considerable sums of money and manipulating inherent suspicion on the part of the Shia clergy that Mossadegh was an un-
reconstructed secularist who would sooner or later challenge their power,
the CIA, by August 1953, had mobilized Iran's irregular and regular
forces against the Iranian prime minister. The shah had fled the country

as unrest reached the boiling point and was only willing to return after the parliament building in Tehran had been surrounded by army troops and Mossadegh himself had surrendered.

Mossadegh was tried for high treason by a military tribunal but spared the death penalty, which would have been the normal punishment. He was exiled to a village far from Iran where he lived under house arrest until his death in 1967.

From the U.S. point of view, Mossadegh was an unstable nationalist fanatic, a man given to ranting public rages, fits of weeping and even fainting. Given the dangerous way the world looked in 1953, it must have seemed too risky to permit him to continue running Iran with such a powerful pro-Soviet Communist Party, the Tudeh, exerting such influence in the country. In Eastern Europe, Soviet tanks had brutally crushed a worker's uprising in Berlin in June; and in Indo-China, the French seemed not to be able to hold their own against an independence war led by the Communist Vietminh. If Iran were to fall within the Soviet orbit, it must have seemed to American policy makers that a geopolitical catastrophe would occur.

But to most Iranians, including those adamantly opposed to the regime of the Islamic Republic today, Mossadegh was a brave, if flawed, national hero. His ouster by forces loyal to the shah might have taken place without any American involvement in Iranian affairs at all. But many Iranians interpreted what happened to Mossadegh as yet another in a long list of national humiliations suffered at the hands of the West. The Mossadegh ouster, to many Iranians, was the CIA at its worst, interfering with and manipulating events in a foreign country in order to foil the patriotic aspirations of the majority of the people. Interestingly, there are some Iranians who dispute this view. Amir Taheri, an Iranian former newspaper editor who has written extensively about Iran since leaving the country in 1980, argues that "in the end, the CIA played only a minor role" in the ouster of Mossadegh.[7]

U.S. democratic administrations have taken a very apologetic view of the American involvement, such as it was, in Mossadegh's ouster. In the year 2000, then-Secretary of State Madeleine Albright publicly expressed regret that Mossadegh had been ousted in a coup. "The coup was clearly a setback for Iran's political development," she said, "and it is easy to see now why many Iranians continue to resent this intervention by America."[8] Recriminations between Iran and the U.S. are likely to continue for decades longer, with the Iranians perennially raising the issue of Mossadegh and the Americans returning relentlessly to the takeover by militants of the American embassy in Tehran in 1979.

The Shah's Return

On the shah's successful return from exile, he seemed to many Iranians to have become a new person. No longer the timid monarch taking refuge from domestic crises or turmoil in his country estates or in foreign exile, Mohammed Pahlavi seems to have concluded that divine approval, what Iranians have traditionally referred to as *farr* ("divine glory"), rested with him. The concept of *farr* extends back to a period even earlier than the age of the Achaemenid kings and is represented in Persian mural reliefs by a crowned birdlike figure hovering over the head of a king. Possession of *farr* somehow made the king more than human, but injustice in a monarch might cause the departure of *farr*. In many ways, the concept of *farr* is reminiscent of China's concept of the Mandate of Heaven, the sense—or absence of it—that a particular dynasty enjoys heaven's favor.

Tightened Control

The shah may have misinterpreted a plot engineered by the CIA and British intelligence as the blessing of divine approval. In fact, after his return from temporary exile in 1953, he worked hard to establish the foundations of an increasingly strident authoritarianism. He made sure that the traditional organs of state power—the police, the army, the gendarmerie—were under tight supervision and control. He also began to rely increasingly on a more ominous organ of state power, the intelligence and security organization known as SAVAK (a contraction of the Farsi phrase *Sazman-e-Ettelaat va Amniyat-e-Keshvar*, "Intelligence and Security Organization of the Country"). SAVAK was initially trained by CIA agents and later received advice and additional training by Israel's foreign espionage agency, Mossad.

SAVAK early on focused on the activities of members of, and sympathizers with, the Tudeh Party. It soon became one of the most feared and hated institutions in Iran, not only because its agents were engaged in everything from censoring poetry to infiltrating Communist cells, but also because it deployed brutal means of incarceration and interrogation. SAVAK's heyday didn't come until the 1970s, when the shah became certain that his most formidable opponents belonged to the Communist underground rather than to the clergy that in fact took over Iran.

Like his father, Reza Khan, Mohammed Reza Pahlavi wanted Iran to be modernized, which in his eyes meant a continuation of efforts to liberate women from all social restrictions and bondages. Yet, though female liberation was an icon of leftist ideology worldwide, the shah was given little credit from his leftist foes for his efforts. He'd already begun to experience student protests in 1962, when angry students demonstrated against him at the University of Tehran. In a foretaste of future repression, the military was called in to crush the protests with great brutality.

Operation Ajax was intended to ensure that Iran did not join the Soviet bloc, and in that sense it succeeded. The U.S. was pleased with the shah's compliance with the policy of keeping him tied closely to the West, but it was deeply disturbed about the heavy-handed repression of Iranian society. The administration of President John F. Kennedy in 1963 prodded the shah to introduce reforms that would dilute the growing opposition to his rule and make it easier for the U.S. to argue in defense of the Iranian regime.

But the shah was already moving in the direction of domestic reform. In January 1963, he announced the White Revolution, a six-point reform program whose centerpiece was land reform, but which included profit sharing in industry, a literacy campaign and a significant move forward in the enfranchisement of women.

The land reform component of the White Revolution was intended to improve the lot of the 75 percent of Iranians who worked as peasants. It did provide immediate relief to many peasants, who were given title deeds to their lands in ceremonies that the shah himself sometimes attended. But though the government did buy the land from landowners at fair prices, the reforms alienated many wealthy landowners—because their wealth was eroded—on whom the shah depended for his political support in the country. The educated middle class was not impressed with the White Revolution's economic prospects, and in any case was more interested in political liberties, which the shah did not want to grant.

Sharp Criticism from the Clergy

Finally, the clergy—ultimately to be the shah's fatal adversary—were displeased because an alteration of economic power in the villages threatened to undermine their power. The clergy, in the form of the shah's future nemesis Ayatollah Ruhollah Khomeini, a Qom-based cleric, was particularly incensed over the issue of women's rights. When in 1962 the shah had made it clear he intended to extend women's rights in the electoral arena as part of the White Revolution, Khomeini cabled the monarch warning that the reform was an attack upon Islam. In March the following year, 1963, Khomeini denounced the entire White Revolution as a danger to the Koran.

The geographical base of his criticism was the city of Qom, one of Shia Islam's "holy" cities, about 100 miles southwest of Tehran. This had long been the center of Shia theological training. The discontent in Qom and the criticism from Khomeini pushed the shah into a sharp crackdown on his clerical opposition. A raid on one of Qom's main theological schools a few days after Khomeini's first denunciations resulted in the deaths of two students. Khomeini used the mourning ceremonies 40 days later as, in effect, the opening broadside in what was to become a life-and-death political duel with the shah.[9]

Ayatollah Ruhollah Khomeini, the man who was to become the glowering symbol of Iran's Islamic revolution, was born in 1902, in a village about 180 miles south of Tehran. His father and both of his grandfathers were Shia clerics. He embarked on theological studies at an early age, and in 1921 moved to Qom to study under a particular cleric, a man ironically known for his lack of interest in politics. Khomeini was interested in mysticism and philosophy, as well as Islamic theology, and lectured for several years at Qom and Najaf (in Iraq). His first emergence to prominence was as a writer opposing the secularization trends of the 1940s.

In June 1963, four days after the speech at the mourning obsequies of the theology students who had been killed, Khomeini launched his most ferocious rhetorical assault yet on the shah. "You miserable wretch," he said, warming up to his topic, "Forty-five years of your life have passed. Isn't it time for you to think and reflect a little, to ponder about where all of this is leading you, to learn a lesson from the experience of your father? I hope to God that you did not have in mind the religious scholars when you said, 'The reactionaries are like an impure animal,' because if you did, it will be difficult for us to tolerate you much longer, and you will find yourself in a predicament. . . . The nation will not allow you to continue this way."[10]

But it was Khomeini that the shah's security services would not allow to continue. Within 24 hours Khomeini had been arrested and confined to house arrest in Qom. The reaction was three days of savage rioting in Tehran, with the shah's palaces and other Tehran locations requiring protection by army tanks. The June rioting spread to other cities in Iran, and by the time it was over some 86 people had been killed.

Khomeini was released from house arrest in the spring of 1964, but remained defiantly hostile to the shah.

The next major issue to arouse his animosity was the U.S. demands that Iran agree to a Status of Forces Agreement (SOFA) that would permit American residents in Iran to be immune from Iranian domestic law. There were tens of thousands of Americans living in Iran, connected with the military aid mission or the petroleum or other businesses. Many of them were insensitive toward, and even openly contemptuous of, Iran's cultural traditions. They would sometimes play music loudly during the deeply serious Shia Ashura holidays and refer slightingly to Iranian culture as "camel culture." Iranians didn't need to know any English to discern the lack of respect. Thus the U.S. government's demand that Iran agree to a SOFA seemed to be an extension of the worst days of old Persia's subordination to foreign powers. Iranians, ever sensitive to foreign pressures and humiliation, exploded once again in protest. The Majlis narrowly passed the measure in October 1964, whereupon Khomeini once again denounced the "slavish" vote of the Majlis. "Does [the Majlis] know what crime has occurred surreptitiously and without the knowledge of the nation?" he thundered. "Does it know that the Assembly at the initiative of the government, has signed the document of enslavement of Iran?"[11]

The Ayatollah Khomeini in Exile

The shah, of course, never replied to the bony-fingered cleric except courtesy of his ever-vigilant security services; in November 1964, they piled Khomeini onto a plane into exile in Turkey, where he was to remain for slightly less than a year. In a curious way, the shah couldn't seem to decide what to do with Khomeini. Other opponents of the regime who had come into the sights of SAVAK had suffered sudden heart attacks at unexpected moments. The shah, however, was more worried about the prospect of Khomeini dead—a potential rallying point of political opposition as a martyr—than Khomeini alive and still inflamed against him. In October 1965, Khomeini was permitted by the new (since 1965), thoroughly secular Iraqi Ba'ath Party regime to continue his exile in the holy Shia city of Najaf, in Iraq. He was to remain there for 13 years.

While in Najaf, Iraq, during late January and early February 1970, Khomeini gave 19 lectures that laid the theoretical foundations on the subject of *Velayat-e Faqih*, a Persian phrase clumsily translated as "Theologian Guide" or "Guardianship of the Jurisconsult." In essence, the system describes a society whose laws are entirely subject to Islamic law, the *sharia*, and the interpretation of those laws defined by Shia clerics knowledgeable in those laws. The ruler of the country in which *Velayat-e Faqih* was operative should be the person considered the most learned in all aspects of Islamic law. *Velayat-e Faqih* prescribes a theocracy resting on the assumption that learned Shia clerics are by definition the men entrusted with the correct interpretation of Allah's politics for society.

Many observers of Khomeini's career have noted that Khomeini was fascinated by the philosophy of Plato, who advocated in *The Republic* an ideal society that was to be governed by "guardians," a privileged elite of philosophers.

Khomeini was not alone in his elaboration of a radical system of governance that would be the antithesis of every constitutional notion ever dreamed up in Europe or North America after the period of the French Enlightenment in the mid-eighteenth century. During the 1970s, opposition to the shah's rule grew in all levels of Iranian society, but especially among the intelligentsia and the middle and lower-middle classes.

An Iranian who came to embody the attempt to fuse Shia theology with Marxism and Third World radical ideas was Ali Shariati (1933-1977). Shariati was exposed to the Marxist ideas of the Tudeh Party in the late 1940s and early 1950s. During the Mossadegh era of the early 1950s, he became a radical nationalist; but after he went to France to study, he linked up with the Algerian National Front, which was fighting the French government to acquire Algerian independence. He deepened his studies in Marxism and became acquainted with Frantz Fanon (1925-1961), author of *The Wretched of the Earth*, the Afro-Caribbean theoretician who attacked European colonialism. Shariati imbibed Marxism through French academics (as did also in the 1950s Cambodia's violent Communist leaders like Pol Pot and Khieu Samphan) but added the gloss that violent revolution for social justice could combine the ideas of Marxism and Shia Islam.

Particularly appealing to many Iranians disturbed by Iran's cultural disjointedness under the pressures of rapid Westernization was the concept of "Westoxification," the idea that something pure in Iranian culture was becoming poisoned by the introduction of entirely alien Western ethos. Shariati was the bridge that enabled many Iranian Communists and leftists to entrust the revolution in Iran to Khomeini, whom they thought they could ultimately control. Of course, in the end, the Islamists controlled and suppressed the leftists, not the other way round.

The Shah's Missteps

But even as leftist political opposition to the monarchy was gathering strength in Iran, so was the shah himself. During five days in October 1971 he organized a lavish celebration of 2,500 years of Persian history near the ruins of Persepolis, the original capital of Cyrus the Great and the Persian Empire. Kings, queens, presidents, diplomats and celebrities flew in for a gargantuan five-and-a-half-hour banquet of roast peacock, quails' eggs and Dom Perignon champagne organized by the staff of Maxim's of Paris, which closed for two weeks so that the 600 guests in Iran could be royally catered to. A sound and light show featuring Iranian soldiers and policemen garbed in the uniforms of different Iranian imperial epochs was another feature of the five-day event, which may have cost as much as $300 million. But it did little to ameliorate the sullen feelings about his regime on the part of many Iranians, much less improve their quality of life.

Not surprisingly, the extravaganza came in for sharp criticism because of the income disparities between rich and poor in Iran. From his aerie in Najaf, Ayatollah Khomeini denounced anyone who participated in the Persepolis events as a "traitor."

The shah, however, was on a roll, and the following year, 1972, he played host to American president Richard Nixon, fresh from his diplomatic triumph in Beijing. (Nixon in that year dramatically ended the U.S.'s 23-year refusal to have any contact with the People's Republic of China. The U.S.-China rapprochement dramatically improved America's geopolitical position in the world vis-à-vis the Soviet Union, its Cold War adversary.)

Oil Revenue and American Friendship

Nixon hit it off with the shah, and the two men discovered they shared similar strategic worldviews on the Soviet Union and the significance of the Persian Gulf in global politics. In Iran, income from oil was raising living standards throughout the country. When the oil price among petroleum-producing nations rose sharply after the Yom Kippur War (between Israel and Egypt and Syria) of October 1973, Iran's national income rose in a spectacular way. In the course of a year the price of oil changed from $3 a barrel to $11 a barrel. Iran's national revenue from oil rose in the period 1972-1974 from $3.4 billion to $17.4 billion. Iranians now had the highest per capita income in the entire Third World.

The massive infusion of wealth fueled the shah's ambitions to become a regional superpower. With the encouragement of President Nixon, who saw the shah as America's policeman in the Persian Gulf, Iran began to acquire massive amounts of high-level American military technology. The transfer of military technology required the presence of some 50,000 Americans, about half of them from the American military. Many of the American helicopter pilots training the shah's spanking new air force had been U.S. Army chopper pilots in South Vietnam before the country abruptly fell to the Communist North in April 1975.

Meanwhile, the shah was making it clear that his idea of Persian greatness was not especially Islamic. He abolished the Islamic calendar and replaced it with a system that recalled the greatness of Persia's ancient empire. On the radio, the poems of the national poet Ferdowsi were often broadcast; statues of the shah went up all over the country. The secret police agency SAVAK was actively identifying radical opponents of the regime, arresting them and sometimes torturing them. More ominously, from time to time, opponents of the regime expired from sudden and unexpected heart attacks. Many thought these were induced clandestinely by agents of SAVAK. One regime opponent who died in this way in 1977, having been incarcerated in Iran for more than a year and then released to England, was Ali Shariati.

An Emerging Revolt

The following year, however, marked the beginning of what turned into a surprisingly sudden collapse of the shah's system. From January 1978 onwards there were strikes and demonstrations that paralyzed the country. Politically, the shah had not succeeded in persuading a significant part of his population that his secular, modernizing policies were good for Iran overall. True, there had been a great increase in wealth at all levels of the country. But the gap between rich and poor, and the perception that the rich elite of Tehran was out of touch with the lives of ordinary Iranians, was flammable material in the mundane but often pious world of the bazaars.

Cassette tapes of the sermons of Khomeini denouncing the shah were passed from hand to hand, creating a climate of discontent at the deepest level of society. To make matters worse, leftists, who certainly had nothing to gain if Iran became governed by Khomeini's *Velayat-e Faqih,* naively thought they were on the same side as the emerging revolt of traditional-ist Shia clerics against the shah's regime. The shah himself made it easier for them; he was an insecure man, alternately convinced that he was a di-vinely approved monarch of the ancient Persian type or the only man in the modern era who could restore Iran to its destined greatness.

During the 1960s and early 1970s, it had been the Left who set the pace of political opposition to the shah, the Tudeh Party continuously playing a major role. But in the second half of 1977, Islamic radical stu-dents began smashing windows and burning buses in the vicinity of the University of Tehran, the bastion of intellectual secularism established by the shah's father. Their demands were entirely contrary to the secular spirit of the University of Tehran in its original formulation: they demanded that women on campus be segregated.

The following year, 1978, violent opposition to the shah's regime in-creasingly came from Islamists, all of whom looked to their idealized leader Khomeini. A large demonstration in downtown Tehran in early Sep-tember 1978 coincided with the end of the Islamic fasting month of Ra-madan. Violence broke out, and the shah declared martial law. A few days later, another demonstration took place, this one suppressed by troops who opened fire on the crowds. Those killed in the shooting may have numbered in the hundreds.

While these events were occurring in Tehran, President Jimmy Carter was hosting President Anwar Sadat of Egypt and Prime Minister Men-achem Begin of Israel at Camp David. The talks there eventually led to the Camp David Accords of 1978 and the subsequent Egyptian-Israeli peace treaty of 1979. But as peace was being discussed in Maryland, a real regime crisis was emerging in Tehran. In a remarkable demonstration of generos-ity of spirit, President Sadat took time to phone the shah from the rural U.S. presidential retreat to express his strong political support for the monarch. The U.S. government was stunned and almost uncomprehend-ing of what was taking place in the capital city of its Persian Gulf ally.[12]

Grassroots Momentum for the Cleric

Khomeini, meanwhile, was not only actively encouraging the growing street opposition to the shah from Islamists, he was orchestrating it. An-noyed at his role in stirring up unrest in his homeland from the safe haven of Najaf, Saddam Hussein began to limit Iranian contacts with him. In

October 1978, Khomeini flew from Iraq to a new exile in a suburb of Paris called Neauphle-le-Château. There he held court to the world's media and to a procession of Iranian political exiles, who increasingly saw in him the cure to all of Iran's problems.

During November, the shah vacillated whether to resign as monarch, establish a military regime or attempt to pull together a conciliatory national government. On November 6, he did install a military government, but it was strikingly indecisive in cracking down on the strikes and demonstrations that had tormented Iran for much of the previous year. About 1,000 soldiers were deserting from the military every week. The shah toyed with the idea of abdicating. In early December 1978, perhaps as many as 10 percent of the entire country joined in demonstrations against him.

With the U.S. unclear what was really happening in Tehran, the shah was not getting clear advice from one of the few governments that had continued to express support for his rule. On January 16, 1979, he and his wife and associates left Iran. He flew first to Egypt where he was warmly welcomed by Sadat. He was now, however, suffering from an advanced stage of pancreatic cancer. After months of wandering among different countries—Morocco, the Bahamas and Mexico—he was admitted into the U.S. for medical treatment in October 1979. By then, however, the situation on the ground in Iran had changed so drastically that his presence in the U.S. became an incendiary symbol of American domination of the affairs of Iran, as alleged by the supporters of Khomeini.

A New Islamist Regime

The Ayatollah descended upon Tehran on February 1, 1979, in an Air France Boeing 747 to a rapturous welcome. A caretaker government left in place by the shah had said that it would welcome Khomeini back to Iran. There was nevertheless street fighting between troops loyal to the shah and those supporting Khomeini, and the shah's regime finally collapsed 11 days after the return of Khomeini.

While in exile in Iraq, Khomeini had made no secret of his intention to establish an Islamic government in Iran. When he put the idea before Iranians in a referendum in April 1979, they supported it overwhelmingly. A provisional government of Iran had been established after the arrival of Khomeini and was led by a prime minister called Mehdi Bazargan. He was a personally pious Shia Muslim, but he sought to implement the rule of law and to provide Iranians with an option for secular government.

Khomeini completely outmaneuvered him and effectively established a parallel government structure ruled entirely by the mullahs and enforced by paramilitary forces loyal to the concept of absolute Islamic rule.

In April 1979, a Revolutionary Guard Corps was formed to protect the Islamic revolution against challenges to its authority from leftists who were now becoming disenchanted with Islamic rule. Parallel with this, the Islamists established revolutionary tribunals that set about tracking down former officials of the shah's regime, arresting them and summarily executing them. Censorship was imposed on cultural and literary expressions that showed any sympathy to the West. In a series of skirmishes with the new religious regime emerging in Tehran, the leftists who had so stalwartly led the opposition to the shah during the 1960s and 1970s found themselves sidelined and suppressed.

The political order of the regime that Khomeini imposed on Iran turned the country into the Islamic Republic of Iran. Though it has a parliament, the Majlis, and an elected president, it is in fact governed by the Supreme Ruler. Until his death in 1989, that person was Khomeini. Since Khomeini's death, however, the position has been held by Ayatollah Ali Hoseyni Khamenei (born in 1939). The Supreme Leader is elected by the Assembly of Experts, a group of 86 Islamic scholars. The Supreme Leader appoints the heads of the armed forces and many senior civil positions. But he also has significant additional powers.

After the Supreme Leader, there is the Council of Guardians, a 12-member body that can decide who may or may not stand for political office. Because six of the members are directly selected by the Supreme Leader, and six others are selected by the Majlis (parliament), with the Supreme Leader's assent, Khamenei in effect can veto anyone who wants to run for political office. The members of the Majlis are 290 in number and are elected for four-year terms. The president of Iran is elected by popular suffrage and is the highest official in the executive branch *after* the Supreme Leader. The president selects the heads of government departments, the Council of Ministers. Yet selection of the ministers of intelligence and defense require explicit approval by the Supreme Leader.

IRGC—A Necessary "Club" Membership

Iran is governed in a curious way by state organs that function similarly to their analogous government agencies in other countries, and by revolutionary bodies that operate in parallel, but often quite separately from official state institutions. For example, one of the most important institutions in Iran today belongs in the revolutionary category: the Iranian Revolutionary Guard Corps (IRGC). Membership in this organization is often the fast track to a well-paid job or access to hard-to-obtain goods and services. In a sense, membership in the IRGC is analogous to membership in the Communist Party of the Soviet Union, whose senior elite comprised a *nomenklatura* of privileged leaders in a society from which, supposedly, class privilege had been banned.

By 2005, the newly elected president of Iran, Mahmoud Ahmadinejad, as well as half his cabinet, were members of the IRGC. In the March 2008 legislative elections, nearly a third of the seats in the Majlis belonged to IRGC members.

The IRGC controls three important facets of Iran's foreign policy: its development of missiles and nuclear technology, its export of revolution, and a vast potential army of paramilitary supporters called *Baseej*. After coming to power in 1979, Khomeini dreamed of an army of 20 million Iranians. To implement this, his then prime minister, Mehdi Bazargan, created the *Pasdaran* ("Guardians"), who in turn controlled the *Baseej Mustafadafeen* ("Mobilization of the Dispossessed") to handle national conscription. The *Baseej* today consists of a force of 400,000, with other conscripts in national service being deployed in different parts of the IRGC. The *Pasdaran* is considered to comprise about 125,000 members.

Legacy of Hatred and Violence

In the years before he returned from exile in triumph to Tehran, Ayatollah Khomeini made no secret of his hatred for the U.S. This fact apparently went over the heads of both American professional diplomats and ambassadorial appointees of the administration of President Carter in the late 1970s. Carter's ambassador to the U.N. Andrew Young referred to Khomeini as a "twentieth-century saint," while the American ambassador to Tehran at the time of the Khomeinist revolution described him as "a Gandhi-like figure."[13] That there was absolutely nothing saintly or Gandhi-like about Khomeini became finally clear to Americans on November 4, 1979.

That morning, hundreds of Iranians, supposedly "students," invaded the compound of the U.S. Embassy and took hostage what was to become a total of 52 embassy personnel. Khomeini had not publicly asked the students to do this, though they had for weeks been conducting demonstrations in front of the embassy. But once the die was cast, Khomeini lent his public approval to the brazen violation of diplomatic immunity. The students claimed that their move had been provoked by the U.S. decision to admit the shah for medical treatment.

The hostage situation in Tehran overshadowed the administration of President Jimmy Carter until the day he left office. It demonstrated that the global superpower was virtually impotent in the face of mob violence in a Third World country. When the U.S. military attempted a hostage rescue in April 1980, that mission went tragically awry, resulting in the cancelation of the mission and the deaths of eight American service personnel, reinforcing the impression of American powerlessness. The hostages were eventually held for a total of 444 days and were released only minutes after Carter had left office and Ronald Reagan had taken the oath as the new president of the U.S. on January 20, 1980.

Meanwhile, the Khomeinist regime was going through the process of eating its children, as all violent revolutions do. In the months between June and November 1981, a reign of terror started during which a total of 1,800 people were executed for various political and religious crimes. The youngest was a 12-year-old girl.[14] Iranian journalist-in-exile Amir Taheri estimates that, since 1979, more than 100,000 Iranians may have been executed.[15] That total is impossible to confirm. What is not is Khomeini's obsession with death in the cause of Islam. "To kill and be killed," the Ayatollah said in an often-repeated mantra, "are the supreme duties of Muslims."[16]

Khomeini in many of his speeches and writings openly justified actions that most people would categorize as terrorism. In one passage he wrote, "Those who say that Islam should not kill, don't understand [it]. Killing is a great [divine] gift that appears [to man]. A religion that does not include [provisions for] killing and massacre is incomplete."[17]

The victims of this philosophy within Iran were always people who had opposed the regime or some aspect of its policies, and they were not limited to Iranians in Iran. Prime Minister Shapour Bakhtiar, who had been appointed prime minister by the shah just before Khomeini's return, was forced out by the new regime and fled Tehran for Paris. He was assassinated in August 1991, in his apartment, by Iranians either dispatched for that purpose by the Ayatollah's regime or those sympathetic to it. Two of the assassins escaped to Iran but one was apprehended in Switzerland and sentenced to life in prison for the crime.

Iranian death squads have assassinated at least 127 of the regime's opponents in a total of 16 foreign countries. In April 1997, a Berlin court officially named four senior Iranian officials, including the then (and current) "Supreme Ruler" of Iran, Ali Khamenei, and former president Hashemi Rafsanjani, as complicit in the murder in Berlin of two Kurdish political opponents of the Islamic Republic and two interpreters. In 2007, a court in Buenos Aires, Argentina, also named senior Iranian officials as implicated in the 1994 bombing of an Argentine Jewish center in which 86 people died. The bomb had been set by an Argentina-based branch of Hezbollah, the pro-Iranian terrorist group based in Lebanon.

The regime's vindictiveness cannot be excused at all, but a factor in it may have been Iran's epic eight-year struggle with Iraq. When Iraq ordered forces to invade Iranian Khuzestan in September 1980, anticipating a quick victory over the Iranians, Saddam unleashed a train of events in Iran that were to torment the country. From September 1980, when Iraq first attacked, until August 1988, when Khomeini reluctantly consented to a U.N.-mandated cease-fire, Iran was locked in one of the most brutal regional wars of the twentieth century. The fighting seesawed back and forth, with the early advantage going to Iraq; and then as Iran's superior numbers and murderous use of children as volunteer martyrs came into play, tipping back towards Iran.

Iran in 1986 succeeded in capturing Iraq's strategic Fao Peninsula on the Persian Gulf, but Iraq was able to recover it. The Iraqis had the advantage of more numerous equipment and ammunition; the Iranians the advantage of numbers and the fanatical commitment of *Baseej*, teenage and pre-teenage volunteers who were rewarded for their Islamic zeal by having plastic keys (to paradise) hanging round their necks. To compensate for Iran's inadequacy of equipment and ammunition, these youngsters were willing to walk through minefields and be blown up in order to provide safe passage for Iranian armor and conventional soldiers.

At another stage of the war, the vicious "war of the cities" began in 1985, and intensified in 1986. Both sides launched Scud missiles against each other's capitals, though Iraq had more of these to deploy. As many as one-quarter of Tehran's population may have fled the city during this phase of the war.

The U.S. had decided early on in the war that it did not want Iraq to lose to Iran. The stakes were too high of revolutionary Islamic fervor stoked by Iran running amok in the Arab Gulf states. (After the Israeli invasion of Lebanon in 1982, however, Iranian *Pasdaran* units deployed to Lebanon's Bekaa Valley to train the forces of Lebanon's Hezbollah.) America supplied intelligence and other military resources to Iraq. But in 1987, with oil tankers off Kuwait and other Arab states coming under attack from Iranian aircraft, the U.S. offered to third-country ships the opportunity of flying the American flag and therefore acquiring American military protection against attack by Iranian missile boats or aerial attack. Hundreds of commercial vessels were damaged in these "tanker wars," though the U.S. navy succeeded in reducing them to a minimum.

The climax to the American challenge to Iran came when an American cruiser, the *USS Vincennes*, shot down a civilian Iranian airliner with significant loss of life in July 1988. The U.S. apologized for the loss of Iranian civilian life and paid financial compensation to Iran, but, ironically, the action may have tipped the balance within Tehran's government leadership in favor of accepting the U.N.-ordered cease-fire. Iran did not want full-scale hostilities with the U.S.

When the cease-fire finally came in August 1988, the losses suffered on both sides were staggering, though they were far worse for the Iranians. In financial terms Iran had suffered damage amounting to close to $87 billion. But in the numbers of lives lost, it suffered far more heavily than Iraq; perhaps almost a million Iranians died in the war and hundreds of thousands were maimed and wounded, with many of the wounded soldiers still experiencing today the effects of having been exposed to Iraqi mustard gas in combat. Iraq was estimated to have from a quarter to half a million killed and wounded.

Khomeini had said that accepting the cease-fire was like "drinking the cup of poison." Throughout the war he had wanted nothing less than the total defeat of Iraq and destruction of Saddam Hussein. But in February 1989, Khomeini reminded the world why so much of it had wanted Iraq to win the war that had just ended. That month, Khomeini issued a *fatwa* calling for the murder of British novelist Salman Rushdie. His novel *The Satanic Verses* offended Khomeini and much of the Muslim world because it alluded to an incident in the life of Mohammed when the Islamic prophet had been tempted to write verses that appeared to call for the worship of three Meccan deities. Essentially, Rushdie called into question the authenticity of the Koran. Because Rushdie had been born in India to Muslim parents, many Muslims were outraged that, in writing in a derogatory way about Mohammed, he had become an "apostate" from

Islam. Under *sharia*, the penalty for apostasy from Islam is death. Khomeini's *fatwa* was boosted by a substantial financial reward by Iran to anyone killing Rushdie, who for a decade had to live virtually underground under police protection.

Khomeini's ugly appeal to murder did lasting damage to Iran's reputation as a country that honored justice and international order, not to mention freedom of literature. Great Britain broke off diplomatic relations with Iran and did not restore them for a decade. When it did so in 1998, Iranian president Mohammad Khatami, as a condition for the restoration, said that Iran would not "support or hinder" assassination attempts against Rushdie. The Iranian government, however, has continued since then at various times to reaffirm the fatwa. In 2005, Supreme Leader Ali Khamenei did so publicly when addressing Iranian pilgrims about to embark on the *haji*, the pilgrimage to Mecca.

Since Khomeini's coming to power in 1979, Iran has occasionally given the impression of moving in a more moderate political direction. In May 1997, Mohammad Khatami (born in 1943) won 70 percent of the votes cast in the presidential election. He ran on a platform of democratic reform, which no doubt accounted for his stunning electoral success. But though he was reelected in 2005, conservatives in the Islamic republic banned reform-supporters of which it disapproved from running for the Majlis. Advocates of greater tolerance in political and cultural life in Iran were greatly disappointed. They were surely even more disappointed by the man who won the 2005 elections, Mahmoud Ahmadinejad, the mayor of Tehran.

Ahmadinejad on the Global Scene

Mahmoud Ahmadinejad is a populist whose radicalism goes back to the earliest days of the Khomeini revolution (with six of the American hostages asserting that Ahmadinejad participated in interrogations of them during the hostage crisis of 1979-1981). Ahmadinejad has been easily the most conspicuous and radical of Iran's leaders in the international arena. In 2005, he spoke at a Tehran conference called "World Without Zionism" at which he said that Israel needed to be "wiped from the pages of history." Some translations of this speech quoted Ahmadinejad as calling for Israel to be "wiped off the map." But since Ahmadinejad in another speech called for Israel to be moved to Europe, there can be little doubt that he seeks the elimination of the Jewish state of Israel.

In conjunction with this inflammatory call, Ahmadinejad has taken to asserting that the Holocaust of Europe's Jews during World War II was "a myth." In a 2006 letter to German chancellor Angela Merkel, he asserted that the Holocaust might have been invented "to embarrass Germany."[18] Such crude ignorance was visible to an American audience when, during a visit to the U.N. in 2007, he accepted an invitation to speak at Columbia University. He was asked about the treatment of gays in Iran—universally regarded as extremely intolerant—and replied, to incredulous guffaws in the audience, "We don't have homosexuals like in your country."[19]

Ahmadinejad may be uneducated and indeed ignorant, but he is clever and extremely ambitious for his country. He has consistently defended Iran's nuclear program, insisting that it is for civilian use only. What is not disputed, however, is that Iran has committed itself to becoming a "superpower in missiles." It is already the ninth nation in the world to have launched its own satellite into space, and it possesses ballistic missiles believed capable of reaching any destination in the Middle East, including, of course, Israel. Yet Iran is also believed to be building a heavy water plant at Arak, west of Tehran, supposedly in order to produce plutonium for a nuclear power plant employing plutonium. The only thing is, Iran does not have such a power plant. Iran *did* cease its nuclear enrichment program in 2003, but then resumed it in 2005, possibly at the insistence of the IRGC leadership.

In the spring of 2009, there were repeated stories from Israel that the Israeli Air Force had been rehearsing for a possible massive air attack on Iran's nuclear facilities and other targets. Presumably, the Obama administration would strongly discourage this. It might even penalize Israel by suspending military and economic relations if such an attack went ahead. But the U.S. military has been concerned with evidence of Iranian Pasdaran support of insurgents in Iraq. It is highly likely, at least, that the U.S. has contingency plans for some possible future military confrontation with Iran. Iran has complained of over-flights of its territory by American UAVs (Unmanned Aerial Vehicles), presumably to conduct intelligence surveillance.

Iran, however, is something of a schizophrenic nation, with its regime committed to a ferocious anti-U.S., anti-Western and anti-Israeli policy, while a large portion of its population remains resolutely pro-American. The U.S.-Iranian relationship is without question a Middle Eastern version of the Cold War, with one important difference: the Soviets always expressed horror at the prospect of a global nuclear exchange with the U.S. The Islamic Republic of Iran, apparently, or at least the Islamic revolutionary zealots who guide its policy, seem less alarmed by the prospect of a massive military clash than the possibility that the regime itself might explode from all the discontent being expressed within it.

8

SAUDI ARABIA AND BEYOND

If you look at any map of the Middle East, there is no getting away from
Saudi Arabia. It dominates the Arabian Peninsula, that huge landmass
washed by the waters of the Red Sea on the West and the Persian Gulf on
the East. Its massive land area, 830,000 square miles, is larger than Iran
and Iraq put together, and one-fifth the size of the United States. Saudi
Arabia's geographical dimensions, however, are dwarfed by its economic
and religious characteristics. It is the world's largest producer of oil, containing more than one-third of the world's known reserves, and it is the
birthplace of the world's second most populous religion, Islam (with approximately 1.3 billion adherents; the total of all denominations of Christians in the world is approximately 2.17 billion).

Together, oil wealth and Islamic fervor have made Saudi Arabia a key
player in the Middle East. Although Saudi Arabia, at a population of 28
million—5.5 million of whom are foreigners—has fewer inhabitants than
Iran, Iraq and Egypt, its influence in the region and the world is proportionate to its size and wealth.

Friend or Foe?

Saudi Arabia's relationship with the U.S. is complex. It has been a nominal ally of the U.S. since an ailing President Roosevelt met with King Abdul Aziz ibn Saud in February 1945, aboard a U.S. naval warship on Egypt's
Great Bitter Lake. Saudi Arabia has been providing oil to the U.S. for seven
decades and exerts such dominance on the global market that by increasing or reducing its oil production it can dramatically affect global petroleum prices.

In 1991, Saudi Arabia invited the U.S. into its territory as a place from
which to launch the attack on Iraqi forces occupying Kuwait. Saudi Ara-

bia's conservative monarchy has also for six decades been a bulwark against pan-Arab radicalism, standing up to Egypt's bullying of the Arab world during the 1950s and 1960s and consistently siding with the U.S. during the American confrontation with the Soviet Union during the Cold War (approximately 1946-1991).

SAUDI ARABIA

Source: Central Intelligence Agency

Yet Saudi Arabian citizens comprised 15 of the 19 hijackers who participated in the 9/11 terrorist attacks in the U.S. in 2001. Osama bin Laden is a Saudi, and Saudi Arabian oil dollars in gargantuan sums—by some estimates, up to $100 billion—have been deployed to fund Islamic centers all over the world with pronounced anti-Western and intolerant teaching.

Saudi Arabia was one of only two countries that recognized the Taliban's rule of Afghanistan (the other was Pakistan).

The expression of Islam that dominates the Saudi Islamic religious scene is known by some of its admirers as Salafism, and by its detractors as Wahhabism. This is a uniquely Saudi expression of the faith and it is uniquely repressive. It prohibits women from voting, from traveling outside of Saudi Arabia without permission of a husband or a male relative, and even from driving a car in public (no other country in the world does this). It doesn't allow the practice within its borders of any other world religion, and it imprisons, beats or expels anyone caught doing so, and censors the Internet with the paranoid obsessiveness of China or North Korea. In *The Economist Intelligence Unit Index of Democracy*, Saudi Arabia did so poorly in 2008 that it came in 161 of a total of 167 countries (North Korea was at the bottom of the list).[1]

In religious views, and internal politics, the U.S. and Saudi Arabia are as different from each other as a camel from a king penguin. Yet, like actors in a surrealist play, they have been thrown together by fate and forced to coexist out of reasons of the need for mutual survival. If the United States did not demonstrate overwhelming military power in the Persian Gulf and the near vicinity of Saudi Arabia, the kingdom might succumb very quickly to a determined show of force from a hostile nearby state. (In 1990, only the threat of imminent conquest by the forces of the secular dictator Saddam Hussein persuaded Saudi Arabia to invite U.S. troops onto its sacred soil.) Similarly, if Saudi Arabia were ever persuaded from within or forced by some foreign power to turn off the spigot of its oil supplies to the U.S., the American economy might suffer a catastrophic collapse.

How did this come to be?

The Draw of Mecca

Long before the birth of Islam in Arabia (it didn't become *Saudi* Arabia until 1932), the Arabian peninsula was a largely empty, parched land inhabited by ethnic Arabs who lived mostly in nomadic communities that traveled constantly. In the first centuries of the Christian era, there were communities of Christian tribes and Jewish tribes living there as well. A well-traveled trade route between the empires of Byzantium and Persia induced some nomadic tribes to settle in and around small cities that sprang up to host the trade. One such important location was the town of Mecca, located about 45 miles inland from the port of Jeddah, which itself is roughly halfway down the Red Sea coast of the Arabian Peninsula.

In the sixth century, Mecca came under the control of the Quraysh tribe. The desert tribes were polytheistic, with each one tending to have its own deities. These were often represented by small statues and carried with the tribes when they traveled.

Since there was frequent rivalry and fighting among the tribes, there was a general agreement on the need for a sacred space in different parts of the land within which fighting would be banned. Mecca was an important trade entrepot, and so one such space was designated there called the Ka'aba, a cube of black granite that stands approximately 43 feet high with sides 36 and 42 feet in height, respectively. The Ka'aba, which today is shrouded by a black and gold curtain, in pre-Islamic times was the location of representations of at least 369 different deities worshiped by various Arabian tribes. The biggest idol was Hubal, a deity represented by a human figure carved of red agate. But the god of the Ka'aba was Allah, accepted by visitors to the Ka'aba as the preeminent deity in place.

The Quraysh ensured that the "cease-fire" rules of peaceful coexistence among different tribal deities and their supporters prevailed within Mecca. It was, of course, essential for successful trade with the rest of the region. Several of the merchants in Mecca had trade caravans that went as far north as modern Syria.

Mohammed's Early Years

Mohammed, the founder of the religion of Islam (the Arabic word for "submission") was the great-grandson of a significant Quraysh trader and was born in Mecca in AD 570. But Mohammed did not have a conventional childhood. His father, Abdullah, died before he was born and his mother died when he was six. Mohammed was then taken under the wing of his grandfather until he, too, died. Mohammed then spent his childhood and adolescence under the care of his uncle, Abu Talib.

Mohammed as a young man was scarcely literate, but he was quick-witted, had a reputation for honesty in business and was also diligent. He caught the eye of a wealthy widow businesswoman, Khadijah, who hired him to manage her trade caravans north into Syria, which at that time was ruled by the Byzantine Empire (which was Christian, of course). She also seems to have been an admirer of the young man in other ways; for in 795, when he was 25 and she was 40, she proposed marriage. Since she reputedly still had good looks and—more important—was very wealthy, Mohammed accepted. It was the beginning of a financially and emotionally prosperous alliance for the young Meccan.

Polytheism was the dominant religious pattern in Mecca and its environs. As we have mentioned, however, there were other religious communities in the Arabian Peninsula: tribes of Jews and tribes of various Christian and almost-Christian groups. Khadijah's cousin was Waraka ibn Nofal, a bishop of the Ebionite church, a Jewish-Christian sect that believed in observing Jewish laws and rites and viewing Jesus as the Messiah but not divine. (The Ebionites were not accepted as orthodox by either the Catholic or the Orthodox branches of Christendom.) It could possibly have been in some form of Ebionite ceremony that Mohammed was married. What is probable is that, through his observations while traveling out of Arabia with commercial caravans, and through contacts with different religious communities that had representatives in Mecca, Mohammed began to learn something of both Judaism and Christianity. Almost certainly, however, he never received a clear teaching of the doctrines of either faith.

The Birth of Islam

In the year 610, Mohammed was conducting a form of spiritual retreat in a cave on Mount Hira, outside Mecca. This was not unusual for a spiritually minded Meccan to do, especially if he was comfortable being alone and contemplating spiritual things. Mohammed was almost certainly familiar with Arabian kahins, soothsayers who operated like shamans and believed themselves to be inspired by familiar spirits. When uttering prophecies in this possessed state, kahins would speak in a sort of breathless rhyming prose.

Mohammed himself had something of a phobia of kahins, but regardless of his view of them, on the night of what became known as 26-7 Ramadan, a month in the lunar Muslim calendar, the Night of Power, he had a spiritual encounter that changed his life, and indeed, in the long run, that of the world.[2] He felt a fearful presence that pressed against him and uttered, "Recite!"

"What shall I recite?" Mohammed answered, the implication of that reported phrase being that he was actually illiterate (which pious Muslims do indeed believe). Having given this answer twice to the "Recite!" command, he felt physical pressure again and started to recite what would become accepted as the first of the revelations of the Koran, Islam's sacred text. Sura 96:1-5, believed to be an exact narrative of the encounter on the Night of Power, reads:

> Recite in the name of your Lord who created—created man from clots of blood. Recite! Your Lord is the Most Bountiful One, who by the pen taught man what he did not know.[3]

Mohammed reported later that he both saw and heard the presence, who identified himself as the angel Gabriel. But scholar Malise Ruthven, a thoughtful and insightful observer of Islam, reports that Arabian poets of Mohammed's day and earlier on several occasions also reported being assaulted by a spiritual presence and being "forced" to utter verses that the poet had not previously been aware of.[4]

Mohammed was apparently terrified of what he had experienced, and sought consolation from his wife, Khadijah, who covered him with a blanket as he shivered. She, however, seemed to believe that he had been favored by Allah (God) and that what had taken place was a good thing.

The Night of Power, as the Ramadan date of Mohammed's first revelation is always referred to, was the first of a lifetime of revelations that Mohammed received. The later revelations were practical-sounding pieces of advice, often as practical guidance for what to do in a particular political situation, and would come to him in quite natural settings—sitting on horseback, for example, or in mid-conversation—but the first revelations were often agonizing, accompanied by perspiration, or foaming at the mouth, rolling on the ground or even bouts of unconsciousness. These phenomena convinced many of the early Christian commentators on Islam to believe that Mohammed suffered from epilepsy, a notion that has received close attention from an American physician who has made a lifetime study of epilepsy.[5]

From 610 to 613, Mohammed did not go public with his revelations, confining them to his wife, Khadijah; to Ali ibn Abi Talib, his first cousin (the same Ali who is considered the founder of the Shia tradition); a prominent merchant, Abu Bakr (who became the first caliph after Mohammed died) and a Christian freedman.

The early revelations deal with the grandeur of Allah and his uniqueness and power and the need for humans to thank Allah when they worship him. They also included references to a day of judgment of all people. For Arabs living in Mecca, the monotheistic message that Mohammed was receiving would not have been too radical. Some Arabs had accepted the reality of monotheism already. But a Day of Judgment, when men and women would be literally constituted into physical form again from their bones, in order to be judged for their actions, was definitely novel, and to many contemporary Arabs in Mecca both a ridiculous and offensive idea. After 613, when Mohammed became increasingly open about the revelations he was receiving, his references to divine judgment were often those most seriously resisted by the inhabitants of Mecca.

Mohammed's earliest followers were his wife, Khadijah; Ali, his cousin (and later his son-in-law); and a local merchant, Abu Bakr. Gradually, others in the Meccan community were drawn to Mohammed's preaching of the oneness and uniqueness of Allah, the need to submit to him, and the equality of all people under Allah. It was an attractive message to the poorer classes of society, but it was irritating to the established families of Mecca. The small, but growing community assembled for prayer in the open in Mecca, and were often ridiculed by other Meccans.

As long as Mohammed was under the patronage of his uncle, Abu Talib, he was protected. But in 615, Mohammed received a revelation that he was to denounce the pagan deities that the inhabitants of Mecca had been worshiping since time immemorial. The wealthy Meccan families responded with a boycott of the Hashim clan from which Mohammed came. This lasted until 619. By then, however, both Khadijah and Mohammed's protector, Abu Talib, had died.

The evolving message of Mohammed's revelations, which were later collected from those who had heard them, memorized them or written them down as the Koran asserted that Mohammed was simply warning people to return to the original revelations of God as first presented to the Hebrews. There were 124,000 prophets who had been sent by God, Mohammed proclaimed (not in the Koran, but in a *haddith*, or sayings or anecdote attributed to him), and he was the final prophet. Later, he was to be described as the "seal" of the prophets. According to Islam, biblical figures who were prophets included Adam, Moses, David, Elijah, and Jesus. In this respect, Mohammed treated the Hebrew Scriptures and the Christian New Testament as the revelation of God that had originally come down but that had been rejected or misrepresented. (Jews and Christians, Muslims assert, have misrepresented their own true Scripture.)

Mohammed's denunciations of polytheism and his warnings about the Day of Judgment were now grating on the ears of many Meccans. When a delegation of representatives, in 620, arrived from Yathrib, a city 280 miles north of Mecca, asking his help in bringing order into a very turbulent urban community, he listened carefully. Some of the visitors became Muslim and they assured him that if he migrated to Yathrib, which was later renamed Medina, he would be welcome there.

In the year 622, he and a group of his followers did indeed migrate from Mecca to Medina. The year marks the beginning of the Muslim calendar, for its Arabic term is *hijra* ("migration"). In Medina, the Muslim community increased with the addition of many Medinans. Muslims came to call themselves the *umma* ("community"), a term that denotes not just a local congregation of Muslims, but the global Muslim community.

In Medina, Mohammed's diplomatic skills were called up to mediate arguments among various tribal factions. Three Jewish tribal groups in Medina, however, the Qaynuqah, Nadir and Qurayzah, resolutely refused to accept Mohammed as a biblical prophet according to their own standards of prophecy. This was a great disappointment to Mohammed, who in 624 changed the *qibla,* the direction of prayer, from Jerusalem to Mecca.

Meanwhile, the Muslim community in Medina both supported itself and obtained practice in battle by raiding passing merchant caravans.

Since many of these belonged to the Meccan merchants, the Meccans decided they needed to be rid of the upstart prophet and his followers. From 624 until 628 the Meccans fought a series of battles with the Muslims. These battles have become iconic milestones on the march of triumph of Islam, with names like the Battle of Badr (624), the Battle of Uhud (a Muslim defeat in 625) and the Battle of the Trench (627). In 628 Mohammed signed a peace treaty with the Meccans, the Treaty of Hudaibiya, which guaranteed for a 10-year period that Muslims would be able to make a pilgrimage to Mecca.

Meanwhile, the Jews of Medina were increasingly cooperating with the Meccans, who wished to destroy the Islamic *umma* completely. Two of the tribes were allowed by Mohammed to leave with what possessions they could take with them on a camel. But when Mohammed learned that the third, the Qurayzah, had sided with the Meccans at the Battle of the Trench, he was merciless. All 700 male tribal members, after they had surrendered, were beheaded, their heads thrown into trenches specially dug for the occasion. The massacre marked the beginning of a sad history of Muslim attitudes toward the Jews. Though Mohammed considered that Christians and Jews were "People of the Book," and thus entitled to treatment better than polytheists, when the Muslims conquered communities of Christians and Jews, both of them had to submit to a status of inferiority to Muslims, called *dhimmi* ("protected"). They had to wear special clothes, could not ride a horse among Muslims, had to pay a special tax, could not ring church bells in a Muslim town, could not build new churches or even make repairs on old ones. In practice, for most of Muslim history, Jews were treated better than they were in most Western countries. After the French Enlightenment, however, the status of Jews in Europe improved dramatically, while that of Jews in the Muslim world continued to be one of subordination and sometimes open humiliation.

In 629, Mohammed and a band of 2,000 Muslims made a pilgrimage to Mecca, which they entered peacefully. According to the terms of Hudaibiya, the city was empty of people. Mohammed performed the *tawaf*, a pre-Islamic pagan ritual of circling the Ka'aba cube, which the Muslims adopted as part of the *hajj* (pilgrimage to Mecca) ritual. Then he returned to Medina.

The Muslim community was by now far more powerful than any coalition that the Meccans could assemble. The writing was on the wall for the Meccans. After negotiations with Meccan leaders, Mohammed entered Mecca in triumph in 630 with 10,000 Muslims. There was little resistance.

On performing once more the *tawaf* on a camel, he touched with a stick the black stone, an object of reverence for Muslims who believe that it dates back to Adam and Eve. The stone, believed by some to be a fallen meteorite, is about 12 inches across and is today set in a silver frame.

The Five Pillars of Islam

Though many of the Meccans doubtless became Muslims for opportunistic reasons, there was soon worked out what became the basic features of Islamic belief and behavior, the so-called Five Pillars of Islam. These are:

1. The *shahadah*, or the profession of faith ("there is no God but God, and Mohammed is his prophet");
2. *Salat*, or prayer five times a day, facing Mecca;
3. *Zakat*, or tithing, traditionally a 2.5 percent annual levy in income and capital;
4. *Sawm*, fasting during the month of Ramadan; and
5. *Hajj*, the commitment of every Muslim to make the pilgrimage to Mecca at least once in a lifetime.

In a continuation of pagan traditions, Muslims were permitted to have up to four wives, with the proviso that each wife must be treated equally. Mohammed himself had far more than that—at least 11, and possibly as many as 14. He had been faithful to Khadijah until her death in 619, but after this seemed to make some marriage decisions for political reasons as well as personal ones. It is interesting that none of the wives Mohammed married after Khadijah's death is mentioned in the Koran. The youngest of Mohammed's wives, and his favorite, was Ayisha, whom Mohammed married in 623 when he was 53 and she was 6 (yes, 6, that is not a typo). The marriage was consummated when Ayisha was 9.

In 632, Mohammed, still based in Medina, made his last pilgrimage to Mecca and died shortly after his return from it. His Muslims had already conquered almost every pagan tribe in Arabia, and joining the *umma* had turned a disparate collection of squabbling nomadic tribes and clans into a disciplined, totally committed, indeed fanatical community.

The first major crisis for the new community was who would be the successor—*khalifa*, or "caliph"—to Mohammed as leader of the Muslims. At this point, the Quraysh tribe asserted itself and selected one of its own, Abu Bakr. The Muslims were now committed not only to bringing the entirety of the Arabian Peninsula under their control, but exporting their faith beyond their borders as well. The desert skills of the Arab horseman and the intense commitment of his new faith overcame even powerful resistance. By 633, the Arabs had poured out of the Peninsula into Syria and Mesopotamia. In 636, they defeated the Byzantines at Yarmuk, which opened the way for the conquest of Jerusalem. The first victory over the Persians had been accomplished the year before that.

Arab-Muslim Dominance

The first four caliphs were called by later generations of Muslims the *Rashidun*, "the rightly guided." Abu Bakr died of natural causes in 634, but the next three caliphs were all murdered: Omar in 644, Uthman in 656, and Ali in 661. Ali's death, of course, was the decisive event that led to the split between Sunni and Shia, as we saw in the previous chapter.

During the rule of the *Rashidun*, the tide of Muslim conquest continued rapidly. It was under the third caliph, Uthman, that the Koran was finally edited in the form that we have today. Muslims believe that the Koran was literally dictated by God, through the angel Gabriel, and that its original form was in the Arabic language. That is why modern translations of the Koran are often referred to by pious Muslims as "an interpretation."

By 636, Muslims had overrun Syria; captured Jerusalem by 638; and Alexandria in Egypt by 641, opening the door to the whole of Egypt and then the entire north African littoral. In accomplishing these conquests, entire long-established Christian communities were displaced or wiped out. Some of them, notably Carthage, the home of St. Augustine, had occupied positions of prominence in the Christian world.

By 711, the Arabs had crossed the Straits of Gibraltar into Spain; and by 715, the Visigoths who ruled the country had been conquered. This marked the beginning of nearly eight centuries of Muslim Arab rule that ended only when the Spanish King Ferdinand defeated the Muslims in 1492 and expelled them from Spain. The Arabs, in 718, crossed the Pyrenees into France, conquering Narbonne and putting to death the entire male adult population. The Arab-Muslim advance was stopped in France only in 732, when the Frankish warrior Charles Martel defeated the Arabs near Poitiers.

As noted earlier, the Arabs were crushingly defeated by the Mongols who sacked Baghdad in 1258, putting an end to the flourishing Abbasid dynasty. But the Muslim advance into Europe was not over. It was merely taken over by the Ottoman Turks, who had set their own stamp on the Middle East in 1517.

The Ottomans conquered the Byzantine Empire of Constantinople in 1453, and by 1529 were at the gates of Vienna. They were stopped there that year, but returned in great force in 1683, when they were definitively turned back and began the long decline as a European imperial power. The date of their defeat was September 11, a fact certainly known to Osama bin Laden. The Ottomans remained substantially—but not wholly, as we have already seen—in control of the Arab Middle East until the end of World War I.

I use the word "substantially" because of a development in Arabia that was to play a role in turning the Arabian Peninsula into Saudi Arabia. This was the sudden and violent rise of Wahhabism, a puritanical Islamic reform movement that swept away all opposition until it became the official version of Islam in Saudi Arabia and by extension the preferred expression of Islam wherever Saudi petro-dollars were successful in spreading Islamic influence.

Mohammed Ibn Abdul Wahhab (1703-1792) was a Muslim preacher and theologian who had spent some years studying in Basra. Returning home to Najd in Arabia, in 1740, he began to preach a strict implementation of *sharia* that required adulteresses actually to be stoned to death (a punishment specified in the Koran but not always implemented in Muslim communities) and the practice of worshiping graves and shrines of famous Muslims to be stopped.

Disapproval of the changes in law caused Wahhab to be forced out of his hometown. He was invited into a nearby provincial capital, Da'iriya, by its ruler Muhammad ibn Saud. He and Saud, in 1744, committed to a pact whereby Saud would enforce Wahhab's rules wherever he could secure political power, and Wahhab would recruit his zealous and militant followers to provide martial assistance in enlarging Saud's fiefdom. Beginning in the second half of the eighteenth century the Wahhab-Saudi alliance steadily expanded, with some temporary setbacks, until King Abdul Aziz ibn Saud established the Kingdom of Saudi Arabia in 1932.

The Wahhabis were a ferocious and fanatical band that behaved with murderous brutality toward any community in Arabia or the Gulf region that opposed their rule. They were particularly hostile to the Shia, and in 1801 and 1802, they captured Karbala and Najaf in (modern-day) Iraq, massacring Shia by the thousands. In 1802 and 1803 (some sources say

1803 and 1804), they captured Mecca and Medina. There they demolished the tomb of Fatimah, Mohammed's daughter, as they had relentlessly destroyed tombs and shrines from Muslim history wherever they had previously conquered.

The Wahhabis preached *tawhid* ("the unity of God") and moral reform. They particularly praised the writings of Ibn Taymiyya (1263-1328), a Muslim scholar who stressed the importance of *jihad* (literally "struggle"). Though jihad can have the meaning of struggle against one's own sinfulness, throughout most of Islamic history it denoted struggle, and actual military combat, against non-Muslims.

The Wahhabis approved of Ibn Taymiyya's denunciations of the Mongols—nominally Muslim by 1300—as living in *jahiliyya*, the state of ignorance that Muslims believe had been the condition of Arabia before the coming of Mohammed. The Wahhabis introduced the burning of books considered by them offensive to Muslims (actually books had been burned in the city of Cordoba in Muslim Spain several centuries earlier) and they executed anyone they captured who had spoken or written against them. In many respects, in their fanaticism and zeal for conquest they were a throwback to the first generation of Muslims who stormed out of Arabia.

The Wahhabis were finally crushed by Ibrahim Pasha, the son of Muhammad Ali who ruled Egypt in the name of the Ottomans. In the year 1818, the Egyptian army destroyed the ibn Saud capital of Dar'iya. Mecca and Medina were also reconquered by the Ottomans and returned to non-Wahhabi control.

By the 1860s, however, the Saud family had recovered some of its fortunes and established a new capital in Riyadh (which is the current capital of Saudi Arabia). What emerged in the next few decades, with decisive consequences for the nature of Arabian politics and religion, was a civil war in Arabia in which the two strongest rivals were to be the family of the Hussein bin Ali, hereditary owner of the title "Sharif of Mecca" (and a direct descendant of Mohammed), and the House of Saud with its allies the Wahhabis.

The Ottomans confirmed Hussein as Grand Sharif, but he was ambitious for a much greater Arab domain. This brought him into conflict with the House of Saud. The Saud family had originally been chased out of Riyadh in 1891 by a rival family, the Rashidis, of the province of Nejd in the interior highlands of Arabia, but it recaptured the small town with a tiny band of fighters under the dynamic leadership of the most impressive of the four sons of the family patriarch who had been expelled.

In 1902, Riyadh was recaptured by this young man, Abdul Aziz ibn Saud (*ibn* in Arab means "son of"), then in his twenties, a physically imposing Arab—tall, dignified and immensely vigorous. Ibn Saud (as we will call him) lived a long life (1876-1953) and had an estimated 80 to 100 children by 16 wives (though only four wives at one time; the others were divorced in turn, usually in their thirties). If Saudi Arabia today seems to have a multitude of royal princes, it has something to do with Ibn Saud's productivity as a father.

In the following two years, Ibn Saud recaptured almost all of the Nejd from the rival Rashidis who were initially backed by the Ottomans. When World War I broke out, the British looked around for an Arab ruler who would ally himself with them against the Ottoman Turks. They would have preferred Ibn Saud, but the canny Arab leader was eager to take British money while not actually assisting the British against the Turks or their allies, the Rashidis. Instead, the British entered negotiations with Hussein bin Ali, the Sharif of Mecca, who harbored grandiose ambitions for a great Arab state from the Persian Gulf to the Levant that he would rule once the Ottomans were defeated.

Hussein talked to the British, who then sent a young British officer, T. E. Lawrence ("Lawrence of Arabia"), to coordinate Arab guerrilla raids against the Turks. In June 1916, Hussein raised the flag of the Arab revolt and swiftly captured Mecca from the Turks. His son Faisal (later to be the King of Iraq) worked with the British to expel the Turks from the Arabian Peninsula and then to capture the port of Aqaba, on the Red Sea, as a means of supporting the British advance into Palestine against the Turks.

Faisal's father, Hussein bin Ali, ruled over a large portion of eastern Arabia called the Hejaz. But Ibn Saud had gathered a new version of the eighteenth-century Wahhabi warriors called the *Ikhwan,* a fanatical group of desert fighters inspired by dreams of renewing Wahhabism's goal of controlling the whole of the Arabian Peninsula. With this militia at his side, Ibn Saud whittled away at Hussein's control of the Nejd until he was forced by the *Ikhwan* successes to resign. He was to go into an embittered exile in Cyprus.

Ibn Saud now controlled the two holy places of Islam, Mecca and Medina. His *Ikhwan* warriors had been conducting raids into the new Kingdom of Iraq in the early 1920s and had been repelled by British aircraft and armored cars. In the late 1920s, they rose against Saud himself because of what they considered his too close associations with infidel foreigners.

Their rebellion was crushed by the king. In September 1932, Abdul Aziz ibn Saud was proclaimed monarch of the united Kingdom of Saudi Arabia.

Saud ruled with moderation and dignity. He seemed to dazzle Americans who visited him. Charles R. Crane, an American philanthropist and explorer, the first American Saud met, described him this way in 1931: "When at rest," he wrote in his diary, "his face is immobile and usually overcast, as though with some permanent sadness. But all of a sudden the subject moves him, or a secretary glides in with some whispered message, and his features light up with excitement or curiosity."[6]

Modern Oil Boom

Undoubtedly the single most important event that led to Saudi Arabia's dramatic prominence in the twentieth century was the discovery of oil. Ibn Saud granted a concession to Standard Oil of California in his eastern territories in 1933, but oil was not discovered in commercial quantities until 1938. Because of the intervention of World War II, it was only in the 1950s that the Saudi kingdom began to acquire vast wealth and flex its muscles in the international community.

Ibn Saud died in 1953, and was succeeded by King Saud. There was, however, a serious rivalry with his younger brother, Prince Faisal, who held the title of President of the Council of Ministers. When the king became involved in a plot to assassinate Egyptian president Nasser in 1958, the Saudi *ulama* and a consensus of royal princes intervened and temporarily removed him from power. When the Yemenite emirate was overthrown in 1962, and the Egyptians intervened to support the new republican regime, Saud was once more removed from office and his younger brother took over for good. In Saudi Arabia, as it happened, slavery was not legally banned until that year.

Faisal, now king, stressed traditional, conservative, religious Arabism, not the Egyptian secular, socialist and pan-Arabist version. Even before he became king, he established the Muslim World League (MWL) in 1962, dedicated to reviving Wahhabism and to spreading it globally. The MWL raised money for mosques around the world and for "wahhabizing" as many existing Islamic centers as possible. The overwhelming majority of the funding for the MWL came from Saudi Arabia, which was able to use the League as an instrument of Saudi foreign policy.

Faisal, on becoming king, gave over control of Saudi education to Wahhabi clerics. The cold war between Saudi religious conservatism and

Egyptian Arab secularism seemed to have shifted when Egypt and Syria were decisively defeated in the Six-Day War in 1967. By comparison with the Egyptian and Syrian humiliation, Saudi Arabia's prestige and influence grew significantly, along with the increasing power of its oil-based financial wealth.

In 1969, Faisal secured a diplomatic triumph for Saudi Arabia by convening the first meeting of Islamic heads of state in Rabat, Morocco. But it was the 1973 Yom Kippur War that thrust Saudi Arabia front and center not just in Middle East politics, but on the world scene. In the first successful demonstration of the "oil weapon," the Organization of Petroleum Exporting Countries (OPEC) decided on a drastic hike in the price of petroleum in the weeks following the war. The oil crisis of late 1973 seriously disrupted economic life in the Western world, but it was a bonanza for Saudi Arabia and the other OPEC countries, including, of course, Iran. There was a quadrupling of the price of oil in the period from 1973 to 1974, which turned Saudi Arabia by 1975 into the global economic power with financial reserves greater than those of the U.S. and Japan combined. By the end of 1975, Saudi Arabia was receiving $25 billion in oil revenues. Its foreign aid program amounted to 10 percent of its national income, a higher percentage of foreign aid than that of any other country in the globe. Much of the aid went into funding Islamic education projects and the building of new mosques.

King Faisal was assassinated by a deranged relative in 1975, but the transition in leadership took place smoothly. Faisal was succeeded by King Khaled, but most of the significant administration of the country was handled by Crown Prince Fahd. When Khaled died in 1982, Fahd became king and continued with his vigorous handling of the kingdom's administration. Saudi Arabia had meanwhile entered on a massive program of infrastructure construction that ate into its huge reserves.

By 1979, the Islamic revolution had occurred in Iran. By November of that year its repercussions were heard dramatically in Mecca, where several hundred rebels, proclaiming that they were following the new Mahdi, seized the grand mosque and were only ejected after nearly two weeks' fighting and the deaths of hundreds of rebels, civilians and soldiers. A persistent rumor held that the final clearing of the underground corridors of the mosque was accomplished only with the help of French commandoes, whose entry into Mecca itself could only be tolerated by the Saudis if the French troops were willing to submit to conversion to Islam. They did.[7]

Though the Saudi *ulama*, at the request of King Khaled (who succeeded Faisal after his 1975 assassination), roused themselves to condemn the attack on the Grand Mosque, they had nothing negative to say about the ideology of the two Saudis who had organized it, Muhammad al-Utaibi and Muhammad ibn Abdullah al-Qahtani. Both men had studied at the deeply conservative, pro-Wahhabi institution the Islamic University of Medina. Al-Utaibi had served for 18 years in the Saudi National Guard, the Saudi security force that evolved from the *Ikhwan* after Ibn Saud formally dissolved it late in the 1920s. Both men had absorbed a deepening anti-foreignism in Saudi religious thought that had developed as a reaction against the influx of foreigners into the Saudi kingdom in consequence of the oil boom.

Jihadism in the Last 30 Years

A bitterly anti-Western book had been written by two professors at the Islamic University of Medina, the institution attended by both men. Called *The Methods of the Ideological Invasion of the Islamic World,* the book railed against capitalism, democracy and freedom.[8] Other books warned against the dangers of Christianity, and after the Grand Mosque attack in 1979, far from repudiating the anti-Western ideology that had inspired al-Utaibi, the Saudi authorities seemed to appropriate it.

One of the Saudi *ulama* who had provided the Saudi monarchy with theological backing to kill, if necessary, the Grand Mosque hijackers while retaking the mosque from them was Sheikh Abdul Aziz bin Baz, later to become Grand Mufti of Saudi Arabia. Bin Baz had written in 1974 that Christianity was a form of blasphemy and that there could never be any friendly connection between Islam and Christianity.[9] He also wrote, "According to the Koran, the *Sunnah* (Islamic tradition), and the consensus of Muslims, it is a requirement of Muslims to be hostile to the Jews and the Christians and the other *mushrikun* ('polytheists')." Bin Baz laid great importance on *jihad* ("struggle") and he specified that he meant *jihad* by the sword.[10] *Jihad* is sometimes mistranslated "holy war," and defenders of the use of the term by Muslims often insist that there is "a lesser jihad" and "a greater jihad," with the second of these phrases referring to a moral struggle by individual Muslims against their own sinfulness, to which we have already referred.

Jihad in the military sense assumed a prominent place in Saudi thinking at the end of 1979, when the Soviets invaded Afghanistan. For many

Saudis, it was a classic case of an infidel, atheistic great power invading the Muslim *umma*. The case of righteous *jihad* was, on the face of it, overwhelming to most Muslims, and Saudi Arabia was at the forefront of Muslim nations who both denounced the invasion and who served as a conduit for American military and financial aid to counter it.

The most significant early recruiter of Saudis to participate in the Afghan struggle was not, however, a Saudi, but a Palestinian living in Saudi Arabia, Abdullah Azzam (1941-1989). Azzam had a slogan, "jihad and the rifle alone; no negotiations, no conferences, no dialogues."[11] One of the most energetic leaders of Arab jihadists, Azzam began actively mobilizing Arabs from both Saudi Arabia and several other countries who began crowding into Peshawar, in Pakistan, to fight the Soviets.

Azzam was a dynamic speaker who frequently returned from Pakistan to Saudi Arabia, where he stayed in a guesthouse belonging to an equally jihad-orientated young Saudi, Osama bin Laden. Bin Laden had joined the Muslim Brotherhood while in high school in Jeddah. When he went to attend college at King Abdul Aziz University in Jeddah, he discovered the works of Sayyid Qutb, the Egyptian Islamist whose book *Milestones* has shaped the thinking of virtually every Muslim radical who has subsequently engaged in *jihad*. Saudi Arabia was heavily populated by professors who had been run out of Egypt and other Arab states for being too Islamist. One of the Islamists whose lectures bin Laden attended in Jeddah was Mohammed Qutb, Sayyid Qutb's brother.

Bin Laden was to turn from fighting the Soviets to plotting against the Americans once the Soviets had withdrawn from Afghanistan in 1989. This is not the place to fill in the details of his career, which is still in progress. Bin Laden is believed currently to be hiding out somewhere in the Pakistan-Afghanistan border area. What is important to note is that bin Laden's hatred of the Americans specifically stemmed from the next challenge to affect Saudi Arabia after the Soviet invasion of Afghanistan, the Iraqi occupation of Kuwait in 1990. It was the presence of American troops on the soil of the homeland of the sacred places of Islam—Mecca and Medina—that finally inflamed bin Laden to start Al-Qaeda at the beginning of the 1990s.

It was certainly discomfiting to Saudis to be suddenly swamped by hundreds of thousands of foreigners, many of whom, in the case of the Americans certainly, were composed of both Jews and committed Christians. The U.S. military went to great lengths to respect the sensibilities of

Saudis, preventing the wearing of crosses by chaplains or any other Americans in uniform, apologizing profusely when Franklin Graham's organization, Samaritan's Purse, sent thousands of Arabic-language Bibles to American service personnel for possible distribution among Saudis and other Arabs.

The commanding general, Norman Schwarzkopf, ordered his military chaplains to confiscate any such Bibles they found. Some of the chaplains may even have obeyed the order. I was in Dhahran, Saudi Arabia, during the Desert Shield period of the build-up of American forces prior to the actual war. Many foreign cab drivers (mostly from the Indian subcontinent) spoke gleefully of a confrontation they said had taken place between a member of the Saudi religious police, the *mutawwa*, and an American female army captain when she drove her Humvee military vehicle into the parking lot of a Dhahran supermarket. (Words were apparently exchanged over his and her perceptions of a female's right to drive, and the *mutawwa* agent began to tap her with his long cane. At this point, she drew her sidearm and pointed it at him, which caused him to back off. Nothing was hurt other than pride.) The story may have been apocryphal, but it revealed the extent to which many foreigners in Saudi Arabia, even if they are not Christians, are conscious of the disdain with which they are regarded. During Desert Shield and Desert Storm, most Saudis gritted their teeth at the inconvenience of requiring so many foreigners to protect their homeland from a fellow-Arab invader.

But not Osama bin Laden. He issued two *fatwas*, religious rulings, in succession denouncing the American presence. The first document, released to a London-based Arabic newspaper in 2006, was called, "Declaration of War Against the Americans Occupying the Land of the Two Holy Places." It made clear that central to his thinking was hatred of everything America stood for: "Terrorizing you, while you are carrying arms on our land, is a legitimate and morally demanded duty. . . . It is the duty now on every tribe in the Arab Peninsula to fight, *Jihad*, in the cause of Allah to cleanse the land from those occupiers."[12] Earlier in the same year, a bomb had been exploded at a housing complex in Khobar, Saudi Arabia, near Dhahran on the northeast coast, which killed 19 American servicemen and 1 Saudi. Though Osama bin Laden claimed credit for having inspired the bombing, the organizing unit called itself Hezbollah Al-Hijaz ("Hezbollah in the Hejaz"), which suggested an Iranian connection on the part of the terrorists, rather than an Al-Qaeda connection. In June 2001, in an

Alexandria, Virginia, court, 13 Saudis and 1 Lebanese were indicted *in absentia*, for the attack.

The second fatwa, in 1998, repeated some of the accusations against America for "occupying the lands of Islam in the holiest of places," but added the stricture that it was a "ruling to kill the Americans and their allies—civilians and military," and that this was "an individual duty for every Muslim who can do it in any country in which it is possible to do it."[13] The chilling seriousness of the call to murder was made apparent in August 1998, when massive bombs exploded almost simultaneously at the U.S. embassies in Kenya, Nairobi, and Dar es Salaam, Tanzania, killing 223 people in both cities and injuring an estimated 4,000 more. In the subsequent American indictment of suspected organizers of the attack, Osama bin Laden and his Egyptian second-in-command, Ayman al-Zawahiri, were both mentioned. To give the Saudis credit, they had stripped bin Laden of his Saudi citizenship in 1994, by which time he was already in Sudan. He would move to Afghanistan two years later.

A string of terrorist attacks against Americans—the 1996 Khobar Towers in Saudi Arabia; the 1998 bombings at the east African embassies; the attack on the *USS Cole* in Aden in 2000—all indicated that Al-Qaeda, having started its life in the early 1990s, was ramping up its program to attack the U.S. and kill Americans and their allies wherever and whenever in the world they could. The ultimate climax of that campaign, of course, was the 9/11 attacks in New York and Washington in 2001. Of the 19 hijackers of the aircraft that crashed into the World Trade Center Towers and the Pentagon that morning, as we have mentioned, 15 were Saudis. Saudi diplomats and government officials were understandably embarrassed by this news and certainly cooperated to a degree with U.S. authorities in closing down financial pipelines to Al-Qaeda and Saudi "charitable" organizations that raised money for Islamic *jihadists*.

They have in the years since 9/11 made determined and successful efforts to suppress terrorist cells operating within Saudi Arabia *and seeking to strike at Saudi royal power*. The poison that kept being pumped into the Saudi religious environment by the Saudi ulama, however, scarcely lessened at all. Crown Prince (later King) Abdullah issued a warning to the Saudi clerical establishment, but anti-Jewish and anti-Christian diatribes continued to pour out of mosques in the Saudi kingdom. As recently as the spring of 2009, an interview with a Saudi cleric made clear that Christians and Jews had no religious rights whatever in Saudi Arabia. "The prophet's Guidance . . . dictates," said Sheikh Adel Al-Kalbani, imam of the Ak-Haram Mosque in Mecca, "Drive the Jews and the Christians out of the Arabian Peninsula. . . . They should be allowed to live here only if their presence is essential."[14]

The approval of terrorism was not limited to statements emerging from mosques. In early May 2002, in Kuala Lumpur, Malaysia, Saudi Arabia's Minister for Islamic Affairs, Sheikh Saleh al-Sheikh, disagreed with a Malaysian deputy prime minister that suicide bombing was not a legitimate way to win holy war. "The suicide bombings are permitted," the sheikh said, and "the victims are considered to have died a martyr's death."[15]

We have already mentioned the Saudi connection to Afghanistan during the war against the Soviets. The country of Afghanistan does not lie geographically within the Middle East, but it does have a strong connection with Saudi Arabia. The Saudis financed a great deal of the anti-Soviet fighting during the 1980s, and they injected much of their religious ideology into key Afghan resistance groups. The faction most influenced by Saudi Wahhabism, however, was the one that came to power in 1996, was dislodged from Kabul by the U.S. and its Afghan Northern Alliance allies in 2001, and is still fighting to regain power, namely the Taliban.

There are several reasons why the Taliban version of *sharia* has always been so severe. When they controlled Kabul, the Taliban prohibited any education whatsoever for women, and the appearance of women in public if they didn't wear the full *chador* that completely covers them. They also banned kite flying, satellite dishes, musical instruments, tapes, computers, VCRs, TVs and any device that can produce music. Strict practitioners of Wahhabism ban all forms of musical expression. Some of the Taliban severity can be attributed to Afghan tribal traditions, but the Wahhabi influence is palpable.

Currently, it is the Pakistani government that is bearing much of the brunt of Taliban insurgency, for Taliban military units were for a time granted de facto control of Pakistan's strategic Swat Valley. The area in the Northwest Frontier Province of Pakistan is close to Afghanistan, but not actually adjacent to it. Nevertheless, when the Taliban took control of the area in December 2008, they proceeded to impose similar restrictions on ordinary Pakistanis that they had imposed while in power in Afghanistan. All education for girls and women was banned and several schools were actually destroyed. During the war against the Soviets, all of the military assistance to the Afghan rebels, whatever its original source, was channeled through the largest of Pakistan's intelligence organizations, the Inter-Services Intelligence (ISI). In fact, the ISI actually trained thousands of Afghan mujahedeen and guided them operationally against the Soviets.

The ISI has become very controversial within Pakistan today, especially now that the country is back under democratic rule. It is believed to be riddled with sympathizers not only of the Taliban but also of Islamic activists within Pakistan. Whether the ISI is firmly under control of the elected government of Pakistan today may not become clear for some time. After the Mumbai hotel terrorist attacks in 2008, however, Pakistan admitted that several of the anti-India terrorist training camps had operated on Pakistan territory with the connivance of some Pakistani military and intelligence officials.

Sudan's Struggles

But while Pakistan is beyond the geographical limit of this book, Sudan isn't. Sudan is clearly in the Middle East, though it is the largest country in Africa. Sudan is a gigantic territory, even larger than Saudi Arabia, and fully one-quarter of the size of the U.S. It has for several years had a few unenviable distinctives: the second most unstable country in the world (the first being Iraq), with one of its regions, Darfur, a virtual synonym for human rights abuses and genocide. In July 2008, the International Criminal Court in the Hague, Netherlands, issued the first indictment for crimes against humanity of any sitting head of state, Sudanese president Omar al-Bashir.

Sudan's history has been linked with that of Egypt for nearly 3,000 years, the two countries' ruling dynasties periodically conquering each other. Islam took several years to penetrate Sudan, and never completely overran the country, a cause for much of the violence and anguish that has characterized life in Sudan over the past half century. The "African" portion of the country, populated more by black Africans than Arabs, has remained resistant to Islamicization efforts by successive Sudanese governments.

Sudan first came significantly into focus in the politics of the great powers of the West when Ibrahim Pasha, the son of Egypt's Muhammad Ali (the same Ibrahim Pasha who conquered the Wahhabis in Arabia in 1820) brought Sudan under the control of Egypt in 1820. After the British took over Egypt in 1882, however, for much of the next century Great Britain and Egypt tussled over who should control Sudan. Egypt claimed it for most of the nineteenth century.

In the 1880s, the rise of a Sudanese leader claiming to be Islam's Mahdi, one Muhammad Ahmad ibn Sayyid Abd Allah, led to one of the more remarkable episodes in British imperial history in the late nineteenth century, the war with the "Dervishes of Sudan." A renowned British military officer, Major-General Charles Gordon (sometimes referred to as "Chinese Gordon" for his role in helping China's Qing dynasty suppress the Taiping rebellion), was killed in 1885 by the Mahdi's forces in Khartoum. Three years before his death in Sudan, Gordon, a devout evangelical Christian, had lent his name to a site outside Jerusalem that came to be known as "Gordon's Calvary." Today it is the alternative site of the crucifixion and resurrection of Christ, known as the Garden Tomb.

It wasn't until 11 years later that the British responded forcefully, and finally crushed the Mahdi at the Battle of Omdurman in 1898. The battle was significant in that one of the young British officers taking part was the youthful (then 23) cavalry officer, Winston Churchill.

The British ruled Sudan from 1899, and only agreed to Sudanese independence after the Egyptian government of Gamal Abdel Nasser challenged Britain to do so in 1954. Sudan became independent in 1956.

Even before then, however, a civil war had begun which was to last initially until 1972, and then later for decades longer. The issue was—and is—Sudan's ethnically contradictory composition of the ethnically Arab northern part of the country, which was overwhelmingly Muslim, and the ethnically African southern portion of Sudan, which was mainly either animist or Christian. A peace treaty between north and south, called the Addis Abbaba Accord, granted a significant amount of autonomy to the south. But when General Gaafar Nimeiry, who had seized power in a military coup in 1969, decided to impose *sharia* over all of Sudan in 1983 and tore up the autonomy agreements with the south ("I am 300 percent the constitution," he said, "I do not know of any plebiscite because I am mandated by the people as president"), the south took up arms. A military wing called the Sudanese People's Liberation Army, originally supported by the Soviet Union but increasingly pro-U.S. later on, took up arms against the north. The resulting renewed civil war, with accompanying famine, was estimated to have cost the lives of 2 million Sudanese.

In 2005, after intensive negotiations between the Khartoum regime and the SPLA, there was a cease-fire and an agreement that southern Sudan would be autonomous for six years, pending an ultimate resolution of constitutional issues. But just as the north-south war was approaching a resolution, an unrelated conflict in Sudan's western region of Darfur was intensifying. In this region, where the forces on both sides were largely black Islamicized Africans, the rebels accused Khartoum of having neglected the region in economic development. The regime responded to the rebellion savagely, employing a malevolent militia of local tribespeople called the *janjaweed*. The violence and *janjaweed* attacks caused the displacement of an estimated 2.5 million civilians. Between 200,000 and 400,000 civilians may have died.

In 2004, U.S. Secretary of State Colin Powell drew attention to the Darfur crisis in a major way by using the term "genocide" to describe it. In 2005, the U.N. Security Council established the United Nations Mission in Sudan (UNMIS) to police the north-south cease-fire. But the U.N. has had no authority from the government in Khartoum to police the Darfur region, and an African Union force of some 7,000 African troops authorized by the African Union Mission in the Sudan (AMIS), was heavily outgunned and outnumbered in Darfur. The Sudanese government has agreed to its being reinforced by military units of any other nation.

A plethora of international organizations such as Amnesty International and Human Rights Watch, meanwhile, plus a galaxy of international celebrities, ranging from Angelina Jolie and Mia Farrow, along with prominent journalists like the *New York Times* columnist Nick Kristof, kept Darfur in the public eye. Other human-rights organizations campaigned for action through the U.N.

In July 2008, the International Criminal Court (ICC), which was established at a founding treaty in Rome only in 2002, published 10 charges of war crimes and crimes against humanity against Sudanese president Omar al-Bashir. In April 2009, the ICC issued an arrest warrant for him for seven counts of these assorted crimes.[16] Sudan, however, doesn't recognize the ICC and it is unlikely that al-Bashir will ever stray onto the territory of countries where the arrest warrant might be executed. Al-Bashir organized immediate street demonstrations in Khartoum to protest the ICC indictment. He said that the ICC could "eat" the warrant.

The Changing Tide of History

We started our journey here in Rome, at the Arch of Titus, where Roman soldiers were depicted looting the Jewish Temple in Jerusalem of its most sacred implements of Jewish religious ritual. Many Muslims believe that the Day of Judgment at the end of time—an Islamic concept as well as a Christian one—is close at hand and will be preceded by the return of Islam to Europe. By "return," they mean the fact that it was expelled from Spain in 1492, and though the Ottoman Turks captured Constantinople from the Christian Byzantine Empire in 1453, they failed to capture Vienna in either 1529 or 1683. Sheik Yussif al-Qaradawi, an Egyptian Muslim scholar who has been known for a popular program on Arabic-language Al Jazeera TV, has his own thoughts on this.

Al-Qaradawi, a member of the Muslim Brotherhood, has asserted that Islam will reconquer Europe and that Rome itself and the Vatican will fall to the Muslims. Referring to a *haddith* that purports to have Mohammed speaking of Rome, Al-Qaradawi said, "This means that the friends of the Prophet heard that the two cities would be conquered by Islam, Romiyya [Rome] and Constantinople, and the Prophet said that '*Hirqil* [Constantinople] would be conquered first.'" Al-Qaradawi predicted that Islam would conquer Rome and all Europe, though he was careful to add that this "conquest" might be through preaching and ideology, and not necessarily through war.[17]

Only historians a long way in the future will be able to determine whether that prophecy associated with Mohammed will be borne out. (I don't personally think it will be.) What is very clear, however, is that it cannot happen unless Jerusalem also falls into the hands of Islam. That is certainly the aspiration of millions of Saudis, and indeed of many Muslims both in the Middle East and in other parts of the world. But the tide of history doesn't always flow in the direction most zealously sought by those who wish to see a particular direction prevail.

Less than three decades ago, the leader of the Soviet Union, Yuri Andropov, was telling his Politburo associates and others that the "co-relation of forces" between Soviet power and the democratic West had now moved to favor the Soviet side. He was wrong, and within less than a decade, the entire Soviet Union had collapsed. There are certainly many Muslim evangelists in Europe today, not to mention a significant percentage of Muslims who are now native to Europe. But Islam is not the fastest-growing religion in the world. Christianity is, and there are far more

Muslims converting to Christianity from Islam around the world than there are Christians who are converting to Islam.

Occasionally, those who wish radical philosophical or ideological change on other civilizations, cultures and religions end up watching their own civilization transformed first—in a direction they would never have wished to see.

APPENDIX A

U.N. SECURITY COUNCIL RESOLUTION 242

November 22, 1967

In 1967, following the Six-Day War in June, the Security Council for the United Nations reviewed the situation in the Middle East. On November 22, 1967, the British Ambassador, Lord Caradon, presented the final draft of the Security Council's resolution on the matter. The resolution was adopted on the same day. This resolution, numbered 242, established provisions and principles that the United Nations hoped would lead to a solution of the conflict. Resolution 242 was to become the cornerstone of Middle East diplomatic efforts in the coming decades.

The Security Council,

Expressing its continuing concern with the grave situation in the Middle East,

Emphasizing the inadmissibility of the acquisition of territory by war and the need to work for a just and lasting peace in which every State in the area can live in security,

Emphasizing further that all Member States in their acceptance of the Charter of the United Nations have undertaken a commitment to act in accordance with Article 2 of the Charter,

1. Affirms that the fulfillment of Charter principles requires the establishment of a just and lasting peace in the Middle East which should include the application of both the following principles:

    (i) Withdrawal of Israeli armed forces from territories occupied in the recent conflict;

    (ii) Termination of all claims or states of belligerency and respect for and acknowledgement of the sovereignty, territorial integrity and political independence of every State in the area and their right to live in peace within secure and recognized boundaries free from threats or acts of force;

2. Affirms further the necessity:

    (i)   For guaranteeing freedom of navigation through international waterways in the area;

    (ii) For achieving a just settlement of the refugee problem;

    (iii) For guaranteeing the territorial inviolability and political independence of every State in the area, through measures including the establishment of demilitarized zones;

3. Requests the Secretary General to designate a Special Representative to proceed to the Middle East to establish and maintain contacts with the States concerned in order to promote agreement and assist efforts to achieve a peaceful and accepted settlement in accordance with the provisions and principles in this resolution;

4. Requests the Secretary-General to report to the Security Council on the progress of the efforts of the Special Representative as soon as possible.

Source: http://www.mfa.gov.il/MFA/Peace+Process/Guide+to+the+Peace+Process/UN+Security+Council+Resolution+242.htm.

UNITED NATIONS GENERAL ASSEMBLY RESOLUTION 181

The U.N. Partition Plan for Palestine
November 29, 1947

The General Assembly,

Having met in special session at the request of the mandatory Power to constitute and instruct a Special Committee to prepare for the consideration of the question of the future Government of Palestine at the second regular session;

Having constituted a Special Committee and instructed it to investigate all questions and issues relevant to the problem of Palestine, and to prepare proposals for the solution of the problem, and

Having received and examined the report of the Special Committee (document A/364)[1] including a number of unanimous recommendations and a plan of partition with economic union approved by the majority of the Special Committee,

Considers that the present situation in Palestine is one which is likely to impair the general welfare and friendly relations among nations;

Takes note of the declaration by the mandatory Power that it plans to complete its evacuation of Palestine by 1 August 1948;

Recommends to the United Kingdom, as the mandatory Power for Palestine, and to all other Members of the United Nations the adoption and implementation, with regard to the future Government of Palestine, of the Plan of Partition with Economic Union set out below;

Requests that

The Security Council takes the necessary measures as provided for in the plan for its implementation;

The Security Council consider, if circumstances during the transitional period require such consideration, whether the situation in Palestine constitutes a threat to the peace. If it decides that such a threat exists, and in order to maintain international peace and security, the Security Council should supplement the authorization of the General Assembly by taking measures, under Articles 39 and 41 of the Charter, to empower the United Nations Commission, as provided in this resolution, to exercise in Palestine the functions which are assigned to it by this resolution;

The Security Council determine as a threat to the peace, breach of the peace or act of aggression, in accordance with Article 39 of the Charter, any attempt to alter by force the settlement envisaged by this resolution;

The Trusteeship Council be informed of the responsibilities envisaged for it in this plan;

Calls upon the inhabitants of Palestine to take such steps as may be necessary on their part to put this plan into effect;

Appeals to all Governments and all peoples to refrain from taking any action which might hamper or delay the carrying out of these recommendations, and

Authorizes the Secretary-General to reimburse travel and subsistence expenses of the members of the Commission referred to in Part 1, Section B, Paragraph I below, on such basis and in such form as he may determine most appropriate in the circumstances, and to provide the Commission with the necessary staff to assist in carrying out the functions assigned to the Commission by the General Assembly.[2]

The General Assembly,

Authorizes the Secretary-General to draw from the Working Capital Fund a sum not to exceed 2,000,000 dollars for the purposes set forth in the last paragraph of the resolution on the future government of Palestine.

PLAN OF PARTITION WITH ECONOMIC UNION

PART I. FUTURE CONSTITUTION AND GOVERNMENT OF PALESTINE

A. Termination of Mandate, Partition and Independence

The Mandate for Palestine shall terminate as soon as possible but in any case not later than 1 August 1948.

The armed forces of the mandatory Power shall be progressively withdrawn from Palestine, the withdrawal to be completed as soon as possible but in any case not later than 1 August 1948.

The mandatory Power shall advise the Commission, as far in advance as possible, of its intention to terminate the mandate and to evacuate each area. The mandatory Power shall use its best endeavors to ensure that an area situated in the territory of the Jewish State, including a seaport and hinterland adequate to provide facilities for a substantial immigration, shall be evacuated at the earliest possible date and in any event not later than 1 February 1948.

Independent Arab and Jewish States and the Special International Regime for the City of Jerusalem, set forth in Part III of this Plan, shall come into existence in Palestine two months after the evacuation of the armed forces of the mandatory Power has been completed but in any case not later than 1 October 1948. The boundaries of the Arab State, the Jewish State, and the City of Jerusalem shall be as described in Parts II and III below.

The period between the adoption by the General Assembly of its recommendation on the question of Palestine and the establishment of the independence of the Arab and Jewish States shall be a transitional period.

B. Steps Preparatory to Independence

A Commission shall be set up consisting of one representative of each of five Member States. The Members represented on the Commission shall be elected by the General Assembly on as broad a basis, geographically and otherwise, as possible.

The administration of Palestine shall, as the mandatory Power withdraws its armed forces, be progressively turned over to the Commission, which shall act in conformity with the recommendations of the General Assembly, under the guidance of the Security Council. The mandatory

Power shall to the fullest possible extent coordinate its plans for withdrawal with the plans of the Commission to take over and administer areas which have been evacuated.

In the discharge of this administrative responsibility the Commission shall have authority to issue necessary regulations and take other measures as required.

The mandatory Power shall not take any action to prevent, obstruct or delay the implementation by the Commission of the measures recommended by the General Assembly.

On its arrival in Palestine the Commission shall proceed to carry out measures for the establishment of the frontiers of the Arab and Jewish States and the City of Jerusalem in accordance with the general lines of the recommendations of the General Assembly on the partition of Palestine. Nevertheless, the boundaries as described in Part II of this Plan are to be modified in such a way that village areas as a rule will not be divided by state boundaries unless pressing reasons make that necessary.

The Commission, after consultation with the democratic parties and other public organizations of the Arab and Jewish States, shall select and establish in each State as rapidly as possible a Provisional Council of Government. The activities of both the Arab and Jewish Provisional Councils of Government shall be carried out under the general direction of the Commission.

If by 1 April 1948 a Provisional Council of Government cannot be selected for either of the States, or, if selected, cannot carry out its functions, the Commission shall communicate that fact to the Security Council for such action with respect to that State as the Security Council may deem proper, and to the Secretary-General for communication to the Members of the United Nations.

Subject to the provisions of these recommendations, during the transitional period the Provisional Councils of Government, acting under the Commission, shall have full authority in the areas under their control including authority over matters of immigration and land regulation.

The Provisional Council of Government of each State, acting under the Commission, shall progressively receive from the Commission full responsibility for the administration of that State in the period between the termination of the Mandate and the establishment of the State's independence.

The Commission shall instruct the Provisional Councils of Government of both the Arab and Jewish States, after their formation, to proceed to the establishment of administrative organs of government, central and local.

The Provisional Council of Government of each State shall, within the shortest time possible, recruit an armed militia from the residents of that State, sufficient in number to maintain internal order and to prevent frontier clashes.

This armed militia in each State shall, for operational purposes, be under the command of Jewish or Arab officers resident in that State, but general political and military control, including the choice of the militia's High Command, shall be exercised by the Commission.

The Provisional Council of Government of each State shall, not later than two months after the withdrawal of the armed forces of the mandatory Power, hold elections to the Constituent Assembly which shall be conducted on democratic lines.

The election regulations in each State shall be drawn up by the Provisional Council of Government and approved by the Commission. Qualified voters for each State for this election shall be persons over eighteen years of age who are (a) Palestinian citizens residing in that State; and (b) Arabs and Jews residing in the State, although not Palestinian citizens, who, before voting, have signed a notice of intention to become citizens of such State.

Arabs and Jews residing in the City of Jerusalem who have signed a notice of intention to become citizens, the Arabs of the Arab State and the Jews of the Jewish State, shall be entitled to vote in the Arab and Jewish States respectively.

Women may vote and be elected to the Constituent Assemblies.

During the transitional period no Jew shall be permitted to establish residence in the area of the proposed Arab State, and no Arab shall be permitted to establish residence in the area of the proposed Jewish State, except by special leave of the Commission.

The Constituent Assembly of each State shall draft a democratic constitution for its State and choose a provisional government to succeed the Provisional Council of Government appointed by the Commission. The Constitutions of the States shall embody Chapters 1 and 2 of the Declaration provided for in section C below and include, inter alia, provisions for:

(i) Establishing in each State a legislative body elected by universal suffrage and by secret ballot on the basis of proportional representation, and an executive body responsible to the legislature;

(ii) Settling all international disputes in which the State may be involved by peaceful means in such a manner that international peace and security, and justice, are not endangered;

(iii) Accepting the obligation of the State to refrain in its international relations from the threat or use of force against the territorial integrity or political independence of any State, or in any other manner inconsistent with the purpose of the United Nations;

(iv) Guaranteeing to all persons equal and non-discriminatory rights in civil, political, economic and religious matters and the enjoyment of human rights and fundamental freedoms, including freedom of religion, language, speech and publication, education, assembly and association;

(v) Preserving freedom of transit and visit for all residents and citizens of the other State in Palestine and the City of Jerusalem, subject to considerations of national security, provided that each State shall control residence within its borders.

The Commission shall appoint a preparatory economic commission of three members to make whatever arrangements are possible for economic co-operation, with a view to establishing, as soon as practicable, the Economic Union and the Joint Economic Board, as provided in section D below.

During the period between the adoption of the recommendations on the question of Palestine by the General Assembly and the termination of the Mandate, the mandatory Power in Palestine shall maintain full responsibility for administration in areas from which it has not withdrawn its armed forces. The Commission shall assist the mandatory Power in the carrying out of these functions. Similarly the mandatory Power shall co-operate with the Commission in the execution of its functions.

With a view to ensuring that there shall be continuity in the functioning of administrative services and that, on the withdrawal of the armed forces of the mandatory Power, the whole administration shall be in the charge of the Provisional Councils and the Joint Economic Board, respectively, acting under the Commission, there shall be a progressive transfer, from the mandatory Power to the Commission, of responsibility for all the functions of government, including that of maintaining law and order in the areas from which the forces of the mandatory Power have been withdrawn.

The Commission shall be guided in its activities by the recommendations of the General Assembly and by such instructions as the Security Council may consider necessary to issue.

The measures taken by the Commission, within the recommendations of the General Assembly, shall become immediately effective unless the Commission has previously received contrary instructions from the Security Council. The Commission shall render periodic monthly progress reports, or more frequently if desirable, to the Security Council.

The Commission shall make its final report to the next regular session of the General Assembly and to the Security Council simultaneously.

C. Declaration

A declaration shall be made to the United Nations by the Provisional Government of each proposed State before independence. It shall contain, inter alia, the following clauses:

General Provision

The stipulations contained in the Declaration are recognized as fundamental laws of the State and no law, regulation or official action shall conflict or interfere with these stipulations, nor shall any law, regulation or official action prevail over them.

Chapter I: Holy Places, Religious Buildings and Sites

Existing rights in respect of Holy Places and religious buildings or sites shall not be denied or impaired.

In so far as Holy Places are concerned, the liberty of access, visit, and transit shall be guaranteed, in conformity with existing rights, to all residents and citizen of the other State and of the City of Jerusalem, as well as to aliens, without distinction as to nationality, subject to requirements of national security, public order and decorum.

Similarly, freedom of worship shall be guaranteed in conformity with existing rights, subject to the maintenance of public order and decorum.

Holy Places and religious buildings or sites shall be preserved. No act shall be permitted which may in any way impair their sacred character. If at any time it appears to the Government that any particular Holy Place, religious, building or site is in need of urgent repair, the Government may call upon the community or communities concerned to carry out such repair. The Government may carry it out itself at the expense of the community or community concerned if no action is taken within a reasonable time.

No taxation shall be levied in respect of any Holy Place, religious building or site which was exempt from taxation on the date of the creation of the State.

No change in the incidence of such taxation shall be made which would either discriminate between the owners or occupiers of Holy Places, religious buildings or sites, or would place such owners or occupiers in a position less favorable in relation to the general incidence of taxation than existed at the time of the adoption of the Assembly's recommendations.

The Governor of the City of Jerusalem shall have the right to determine whether the provisions of the Constitution of the State in relation to Holy Places, religious buildings and sites within the borders of the State and the religious rights appertaining thereto, are being properly applied and respected, and to make decisions on the basis of existing rights in cases of disputes which may arise between the different religious communities or the rites of a religious community with respect to such places, buildings and sites. He shall receive full co-operation and such privileges and immunities as are necessary for the exercise of his functions in the State.

Chapter 2: Religious and Minority Rights
Freedom of conscience and the free exercise of all forms of worship, subject only to the maintenance of public order and morals, shall be ensured to all.

No discrimination of any kind shall be made between the inhabitants on the ground of race, religion, language or sex.

All persons within the jurisdiction of the State shall be entitled to equal protection of the laws.

The family law and personal status of the various minorities and their religious interests, including endowments, shall be respected.

Except as may be required for the maintenance of public order and good government, no measure shall be taken to obstruct or interfere with

the enterprise of religious or charitable bodies of all faiths or to discriminate against any representative or member of these bodies on the ground
of his religion or nationality.

The State shall ensure adequate primary and secondary education for
the Arab and Jewish minority, respectively, in its own language and its cultural traditions.

The right of each community to maintain its own schools for the education of its own members in its own language, while conforming to such
educational requirements of a general nature as the State may impose,
shall not be denied or impaired. Foreign educational establishments shall
continue their activity on the basis of their existing rights.

No restriction shall be imposed on the free use by any citizen of the
State of any language in private intercourse, in commerce, in religion, in
the Press or in publications of any kind, or at public meetings.[3]

No expropriation of land owned by an Arab in the Jewish State (by a
Jew in the Arab State)[4] shall be allowed except for public purposes. In all
cases of expropriation full compensation as fixed by the Supreme Court
shall be said previous to dispossession.

Chapter 3: Citizenship, International Conventions and Financial Obligations
1. Citizenship Palestinian citizens residing in Palestine outside the City of
Jerusalem, as well as Arabs and Jews who, not holding Palestinian citizenship, reside in Palestine outside the City of Jerusalem shall, upon the recognition of independence, become citizens of the State in which they are
resident and enjoy full civil and political rights. Persons over the age of
eighteen years may opt, within one year from the date of recognition of independence of the State in which they reside, for citizenship of the other
State, providing that no Arab residing in the area of the proposed Arab
State shall have the right to opt for citizenship in the proposed Jewish State
and no Jew residing in the proposed Jewish State shall have the right to opt
for citizenship in the proposed Arab State. The exercise of this right of option will be taken to include the wives and children under eighteen years of
age of persons so opting.

Arabs residing in the area of the proposed Jewish State and Jews residing in the area of the proposed Arab State who have signed a notice of intention to opt for citizenship of the other State shall be eligible to vote in
the elections to the Constituent Assembly of that State, but not in the elections to the Constituent Assembly of the State in which they reside.

2. International conventions. The State shall be bound by all the international agreements and conventions, both general and special, to which Palestine has become a party. Subject to any right of denunciation provided for therein, such agreements and conventions shall be respected by the State throughout the period for which they were concluded.

Any dispute about the applicability and continued validity of international conventions or treaties signed or adhered to by the mandatory Power on behalf of Palestine shall be referred to the International Court of Justice in accordance with the provisions of the Statute of the Court.

3. Financial obligations. The State shall respect and fulfill all financial obligations of whatever nature assumed on behalf of Palestine by the mandatory Power during the exercise of the Mandate and recognized by the State. This provision includes the right of public servants to pensions, compensation or gratuities.

These obligations shall be fulfilled through participation in the Joint Economic Board in respect of those obligations applicable to Palestine as a whole, and individually in respect of those applicable to, and fairly apportionable between, the States.

A Court of Claims, affiliated with the Joint Economic Board, and composed of one member appointed by the United Nations, one representative of the United Kingdom and one representative of the State concerned, should be established. Any dispute between the United Kingdom and the State respecting claims not recognized by the latter should be referred to that Court.

Commercial concessions granted in respect of any part of Palestine prior to the adoption of the resolution by the General Assembly shall continue to be valid according to their terms, unless modified by agreement between the concession-holders and the State.

Chapter 4: Miscellaneous Provisions
The provisions of chapters 1 and 2 of the declaration shall be under the guarantee of the United Nations, and no modifications shall be made in them without the assent of the General Assembly of the United Nations. Any Member of the United Nations shall have the right to bring to the attention of the General Assembly any infraction or danger of infraction of any of these stipulations, and the General Assembly may thereupon make such recommendations as it may deem proper in the circumstances.

Any dispute relating to the application or interpretation of this declaration shall be referred, at the request of either party, to the International Court of Justice, unless the parties agree to another mode of settlement.

D. Economic Union and Transit

The Provisional Council of Government of each State shall enter into an undertaking with respect to Economic Union and Transit. This undertaking shall be drafted by the Commission provided for in section B, paragraph 1, utilizing to the greatest possible extent the advice and cooperation of representative organizations and bodies from each of the proposed States. It shall contain provisions to establish the Economic Union of Palestine and provide for other matters of common interest. If by 1 April 1948 the Provisional Councils of Government have not entered into the undertaking, the undertaking shall be put into force by the Commission.

The Economic Union of Palestine
The objectives of the Economic Union of Palestine shall be:

- (i) A customs union;
- (ii) A joint currency system providing for a single foreign exchange rate;
- (iii) Operation in the common interest on a non-discriminatory basis of railways inter-State highways; postal, telephone and telegraphic services and ports and airports involved in international trade and commerce;
- (iv) Joint economic development, especially in respect of irrigation, land reclamation and soil conservation;
- (iv) Access for both States and for the City of Jerusalem on a non-discriminatory basis to water and power facilities.

There shall be established a Joint Economic Board, which shall consist of three representatives of each of the two States and three foreign members appointed by the Economic and Social Council of the United Nations. The foreign members shall be appointed in the first instance for a term of three years; they shall serve as individuals and not as representatives of States.

The functions of the Joint Economic Board shall be to implement either directly or by delegation the measures necessary to realize the objectives of the Economic Union. It shall have all powers of organization and administration necessary to fulfill its functions.

The States shall bind themselves to put into effect the decisions of the Joint Economic Board. The Board's decisions shall be taken by a majority vote.

In the event of failure of a State to take the necessary action the Board may, by a vote of six members, decide to withhold an appropriate portion of the part of the customs revenue to which the State in question is entitled under the Economic Union. Should the State persist in its failure to cooperate, the Board may decide by a simple majority vote upon such further sanctions, including disposition of funds which it has withheld, as it may deem appropriate.

In relation to economic development, the functions of the Board shall be planning, investigation and encouragement of joint development projects, but it shall not undertake such projects except with the assent of both States and the City of Jerusalem, in the event that Jerusalem is directly involved in the development project.

In regard to the joint currency system, the currencies circulating in the two States and the City of Jerusalem shall be issued under the authority of the Joint Economic Board, which shall be the sole issuing authority and which shall determine the reserves to be held against such currencies.

So far as is consistent with paragraph 2(b) above, each State may operate its own central bank, control its own fiscal and credit policy, its foreign exchange receipts and expenditures, the grant of import licenses, and may conduct international financial operations on its own faith and credit. During the first two years after the termination of the Mandate, the Joint Economic Board shall have the authority to take such measures as may be necessary to ensure that—to the extent that the total foreign exchange revenues of the two States from the export of goods and services permit, and provided that each State takes appropriate measures to conserve its own foreign exchange resources—each State shall have available, in any twelve months' period, foreign exchange sufficient to assure the supply of quantities of imported goods and services for consumption in its territory equivalent to the quantities of such goods and services consumed in that territory in the twelve months' period ending 31 December 1947.

All economic authority not specifically vested in the Joint Economic Board is reserved to each State.

There shall be a common customs tariff with complete freedom of trade between the States, and between the States and the City of Jerusalem.

The tariff schedules shall be drawn up by a Tariff Commission, consisting of representatives of each of the States in equal numbers, and shall be submitted to the Joint Economic Board for approval by a majority vote. In case of disagreement in the Tariff Commission, the Joint Economic Board shall arbitrate the points of difference. In the event that the Tariff Commission fails to draw up any schedule by a date to be fixed, the Joint Economic Board shall determine the tariff schedule.

The following items shall be a first charge on the customs and other common revenue of the Joint Economic Board:

(i) The expenses of the customs service and of the operation of the joint services;

(ii) The administrative expenses of the Joint Economic Board;

(iii) The financial obligations of the Administration of Palestine, consisting of:
   • the service of the outstanding public debt;
   • the cost of superannuation benefits, now being paid or falling due in the future, in accordance with the rules and to the extent established by paragraph 3 of chapter 3 above.

After these obligations have been met in full, the surplus revenue from the customs and other common services shall be divided in the following manner: not less than 5 per cent and not more than 10 per cent to the City of Jerusalem; the residue shall be allocated to each State by the Joint Economic Board equitably, with the objective of maintaining a sufficient and suitable level of government and social services in each State, except that the share of either State shall not exceed the amount of that State's contribution to the revenues of the Economic Union by more than approximately four million pounds in any year. The amount granted may be adjusted by the Board according to the price level in relation to the prices prevailing at the time of the establishment of the Union. After five years, the principles of the distribution of the joint revenue may be revised by the Joint Economic Board on a basis of equity.

All international conventions and treaties affecting customs tariff rates, and those communications services under the jurisdiction of the

Joint Economic Board, shall be entered into by both States. In these matters, the two States shall be bound to act in accordance with the majority of the Joint Economic Board.

The Joint Economic Board shall endeavor to secure for Palestine's exports fair and equal access to world markets.

All enterprises operated by the Joint Economic Board shall pay fair wages on a uniform basis.

Freedom of Transit and Visit

The undertaking shall contain provisions preserving freedom of transit and visit for all residents or citizens of both States and of the City of Jerusalem, subject to security considerations; provided that each State and the City shall control residence within its borders.

Termination, Modification and Interpretation of the Undertaking

The undertaking and any treaty issuing therefrom shall remain in force for a period of ten years. It shall continue in force until notice of termination, to take effect two years thereafter, is given by either of the parties.

During the initial ten-year period, the undertaking and any treaty issuing therefrom may not be modified except by consent of both parties and with the approval of the General Assembly.

Any dispute relating to the application or the interpretation of the undertaking and any treaty issuing therefrom shall be referred, at the request of either party, to the International Court of Justice, unless the parties agree to another mode of settlement.

E. Assets

The movable assets of the Administration of Palestine shall be allocated to the Arab and Jewish States and the City of Jerusalem on an equitable basis. Allocations should be made by the United Nations Commission referred to iii section B, paragraph 1, above. Immovable assets shall become the property of the government of the territory in which they are situated.

During the period between the appointment of the United Nations Commission and the termination of the Mandate, the mandatory Power shall, except in respect of ordinary operations, consult with the Commission on any measure which it may contemplate involving the liquidation, disposal or encumbering of the assets of the Palestine Government, such as the accumulated treasury surplus, the proceeds of Government bond issues, State lands or any other asset.

F. Admission to Membership in the United Nations

When the independence of either the Arab or the Jewish State as envisaged in this plan has become effective and the declaration and undertaking, as envisaged in this plan, have been signed by either of them, sympathetic consideration should be given to its application for admission to membership in the United Nations in accordance with article 4 of the Charter of the United Nations.

PART II. BOUNDARIES

A. The Arab State

The area of the Arab State in Western Galilee is bounded on the west by the Mediterranean and on the north by the frontier of the Lebanon from Ras en Naqura to a point north of Saliha. From there the boundary proceeds southwards, leaving the built-up area of Saliha in the Arab State, to join the southernmost point of this village. There it follows the western boundary line of the villages of 'Alma, Rihaniya and Teitaba, thence following the northern boundary line of Meirun village to join the Acre-Safad Sub-District boundary line. It follows this line to a point west of Es Sammu'i village and joins it again at the northernmost point of Farradiya. Thence it follows the sub-district boundary line to the Acre-Safad main road. From here it follows the western boundary of Kafr-I'nan village until it reaches the Tiberias-Acre Sub-District boundary line, passing to the west of the junction of the Acre-Safad and Lubiya-Kafr-I'nan roads. From the southwest corner of Kafr-I'nan village the boundary line follows the western boundary of the Tiberias Sub-District to a point close to the boundary line between the villages of Maghar and 'Eilabun, thence bulging out to the west to include as much of the eastern part of the plain of Battuf as is necessary for the reservoir proposed by the Jewish Agency for the irrigation of lands to the south and east.

The boundary rejoins the Tiberias Sub-District boundary at a point on the Nazareth-Tiberias road south-east of the built-up area of Tur'an; thence it runs southwards, at first following the sub-district boundary and then passing between the Kadoorie Agricultural School and Mount Tabor, to a point due south at the base of Mount Tabor. From here it runs due west, parallel to the horizontal grid line 230, to the north-east corner of the village lands of Tel Adashim. It then runs to the northwest corner of these lands, whence it turns south and west so as to include in the Arab State the sources of the Nazareth water supply in Yafa village. On reaching Ginneiger it follows the eastern, northern and western boundaries of the lands of this village to their south-west comer, whence it proceeds in a straight line to a point on the Haifa-Afula railway on the boundary between the villages of Sarid and El-Mujeidil. This is the point of intersection. The south-western boundary of the area of the Arab State in Galilee takes a line from this point, passing northwards along the eastern boundaries of Sarid and Gevat to the north-eastern corner of Nahalal, proceeding thence across the land of Kefar ha Horesh to a central point on the southern boundary of the village of 'Ilut, thence westwards along that village boundary to the eastern boundary of Beit Lahm, thence northwards and north-eastwards along its western boundary to the north-eastern corner of Waldheim and thence north-westwards across the village lands of Shafa 'Amr to the southeastern corner of Ramat Yohanan. From here it runs due north-north-east to a point on the Shafa 'Amr-Haifa road, west of its junction with the road of I'billin. From there it proceeds north-east to a point on the southern boundary of I'billin situated to the west of the I'billin-Birwa road. Thence along that boundary to its westernmost point, whence it turns to the north, follows across the village land of Tamra to the north-westernmost corner and along the western boundary of Julis until it reaches the Acre-Safad road. It then runs westwards along the southern side of the Safad-Acre road to the Galilee-Haifa District boundary, from which point it follows that boundary to the sea.

The boundary of the hill country of Samaria and Judea starts on the Jordan River at the Wadi Malih south-east of Beisan and runs due west to meet the Beisan-Jericho road and then follows the western side of that road in a north-westerly direction to the junction of the boundaries of the Sub-Districts of Beisan, Nablus, and Jenin. From that point it follows the Nablus-Jenin sub-District boundary westwards for a distance of about three kilometres and then turns north-westwards, passing to the east of the built-up areas of the villages of Jalbun and Faqqu'a, to the boundary of the Sub-Districts of Jenin and Beisan at a point northeast of Nuris. Thence it proceeds first northwestwards to a point due north of the built-up area of Zie'in and then westwards to the Afula-Jenin railway, thence north-westwards along the District boundary line to the point of intersection on the Hejaz railway. From here the boundary runs southwestwards,

including the built-up area and some of the land of the village of Kh. Lid
in the Arab State to cross the Haifa-Jenin road at a point on the district
boundary between Haifa and Samaria west of El- Mansi. It follows this
boundary to the southernmost point of the village of El-Buteimat. From
here it follows the northern and eastern boundaries of the village of Ar'ara
rejoining the Haifa-Samaria district boundary at Wadi 'Ara, and thence
proceeding south-south-westwards in an approximately straight line joining up with the western boundary of Qaqun to a point east of the railway line on the eastern boundary of Qaqun village. From here it runs
along the railway line some distance to the east of it to a point just east
of the Tulkarm railway station. Thence the boundary follows a line halfway between the railway and the Tulkarm-Qalqiliya-Jaljuliya and Ras El-
Ein road to a point just east of Ras El-Ein station, whence it proceeds
along the railway some distance to the east of it to the point on the railway line south of the junction of the Haifa-Lydda and Beit Nabala lines,
whence it proceeds along the southern border of Lydda airport to its
south-west corner, thence in a south-westerly direction to a point just
west of the built-up area of Sarafand El 'Amar, whence it turns south,
passing just to the west of the built-up area of Abu El-Fadil to the north-
east corner of the lands of Beer Ya'aqov. (The boundary line should be so
demarcated as to allow direct access from the Arab State to the airport.)
Thence the boundary line follows the western and southern boundaries
of Ramle village, to the north-east corner of El Na'ana village, thence in
a straight line to the southernmost point of El Barriya, along the eastern
boundary of that village and the southern boundary of 'Innaba village.
Thence it turns north to follow the southern side of the Jaffa-Jerusalem
road until El-Qubab, whence it follows the road to the boundary of Abu-
Shusha. It runs along the eastern boundaries of Abu Shusha, Seidun,
Hulda to the southernmost point of Hulda, thence westwards in a
straight line to the north-eastern corner of Umm Kalkha, thence following the northern boundaries of Umm Kalkha, Qazaza and the northern
and western boundaries of Mukhezin to the Gaza District boundary and
thence runs across the village lands of El-Mismiya El-Kabira, and Yasur to
the southern point of intersection, which is midway between the built-
up areas of Yasur and Batani Sharqi.

From the southern point of intersection the boundary lines run north-
westwards between the villages of Gan Yavne and Barqa to the sea at a
point half way between Nabi Yunis and Minat El-Qila, and south-eastwards

to a point west of Qastina, whence it turns in a south-westerly direction, passing to the east of the built-up areas of Es Sawafir Esh Sharqiya and 'Ibdis. From the south-east corner of 'Ibdis village it runs to a point south-west of the built-up area of Beit 'Affa, crossing the Hebron-El-Majdal road just to the west of the built-up area of 'Iraq Suweidan. Thence it proceeds southward along the western village boundary of El-Faluja to the Beersheba Sub-District boundary. It then runs across the tribal lands of 'Arab El-Jubarat to a point on the boundary between the Sub-Districts of Beersheba and Hebron north of Kh. Khuweilifa, whence it proceeds in a south-westerly direction to a point on the Beersheba-Gaza main road two kilometres to the north-west of the town. It then turns south-eastwards to reach Wadi Sab' at a point situated one kilometer to the west of it. From here it turns north-eastwards and proceeds along Wadi Sab' and along the Beersheba-Hebron road for a distance of one kilometer, whence it turns eastwards and runs in a straight line to Kh. Kuseifa to join the Beersheba-Hebron Sub-District boundary. It then follows the Beersheba-Hebron boundary eastwards to a point north of Ras Ez-Zuweira, only departing from it so as to cut across the base of the indentation between vertical grid lines 150 and 160.

About five kilometres north-east of Ras Ez-Zuweira it turns north, excluding from the Arab State a strip along the coast of the Dead Sea not more than seven kilometres in depth, as far as 'Ein Geddi, whence it turns due east to join the Transjordan frontier in the Dead Sea.

The northern boundary of the Arab section of the coastal plain runs from a point between Minat El-Qila and Nabi Yunis, passing between the built-up areas of Gan Yavne and Barqa to the point of intersection. From here it turns south-westwards, running across the lands of Batani Sharqi, along the eastern boundary of the lands of Beit Daras and across the lands of Julis, leaving the built-up areas of Batani Sharqi and Julis to the westwards, as far as the north-west corner of the lands of Beit-Tima. Thence it runs east of El-Jiya across the village lands of El-Barbara along the eastern boundaries of the villages of Beit Jirja, Deir Suneid and Dimra. From the south-east corner of Dimra the boundary passes across the lands of Beit Hanun, leaving the Jewish lands of Nir-Am to the eastwards. From the south-east corner of Beit Hanun the line runs south-west to a point south of the parallel grid line 100, then turns north-west for two kilometres, turning again in a southwesterly direction and continuing in an almost straight line to the north-west corner of the village lands of Kirbet Ikhza'a.

From there it follows the boundary line of this village to its southernmost point. It then runs in a southerly direction along the vertical grid line 90 to its junction with the horizontal grid line 70. It then turns south-eastwards to Kh. El-Ruheiba and then proceeds in a southerly direction to a point known as El-Baha, beyond which it crosses the Beersheba-EI 'Auja main road to the west of Kh. El-Mushrifa. From there it joins Wadi El-Zaiyatin just to the west of El-Subeita. From there it turns to the north-east and then to the south-east following this Wadi and passes to the east of 'Abda to join Wadi Nafkh. It then bulges to the south-west along Wadi Nafkh, Wadi 'Ajrim and Wadi Lassan to the point where Wadi Lassan crosses the Egyptian frontier.

The area of the Arab enclave of Jaffa consists of that part of the town-planning area of Jaffa which lies to the west of the Jewish quarters lying south of Tel-Aviv, to the west of the continuation of Herzl street up to its junction with the Jaffa-Jerusalem road, to the south-west of the section of the Jaffa-Jerusalem road lying south-east of that junction, to the west of Miqve Yisrael lands, to the northwest of Holon local council area, to the north of the line linking up the north-west corner of Holon with the northeast corner of Bat Yam local council area and to the north of Bat Yam local council area. The question of Karton quarter will be decided by the Boundary Commission, bearing in mind among other considerations the desirability of including the smallest possible number of its Arab inhabitants and the largest possible number of its Jewish inhabitants in the Jewish State.

B. The Jewish State

The north-eastern sector of the Jewish State (Eastern Galilee) is bounded on the north and west by the Lebanese frontier and on the east by the frontiers of Syria and Transjordan. It includes the whole of the Huleh Basin, Lake Tiberias, the whole of the Beisan Sub-District, the boundary line being extended to the crest of the Gilboa mountains and the Wadi Malih. From there the Jewish State extends north-west, following the boundary described in respect of the Arab State. The Jewish section of the coastal plain extends from a point between Minat El-Qila and Nabi Yunis in the Gaza Sub-District and includes the towns of Haifa and Tel-Aviv, leaving Jaffa as an enclave of the Arab State. The eastern frontier of the Jewish State follows the boundary described in respect of the Arab State.

The Beersheba area comprises the whole of the Beersheba Sub-District, including the Negeb and the eastern part of the Gaza Sub-District, but excluding the town of Beersheba and those areas described in respect of the Arab State. It includes also a strip of land along the Dead Sea stretching from the Beersheba-Hebron Sub-District boundary line to 'Ein Geddi, as described in respect of the Arab State.

C. The City of Jerusalem
The boundaries of the City of Jerusalem are as defined in the recommendations on the City of Jerusalem. (See Part III, section B, below).

PART III. CITY OF JERUSALEM[5]

A. Special Regime
The City of Jerusalem shall be established as a corpus separatum under a special international regime and shall be administered by the United Nations. The Trusteeship Council shall be designated to discharge the responsibilities of the Administering Authority on behalf of the United Nations.

B. Boundaries of the City
The City of Jerusalem shall include the present municipality of Jerusalem plus the surrounding villages and towns, the most eastern of which shall be Abu Dis; the most southern, Bethlehem; the most western, 'Ein Karim (including also the built-up area of Motsa); and the most northern Shu'fat, as indicated on the attached sketch-map (annex B).

C. Statue of the City
The Trusteeship Council shall, within five months of the approval of the present plan, elaborate and approve a detailed statute of the City which shall contain, inter alia, the substance of the following provisions:

Government machinery; special objectives. The Administering Authority in discharging its administrative obligations shall pursue the following special objectives:

(i) To protect and to preserve the unique spiritual and religious interests located in the city of the three great monotheistic faiths throughout the world, Christian, Jewish and Moslem;

to this end to ensure that order and peace, and especially religious peace, reign in Jerusalem;

(ii) To foster cooperation among all the inhabitants of the city in their own interests as well as in order to encourage and support the peaceful development of the mutual relations between the two Palestinian peoples throughout the Holy Land; to promote the security, well-being and any constructive measures of development of the residents having regard to the special circumstances and customs of the various peoples and communities.

Governor and Administrative staff. A Governor of the City of Jerusalem shall be appointed by the Trusteeship Council and shall be responsible to it. He shall be selected on the basis of special qualifications and without regard to nationality. He shall not, however, be a citizen of either State in Palestine.

The Governor shall represent the United Nations in the City and shall exercise on their behalf all powers of administration, including the conduct of external affairs. He shall be assisted by an administrative staff classed as international officers in the meaning of Article 100 of the Charter and chosen whenever practicable from the residents of the city and of the rest of Palestine on a non-discriminatory basis. A detailed plan for the organization of the administration of the city shall be submitted by the Governor to the Trusteeship Council and duly approved by it.

Local autonomy. The existing local autonomous units in the territory of the city (villages, townships and municipalities) shall enjoy wide powers of local government and administration.

The Governor shall study and submit for the consideration and decision of the Trusteeship Council a plan for the establishment of special town units consisting, respectively, of the Jewish and Arab sections of new Jerusalem. The new town units shall continue to form part the present municipality of Jerusalem.

Security measures. The City of Jerusalem shall be demilitarized; neutrality shall be declared and preserved, and no para-military formations, exercises or activities shall be permitted within its borders.

Should the administration of the City of Jerusalem be seriously obstructed or prevented by the non-cooperation or interference of one or more sections of the population the Governor shall have authority to take such measures as may be necessary to restore the effective functioning of administration.

To assist in the maintenance of internal law and order, especially for the protection of the Holy Places and religious buildings and sites in the city, the Governor shall organize a special police force of adequate strength, the members of which shall be recruited outside of Palestine. The Governor shall be empowered to direct such budgetary provision as may be necessary for the maintenance of this force.

Legislative Organization. A Legislative Council, elected by adult residents of the city irrespective of nationality on the basis of universal and secret suffrage and proportional representation, shall have powers of legislation and taxation. No legislative measures shall, however, conflict or interfere with the provisions which will be set forth in the Statute of the City, nor shall any law, regulation, or official action prevail over them. The Statute shall grant to the Governor a right of vetoing bills inconsistent with the provisions referred to in the preceding sentence. It shall also empower him to promulgate temporary ordinances in case the Council fails to adopt in time a bill deemed essential to the normal functioning of the administration.

Administration of Justice. The Statute shall provide for the establishment of an independent judiciary system, including a court of appeal. All the inhabitants of the city shall be subject to it.

Economic Union and Economic Regime. The City of Jerusalem shall be included in the Economic Union of Palestine and be bound by all stipulations of the undertaking and of any treaties issued therefrom, as well as by the decisions of the Joint Economic Board. The headquarters of the Economic Board shall be established in the territory City. The Statute shall provide for the regulation of economic matters not falling within the regime of the Economic Union, on the basis of equal treatment and non-discrimination for all members of the United Nations and their nationals.

Freedom of Transit and Visit: Control of Residents. Subject to considerations of security, and of economic welfare as determined by the Governor under the directions of the Trusteeship Council, freedom of entry into, and residence within the borders of the City shall be guaranteed for the residents or citizens of the Arab and Jewish States. Immigration into, and residence within, the borders of the city for nationals of other States shall be controlled by the Governor under the directions of the Trusteeship Council.

Relations with Arab and Jewish States. Representatives of the Arab and Jewish States shall be accredited to the Governor of the City and charged with the protection of the interests of their States and nationals in connection with the international administration of the City.

Official languages. Arabic and Hebrew shall be the official languages of the city. This will not preclude the adoption of one or more additional working languages, as may be required.

Citizenship. All the residents shall become ipso facto citizens of the City of Jerusalem unless they opt for citizenship of the State of which they have been citizens or, if Arabs or Jews, have filed notice of intention to become citizens of the Arab or Jewish State respectively, according to Part 1, section B, paragraph 9, of this Plan.

The Trusteeship Council shall make arrangements for consular protection of the citizens of the City outside its territory.

Freedoms of citizens. Subject only to the requirements of public order and morals, the inhabitants of the City shall be ensured the enjoyment of human rights and fundamental freedoms, including freedom of conscience, religion and worship, language, education, speech and press, assembly and association, and petition.

No discrimination of any kind shall be made between the inhabitants on the grounds of race, religion, language or sex.

All persons within the City shall be entitled to equal protection of the laws.

The family law and personal status of the various persons and communities and their religious interests, including endowments, shall be respected.

Except as may be required for the maintenance of public order and good government, no measure shall be taken to obstruct or interfere with the enterprise of religious or charitable bodies of all faiths or to discriminate against any representative or member of these bodies on the ground of his religion or nationality.

The City shall ensure adequate primary and secondary education for the Arab and Jewish communities respectively, in their own languages and in accordance with their cultural traditions.

The right of each community to maintain its own schools for the education of its own members in its own language, while conforming to such educational requirements of a general nature as the City may impose, shall not be denied or impaired. Foreign educational establishments shall continue their activity on the basis of their existing rights.

No restriction shall be imposed on the free use by any inhabitant of the City of any language in private intercourse, in commerce, in religion, in the Press or in publications of any kind, or at public meetings.

Holy Places. Existing rights in respect of Holy Places and religious buildings or sites shall not be denied or impaired.

Free access to the Holy Places and religious buildings or sites and the free exercise of worship shall be secured in conformity with existing rights and subject to the requirements of public order and decorum.

Holy Places and religious buildings or sites shall be preserved. No act shall be permitted which may in any way impair their sacred character. If at any time it appears to the Governor that any particular Holy Place, religious building or site is in need of urgent repair, the Governor may call upon the community or communities concerned to carry out such repair. The Governor may carry it out himself at the expense of the community or communities concerned if no action is taken within a reasonable time.

No taxation shall be levied in respect of any Holy Place, religious building or site which was exempt from taxation on the date of the creation of the City. No change in the incidence of such taxation shall be made which would either discriminate between the owners or occupiers of Holy Places, religious buildings or sites or would place such owners or occupiers in a position less favorable in relation to the general incidence of taxation than existed at the time of the adoption of the Assembly's recommendations.

Special powers of the Governor in respect of the Holy Places, religious buildings and sites in the City and in any part of Palestine.

The protection of the Holy Places, religious buildings and sites located in the City of Jerusalem shall be a special concern of the Governor.

With relation to such places, buildings and sites in Palestine outside the city, the Governor shall determine, on the ground of powers granted to him by the Constitution of both States, whether the provisions of the

Constitution of the Arab and Jewish States in Palestine dealing therewith and the religious rights appertaining thereto are being properly applied and respected.

The Governor shall also be empowered to make decisions on the basis of existing rights in cases of disputes which may arise between the different religious communities or the rites of a religious community in respect of the Holy Places, religious buildings and sites in any part of Palestine.

In this task he may be assisted by a consultative council of representatives of different denominations acting in an advisory capacity.

D. Duration of the Special Regime

The Statute elaborated by the Trusteeship Council the aforementioned principles shall come into force not later than 1 October 1948. It shall remain in force in the first instance for a period of ten years, unless the Trusteeship Council finds it necessary to undertake a re-examination of these provisions at an earlier date. After the expiration of this period the whole scheme shall be subject to examination by the Trusteeship Council in the light of experience acquired with its functioning. The residents the City shall be then free to express by means of a referendum their wishes as to possible modifications of regime of the City.

PART IV. CAPITULATIONS

States whose nationals have in the past enjoyed in Palestine the privileges and immunities of foreigners, including the benefits of consular jurisdiction and protection, as formerly enjoyed by capitulation or usage in the Ottoman Empire, are invited to renounce any right pertaining to them to the re-establishment of such privileges and immunities in the proposed Arab and Jewish States and the City of Jerusalem.

Adopted at the 128th plenary meeting:

In favor: 33

Australia, Belgium, Bolivia, Brazil, Byelorussian S.S.R., Canada, Costa Rica, Czechoslovakia, Denmark, Dominican Republic, Ecuador, France, Guatemala, Haiti, Iceland, Liberia, Luxemburg, Netherlands, New Zealand, Nicaragua, Norway, Panama, Paraguay, Peru, Philippines, Poland, Sweden, Ukrainian S.S.R., Union of South Africa, U.S.A., U.S.S.R., Uruguay, Venezuela.

Against: 13
Afghanistan, Cuba, Egypt, Greece, India, Iran, Iraq, Lebanon, Pakistan, Saudi Arabia, Syria, Turkey, Yemen.

Abstained: 10
Argentina, Chile, China, Colombia, El Salvador, Ethiopia, Honduras, Mexico, United Kingdom, Yugoslavia.

Source: http://www.mideastweb.org/181.htm; http://www.yale.edu/lawweb/avalon/un/res181.htm#back5.

APPENDIX C

THE PALESTINIAN NATIONAL CHARTER

Resolutions of the Palestine National Council
July 1-17, 1968

Article 1: Palestine is the homeland of the Arab Palestinian people; it is an indivisible part of the Arab homeland, and the Palestinian people are an integral part of the Arab nation.

Article 2: Palestine, with the boundaries it had during the British Mandate, is an indivisible territorial unit.

Article 3: The Palestinian Arab people possess the legal right to their homeland and have the right to determine their destiny after achieving the liberation of their country in accordance with their wishes and entirely of their own accord and will.

Article 4: The Palestinian identity is a genuine, essential, and inherent characteristic; it is transmitted from parents to children. The Zionist occupation and the dispersal of the Palestinian Arab people, through the disasters which befell them, do not make them lose their Palestinian identity and their membership in the Palestinian community, nor do they negate them.

Article 5: The Palestinians are those Arab nationals who, until 1947, normally resided in Palestine regardless of whether they were evicted from it or have stayed there. Anyone born, after that date, of a Palestinian father—whether inside Palestine or outside it—is also a Palestinian.

Article 6: The Jews who had normally resided in Palestine until the beginning of the Zionist invasion will be considered Palestinians.

Article 7: That there is a Palestinian community and that it has material, spiritual, and historical connection with Palestine are indisputable facts. It is a national duty to bring up individual Palestinians in an Arab revolutionary manner. All means of information and education must be adopted in order to acquaint the Palestinian with his country in the most profound manner, both spiritual and material, that is possible. He must be prepared for the armed struggle and ready to sacrifice his wealth and his life in order to win back his homeland and bring about its liberation.

Article 8: The phase in their history, through which the Palestinian people are now living, is that of national (*watani*) struggle for the liberation of Palestine. Thus the conflicts among the Palestinian national forces are secondary, and should be ended for the sake of the basic conflict that exists between the forces of Zionism and of imperialism on the one hand, and the Palestinian Arab people on the other. On this basis the Palestinian masses, regardless of whether they are residing in the national homeland or in diaspora (*mahajir*) constitute—both their organizations and the individuals—one national front working for the retrieval of Palestine and its liberation through armed struggle.

Article 9: Armed struggle is the only way to liberate Palestine. This it is the overall strategy, not merely a tactical phase. The Palestinian Arab people assert their absolute determination and firm resolution to continue their armed struggle and to work for an armed popular revolution for the liberation of their country and their return to it. They also assert their right to normal life in Palestine and to exercise their right to self-determination and sovereignty over it.

Article 10: Commando action constitutes the nucleus of the Palestinian popular liberation war. This requires its escalation, comprehensiveness, and the mobilization of all the Palestinian popular and educational efforts and their organization and involvement in the armed Palestinian revolution. It also requires the achieving of unity for the national (*watani*) struggle among the different groupings of the Palestinian people, and between the Palestinian people and the Arab masses, so as to secure the continuation of the revolution, its escalation, and victory.

Article 11: The Palestinians will have three mottoes: national (*wataniyya*) unity, national (*qawmiyya*) mobilization, and liberation.

Article 12: The Palestinian people believe in Arab unity. In order to contribute their share toward the attainment of that objective, however, they must, at the present stage of their struggle, safeguard their Palestinian identity and develop their consciousness of that identity, and oppose any plan that may dissolve or impair it.

Article 13: Arab unity and the liberation of Palestine are two complementary objectives, the attainment of either of which facilitates the attainment of the other. Thus, Arab unity leads to the liberation of Palestine, the liberation of Palestine leads to Arab unity; and work toward the realization of one objective proceeds side by side with work toward the realization of the other.

Article 14: The destiny of the Arab nation, and indeed Arab existence itself, depend upon the destiny of the Palestine cause. From this interdependence springs the Arab nation's pursuit of, and striving for, the liberation of Palestine. The people of Palestine play the role of the vanguard in the realization of this sacred (*qawmi*) goal.

Article 15: The liberation of Palestine, from an Arab viewpoint, is a national (*qawmi*) duty and it attempts to repel the Zionist and imperialist aggression against the Arab homeland, and aims at the elimination of Zionism in Palestine. Absolute responsibility for this falls upon the Arab nation—peoples and governments—with the Arab people of Palestine in the vanguard. Accordingly, the Arab nation must mobilize all its military, human, moral, and spiritual capabilities to participate actively with the Palestinian people in the liberation of Palestine. It must, particularly in the phase of the armed Palestinian revolution, offer and furnish the Palestinian people with all possible help, and material and human support, and make available to them the means and opportunities that will enable them to continue to carry out their leading role in the armed revolution, until they liberate their homeland.

Article 16: The liberation of Palestine, from a spiritual point of view, will provide the Holy Land with an atmosphere of safety and tranquility, which in turn will safeguard the country's religious sanctuaries and guarantee freedom of worship and of visit to all, without discrimination of race, color, language, or religion. Accordingly, the people of Palestine look to all spiritual forces in the world for support.

Article 17: The liberation of Palestine, from a human point of view, will restore to the Palestinian individual his dignity, pride, and freedom. Accordingly the Palestinian Arab people look forward to the support of all those who believe in the dignity of man and his freedom in the world.

Article 18: The liberation of Palestine, from an international point of view, is a defensive action necessitated by the demands of self-defense. Accordingly the Palestinian people, desirous as they are of the friendship of all people, look to freedom-loving, and peace-loving states for support in order to restore their legitimate rights in Palestine, to re-establish peace and security in the country, and to enable its people to exercise national sovereignty and freedom.

Article 19: The partition of Palestine in 1947 and the establishment of the state of Israel are entirely illegal, regardless of the passage of time, because they were contrary to the will of the Palestinian people and to their natural right in their homeland, and inconsistent with the principles embodied in the Charter of the United Nations, particularly the right to self-determination.

Article 20: The Balfour Declaration, the Mandate for Palestine, and everything that has been based upon them, are deemed null and void. Claims of historical or religious ties of Jews with Palestine are incompatible with the facts of history and the true conception of what constitutes statehood. Judaism, being a religion, is not an independent nationality. Nor do Jews constitute a single nation with an identity of its own; they are citizens of the states to which they belong.

Article 21: The Arab Palestinian people, expressing themselves by the armed Palestinian revolution, reject all solutions which are substitutes for the total liberation of Palestine and reject all proposals aiming at the liquidation of the Palestinian problem, or its internationalization.

Article 22: Zionism is a political movement organically associated with international imperialism and antagonistic to all action for liberation and to progressive movements in the world. It is racist and fanatic in its nature, aggressive, expansionist, and colonial in its aims, and fascist in its methods. Israel is the instrument of the Zionist movement, and geographical base for world imperialism placed strategically in the midst of the Arab homeland to combat the hopes of the Arab nation for liberation, unity, and progress. Israel is a constant source of threat vis-à-vis peace in the Middle East and the whole world. Since the liberation of Palestine will destroy the Zionist and imperialist presence and will contribute to the establishment of peace in the Middle East, the Palestinian people look for the support of all the progressive and peaceful forces and urge them all, irrespective of their affiliations and beliefs, to offer the Palestinian people all aid and support in their just struggle for the liberation of their homeland.

Article 23: The demand of security and peace, as well as the demand of right and justice, require all states to consider Zionism an illegitimate movement, to outlaw its existence, and to ban its operations, in order that friendly relations among peoples may be preserved, and the loyalty of citizens to their respective homelands safeguarded.

Article 24: The Palestinian people believe in the principles of justice, freedom, sovereignty, self-determination, human dignity, and in the right of all peoples to exercise them.

Article 25: For the realization of the goals of this Charter and its principles, the Palestine Liberation Organization will perform its role in the liberation of Palestine in accordance with the Constitution of this Organization.

Article 26: The Palestine Liberation Organization, representative of the Palestinian revolutionary forces, is responsible for the Palestinian Arab people's movement in its struggle—to retrieve its homeland, liberate and return to it and exercise the right to self-determination in it—in all military, political, and financial fields and also for whatever may be required by the Palestine case on the inter-Arab and international levels.

Article 27: The Palestine Liberation Organization shall cooperate with all Arab states, each according to its potentialities; and will adopt a neutral policy among them in the light of the requirements of the war of liberation; and on this basis it shall not interfere in the internal affairs of any Arab state.

Article 28: The Palestinian Arab people assert the genuineness and independence of their national (*wataniyya*) revolution and reject all forms of intervention, trusteeship, and subordination.

Article 29: The Palestinian people possess the fundamental and genuine legal right to liberate and retrieve their homeland. The Palestinian people determine their attitude toward all states and forces on the basis of the stands they adopt vis-à-vis to the Palestinian revolution to fulfill the aims of the Palestinian people.

Article 30: Fighters and carriers of arms in the war of liberation are the nucleus of the popular army which will be the protective force for the gains of the Palestinian Arab people.

Article 31: The Organization shall have a flag, an oath of allegiance, and an anthem. All this shall be decided upon in accordance with a special regulation.

Article 32: Regulations, which shall be known as the Constitution of the Palestinian Liberation Organization, shall be annexed to this Charter. It will lay down the manner in which the Organization, and its organs and institutions, shall be constituted; the respective competence of each; and the requirements of its obligation under the Charter.

Article 33: This Charter shall not be amended save by [vote of] a majority of two-thirds of the total membership of the National Congress of the Palestine Liberation Organization [taken] at a special session convened for that purpose.

English rendition as published in Basic Political Documents of the Armed Palestinian Resistance Movement; Leila S. Kadi (ed.), Palestine Research Centre, Beirut, December 1969, pp.137-141.

Source: http://www.acpr.org.il/resources/pacovenant.html.

THE CHARTER OF THE HAMAS

The Charter of Allah:
The Platform of the Islamic Resistance Movement (Hamas)

In the Name of Allah, the Merciful, the Compassionate

You are the best community that has been raised up for mankind.

Ye enjoin right conduct and forbid indecency; and ye believe in Allah. And if the People of the Scripture had believed, it had been better for them. Some of them are believers; but most of them are evil-doers.

They will not harm you save a trifling hurt, and if they fight against you they will turn and flee. And afterward they will not be helped.

Ignominy shall be their portion wheresoever they are found save [where they grasp] a rope from Allah and a rope from man. They have incurred anger from their Lord, and wretchedness is laid upon them. That is because they used to disbelieve the revelations of Allah, and slew the Prophets wrongfully. That is because they were rebellious and used to transgress. Surat Al-Imran (III), verses 109-111

Israel will rise and will remain erect until Islam eliminates it as it had eliminated its predecessors.

The Islamic World is burning. It is incumbent upon each one of us to pour some water, little as it may be, with a view of extinguishing as much of the fire as he can, without awaiting action by the others.

Introduction

Grace to Allah, whose help we seek, whose forgiveness we beseech, whose guidance we implore and on whom we rely. We pray and bid peace upon the Messenger of Allah, his family, his companions, his followers and those who spread his message and followed his tradition; they will last as long as there exist Heaven and Earth.

O, people! In the midst of misadventure, from the depth of suffering, from the believing hearts and purified arms; aware of our duty and in response to the decree of Allah, we direct our call, we rally together and join each other. We educate in the path of Allah and we make our firm determination prevail so as to take its proper role in life, to overcome all difficulties and to cross all hurdles. Hence our permanent state of preparedness and our readiness to sacrifice our souls and dearest [possessions] in the path of Allah.

Thus, our nucleus has formed which chartered its way in the tempestuous ocean of creeds and hopes, desires and wishes, dangers and difficulties, setbacks and challenges, both internal and external.

When the thought matured, the seed grew and the plant took root in the land of reality, detached from temporary emotion and unwelcome haste, the Islamic Resistance Movement erupted in order to play its role in the path of its Lord. In so doing, it joined its hands with those of all Jihad fighters for the purpose of liberating Palestine. The souls of its Jihad fighters will encounter those of all Jihad fighters who have sacrificed their lives in the land of Palestine since it was conquered by the Companion of the Prophet, be Allah's prayer and peace upon him, and until this very day. This is the Charter of the Islamic Resistance (Hamas) which will reveal its face, unveil its identity, state its position, clarify its purpose, discuss its hopes, call for support to its cause and reinforcement, and for joining its ranks. For our struggle against the Jews is extremely wide-ranging and grave, so much so that it will need all the loyal efforts we can wield, to be followed by further steps and reinforced by successive battalions from the multifarious Arab and Islamic world, until the enemies are defeated and Allah's victory prevails. Thus we shall perceive them approaching in the horizon, and this will be known before long:

> *"Allah has decreed: Lo! I very shall conquer, I and my messenger, lo! Allah is strong, almighty."*

PART I. KNOWING THE MOVEMENT

The Ideological Aspects

Article One. The Islamic Resistance Movement draws its guidelines from Islam; derives from it its thinking, interpretations and views about existence, life and humanity; refers back to it for its conduct; and is inspired by it in whatever step it takes.

The Link Between Hamas and the Association of Muslim Brothers
Article Two. The Islamic Resistance Movement is one of the wings of the Muslim Brothers in Palestine. The Muslim Brotherhood Movement is a world organization, the largest Islamic Movement in the modern era. It is characterized by a profound understanding, by precise notions and by a complete comprehensiveness of all concepts of Islam in all domains of life: views and beliefs, politics and economics, education and society, jurisprudence and rule, indoctrination and teaching, the arts and publications, the hidden and the evident, and all the other domains of life.

Structure and Essence
Article Three. The basic structure of the Islamic Resistance Movement consists of Muslims who are devoted to Allah and worship Him verily [as it is written]: "I have created Man and Devil for the purpose of their worship" [of Allah]. Those Muslims are cognizant of their duty towards themselves, their families and country and they have been relying on Allah for all that. They have raised the banner of Jihad in the face of the oppressors in order to extricate the country and the people from the [oppressors'] desecration, filth and evil.

Article Four. The Movement welcomes all Muslims who share its beliefs and thinking, commit themselves to its course of action, keep its secrets and aspire to join its ranks in order to carry out their duty.
    Allah will reward them.

Dimensions of Time and Space of the Hamas
Article Five. As the Movement adopts Islam as its way of life, its time dimension extends back as far as the birth of the Islamic Message and of the Righteous Ancestor. Its ultimate goal is Islam, the Prophet its model, the Qur'an its Constitution. Its special dimension extends wherever on earth there are Muslims, who adopt Islam as their way of life; thus, it penetrates to the deepest reaches of the land and to the highest spheres of Heavens.

Peculiarity and Independence
Article Six. The Islamic Resistance Movement is a distinct Palestinian Movement which owes its loyalty to Allah, derives from Islam its way of life and

strives to raise the banner of Allah over every inch of Palestine. Only under the shadow of Islam could the members of all regions coexist in safety and security for their lives, properties and rights. In the absence of Islam, conflict arises, oppression reigns, corruption is rampant and struggles and wars prevail. Allah had inspired the Muslim poet, Muhammad Iqbal, when he said:

> When the Faith wanes, there is no security. There is no this-world-liness for those who have no faith. Those who wish to live their life without religion Have made annihilation the equivalent of life.

The Universality of Hamas

Article Seven. By virtue of the distribution of Muslims, who pursue the cause of the Hamas, all over the globe, and strive for its victory, for the reinforcement of its positions and for the encouragement of its Jihad, the Movement is a universal one. It is apt to be that due to the clarity of its thinking, the nobility of its purpose and the loftiness of its objectives.

It is in this light that the Movement has to be regarded, evaluated and acknowledged. Whoever denigrates its worth, or avoids supporting it, or is so blind as to dismiss its role, is challenging Fate itself. Whoever closes his eyes from seeing the facts, whether intentionally or not, will wake up to find himself overtaken by events, and will find no excuses to justify his position. Priority is reserved to the early comers.

Oppressing those who are closest to you, is more of an agony to the soul than the impact of an Indian sword.

> And unto thee have we revealed the Scripture with the truth, confirming whatever scripture was before it, and a watcher over it. So judge between them by that which Allah hath revealed, and follow not their desires away from the truth which has come unto thee. For each we have appointed a divine law and a traced-out way. Had Allah willed, He could have made you one community. But that He may try you by that which he has given you [He has made you as you are]. So vie with one another in good works. Unto Allah, you will all return. He will then inform you of that wherein you differ.

Hamas is one of the links in the Chain of Jihad in the confrontation with the Zionist invasion. It links up with the setting out of the Martyr Izz a-din al-Qassam and his brothers in the Muslim Brotherhood who fought the Holy War in 1936; it further relates to another link of the

Palestinian Jihad and the Jihad and efforts of the Muslim Brothers during the 1948 War, and to the Jihad operations of the Muslim Brothers in 1968 and thereafter.

But even if the links have become distant from each other, and even if the obstacles erected by those who revolve in the Zionist orbit, aiming at obstructing the road before the Jihad fighters, have rendered the pursuance of Jihad impossible; nevertheless, the Hamas has been looking forward to implement Allah's promise whatever time it might take. The prophet, prayer and peace be upon him, said:

> *The time will not come until Muslims will fight the Jews (and kill them); until the Jews hide behind rocks and trees, which will cry: O Muslim! there is a Jew hiding behind me, come on and kill him! This will not apply to the Gharqad, which is a Jewish tree* (cited by Bukhari and Muslim).

The Slogan of the Hamas

Article Eight. Allah is its goal, the Prophet its model, the Qur'an its Constitution, Jihad its path and death for the case of Allah its most sublime belief.

PART II. OBJECTIVES

Motives and Objectives

Article Nine. Hamas finds itself at a period of time when Islam has waned away from the reality of life. For this reason, the checks and balances have been upset, concepts have become confused, and values have been transformed; evil has prevailed, oppression and obscurity have reigned; cowards have turned tigers, homelands have been usurped, people have been uprooted and are wandering all over the globe. The state of truth has disappeared and was replaced by the state of evil. Nothing has remained in its right place, for when Islam is removed from the scene, everything changes. These are the motives.

As to the objectives: discarding the evil, crushing it and defeating it, so that truth may prevail, homelands revert [to their owners], calls for prayer be heard from their mosques, announcing the reinstitution of the Muslim state. Thus, people and things will revert to their true place.

Article Ten. The Islamic Resistance Movement, while breaking its own path, will do its utmost to constitute at the same time a support to the weak, a defense to all the oppressed. It will spare no effort to implement the truth and abolish evil, in speech and in fact, both here and in any other location where it can reach out and exert influence.

PART III. STRATEGIES AND METHODS

The Strategy of Hamas: Palestine is an Islamic Waqf

Article Eleven. The Islamic Resistance Movement believes that the land of Palestine has been an Islamic Waqf throughout the generations and until the Day of Resurrection, no one can renounce it or part of it, or abandon it or part of it. No Arab country nor the aggregate of all Arab countries, and no Arab King or President nor all of them in the aggregate, have that right, nor has that right any organization or the aggregate of all organizations, be they Palestinian or Arab, because Palestine is an Islamic Waqf throughout all generations and to the Day of Resurrection. Who can presume to speak for all Islamic Generations to the Day of Resurrection? This is the status [of the land] in Islamic Shari'a, and it is similar to all lands conquered by Islam by force, and made thereby Waqf lands upon their conquest, for all generations of Muslims until the Day of Resurrection. This [norm] has prevailed since the commanders of the Muslim armies completed the conquest of Syria and Iraq, and they asked the Caliph of Muslims, 'Umar Ibn al-Khattab, for his view of the conquered land, whether it should be partitioned between the troops or left in the possession of its population, or otherwise. Following discussions and consultations between the Caliph of Islam, 'Umar Ibn al-Khattab, and the Companions of the Messenger of Allah, be peace and prayer upon him, they decided that the land should remain in the hands of its owners to benefit from it and from its wealth; but the control of the land and the land itself ought to be endowed as a Waqf [in perpetuity] for all generations of Muslims until the Day of Resurrection. The ownership of the land by its owners is only one of usufruct, and this Waqf will endure as long as Heaven and earth last. Any demarche in violation of this law of Islam, with regard to Palestine, is baseless and reflects on its perpetrators.

Hamas in Palestine: Its Views on Homeland and Nationalism

Article Twelve. Hamas regards Nationalism (Wataniyya) as part and parcel of the religious faith. Nothing is loftier or deeper in Nationalism than waging Jihad against the enemy and confronting him when he sets foot on the land of the Muslims. And this becomes an individual duty binding on every Muslim man and woman; a woman must go out and fight the enemy even without her husband's authorization, and a slave without his masters' permission.

This [principle] does not exist under any other regime, and it is a truth not to be questioned. While other nationalisms consist of material, human and territorial considerations, the nationality of Hamas also carries, in addition to all those, the all important divine factors which lend to it its spirit and life; so much so that it connects with the origin of the spirit and the source of life and raises in the skies of the Homeland the Banner of the Lord, thus inexorably connecting earth with Heaven.

When Moses came and threw his baton, sorcery and sorcerers became futile.

Peaceful Solutions, [Peace] Initiatives and International Conferences

Article Thirteen. [Peace] initiatives, the so-called peaceful solutions, and the international conferences to resolve the Palestinian problem, are all contrary to the beliefs of the Islamic Resistance Movement. For renouncing any part of Palestine means renouncing part of the religion; the nationalism of the Islamic Resistance Movement is part of its faith, the movement educates its members to adhere to its principles and to raise the banner of Allah over their homeland as they fight their Jihad: "Allah is the all-powerful, but most people are not aware."

From time to time a clamoring is voiced, to hold an International Conference in search for a solution to the problem. Some accept the idea, others reject it, for one reason or another, demanding the implementation of this or that condition, as a prerequisite for agreeing to convene the Conference or for participating in it. But the Islamic Resistance Movement, which is aware of the [prospective] parties to this conference, and of their past and present positions towards the problems of the Muslims, does not believe that those conferences are capable of responding to demands, or of restoring rights or doing justice to the oppressed.

Those conferences are no more than a means to appoint the nonbelievers as arbitrators in the lands of Islam. Since when did the Unbelievers do justice to the Believers?

And the Jews will not be pleased with thee, nor will the Christians, till thou follow their creed. Say: Lo! the guidance of Allah [himself] is the Guidance. And if you should follow their desires after the knowledge which has come

unto thee, then you would have from Allah no protecting friend nor helper.
Sura 2 (the Cow), verse 120

There is no solution to the Palestinian problem except by Jihad. The initiatives, proposals and International Conferences are but a waste of time, an exercise in futility. The Palestinian people are too noble to have their future, their right and their destiny submitted to a vain game. As the hadith has it:

> *The people of Syria are Allah's whip on this land; He takes revenge by their intermediary from whoever he wished among his worshipers. The Hypocrites among them are forbidden from vanquishing the true believers, and they will die in anxiety and sorrow.* (Told by Tabarani, who is traceable in ascending order of traditionaries to Muhammad, and by Ahmed whose chain of transmission is incomplete. But it is bound to be a true hadith, for both story tellers are reliable. Allah knows best.)

The Three Circles

Article Fourteen. The problem of the liberation of Palestine relates to three circles: the Palestinian, the Arab and the Islamic. Each one of these circles has a role to play in the struggle against Zionism and it has duties to fulfill. It would be an enormous mistake and an abysmal act of ignorance to disregard anyone of these circles.

For Palestine is an Islamic land where the First Qibla and the third holiest site are located. That is also the place whence the Prophet, be Allah's prayer and peace upon him, ascended to heavens.

> *Glorified be He who carried His servant by night from the Inviolable Place of worship to the Far Distant Place of Worship, the neighborhood whereof we have blessed, that we might show him of our tokens! Lo! He, only He, is the Hearer, the Seer.* Sura XVII (al-Isra'), verse 1

In consequence of this state of affairs, the liberation of that land is an individual duty binding on all Muslims everywhere. This is the base on which all Muslims have to regard the problem; this has to be understood by all Muslims. When the problem is dealt with on this basis, where the full potential of the three circles is mobilized, then the current circumstances will change and the day of liberation will come closer.

You are more awful as a fear in their bosoms than Allah. That is because they are a folk who understand not. Sura LIX, (Al-Hashr, the Exile), verse 13

The Jihad for the Liberation of Palestine is an Individual Obligation

Article Fifteen. When our enemies usurp some Islamic lands, Jihad becomes a duty binding on all Muslims. In order to face the usurpation of Palestine by the Jews, we have no escape from raising the banner of Jihad. This would require the propagation of Islamic consciousness among the masses on all local, Arab and Islamic levels. We must spread the spirit of Jihad among the [Islamic] Umma, clash with the enemies and join the ranks of the Jihad fighters.

The 'ulama as well as educators and teachers, publicity and media men as well as the masses of the educated, and especially the youth and the elders of the Islamic Movements, must participate in this raising of consciousness. There is no escape from introducing fundamental changes in educational curricula in order to cleanse them from all vestiges of the ideological invasion which has been brought about by orientalists and missionaries.

That invasion had begun overtaking this area following the defeat of the Crusader armies by Salah a-Din el Ayyubi. The Crusaders had understood that they had no way to vanquish the Muslims unless they prepared the grounds for that with an ideological invasion which would confuse the thinking of Muslims, revile their heritage, discredit their ideals, to be followed by a military invasion. That was to be in preparation for the Imperialist invasion, as in fact [General] Allenby acknowledged it upon his entry to Jerusalem: "Now, the Crusades are over." General Gouraud stood on the tomb of Salah a-Din and declared: "We have returned, O Salah a-Din!" Imperialism has been instrumental in boosting the ideological invasion and deepening its roots, and it is still pursuing this goal. All this had paved the way to the loss of Palestine. We must imprint on the minds of generations of Muslims that the Palestinian problem is a religious one, to be dealt with on this premise. It includes Islamic holy sites such as the Aqsa Mosque, which is inexorably linked to the Holy Mosque as long as the Heaven and earth will exist, to the journey of the Messenger of Allah, be Allah's peace and blessing upon him, to it, and to his ascension from it.

Dwelling one day in the Path of Allah is better than the entire world and everything that exists in it. The place of the whip of one among you in

Paradise is better than the entire world and everything that exists in it. [God's] worshiper's going and coming in the Path of Allah is better than the entire world and everything that exists in it. (Told by Bukhari, Muslim Tirmidhi and Ibn Maja.)

I swear by that who holds in His Hands the Soul of Muhammad! I indeed wish to go to war for the sake of Allah! I will assault and kill, assault and kill, assault and kill. (Told by Bukhari and Muslim.)

Article Sixteen. We must accord the Islamic [young] generations in our area, an Islamic education based on the implementation of religious precepts, on the conscientious study of the Book of Allah; on the Study of the Prophetic Tradition, on the study of Islamic history and heritage from its reliable sources, under the guidance of experts and scientists, and on singling out the paths which constitute for the Muslims sound concepts of thinking and faith. It is also necessary to study conscientiously the enemy and its material and human potential; to detect its weak and strong spots, and to recognize the powers that support it and stand by it. At the same time, we must be aware of current events, follow the news and study the analyses and commentaries on it, together with drawing plans for the present and the future and examining every phenomenon, so that every Muslim, fighting Jihad, could live out his era aware of his objective, his goals, his way and the things happening round him.

O my dear son! Lo! though it be but the weight of a grain of mustard-seed, and though it be in a rock, or in the heavens, or in the earth, Allah will bring it forth. Lo! Allah is subtle. Aware. O my dear son! Establish worship and enjoin kindness and forbid inequity, and persevere, whatever may befall thee. Lo! that is of the steadfast heart of things. Turn not thy cheek in scorn toward folk, nor walk with pertness in the land. Lo! Allah loves not braggarts and boasters. Sura XXXI (Luqman), verses 16-18

The Role of Muslim Women

Article Seventeen. The Muslim women have a no lesser role than that of men in the war of liberation; they manufacture men and play a great role in guiding and educating the [new] generation. The enemies have understood that role, therefore they realize that if they can guide and educate [the Muslim women] in a way that would distance them from Islam, they would have won that war. Therefore, you can see them making consistent efforts [in that direction] by way of publicity and movies, curricula of education and culture, using as their intermediaries their craftsmen who are part of the various Zionist Organizations which take on all sorts of names and shapes such as: the Freemasons, Rotary Clubs, gangs of spies and the like. All of them are nests of saboteurs and sabotage.

Those Zionist organizations control vast material resources, which enable them to fulfill their mission amidst societies, with a view of implementing Zionist goals and sowing the concepts that can be of use to the enemy. Those organizations operate [in a situation] where Islam is absent from the arena and alienated from its people. Thus, the Muslims must fulfill their duty in confronting the schemes of those saboteurs. When Islam will retake possession of [the means to] guide the life [of the Muslims], it will wipe out those organizations which are the enemy of humanity and Islam.

Article Eighteen. The women in the house and the family of Jihad fighters, whether they are mothers or sisters, carry out the most important duty of caring for the home and raising the children upon the moral concepts and values which derive from Islam; and of educating their sons to observe the religious injunctions in preparation for the duty of Jihad awaiting them. Therefore, we must pay attention to the schools and curricula upon which Muslim girls are educated, so as to make them righteous mothers, who are conscious of their duties in the war of liberation. They must be fully capable of being aware and of grasping the ways to manage their households. Economy and avoiding waste in household expenditures are prerequisites to our ability to pursue our cause in the difficult circumstances surrounding us. Therefore let them remember at all times that money saved is equivalent to blood, which must be made to run in the veins in order to ensure the continuity of life of our young and old.

> *Lo, men who surrender unto Allah, and women who surrender and men who believe and women who believe, and men who obey and women who obey, and men who speak the truth and women who speak the truth and men who persevere (in righteousness) and women who persevere and men who are humble and women who are humble, and men who give alms and women who give alms, and men who fast and women who fast, and men who guard their modesty and women who guard [their modesty], and men who remember Allah much and*

women who remember Allah has prepared for them forgiveness and a vast reward. Sura 33 (Al-Ahzab, the Clans), verse 35

The Role of Islamic Art in the War of Liberation

Article Nineteen. Art has rules and criteria by which one can know whether it is Islamic or Jahiliyya art. The problems of Islamic liberation underlie the need for Islamic art which could lift the spirit, and instead of making one party triumph over the other, would lift up all parties in harmony and balance.

Man is a strange and miraculous being, made out of a handful of clay and a breath of soul; Islamic art is to address man on this basis, while Jahili art addresses the body and makes the element of clay paramount. So, books, articles, publications, religious exhortations, epistles, songs, poems, hymns, plays, and the like, if they possess the characteristics of Islamic art, have the requisites of ideological mobilization, of a continuous nurturing in the pursuance of the journey, and of relaxing the soul. The road is long and the suffering is great and the spirits are weary; it is Islamic art which renews the activity, revives the movement and arouses lofty concepts and sound planning. The soul cannot thrive, unless it knows how to contrive, unless it can transit from one situation to another. All this is a serious matter, no jesting. For the umma fighting its Jihad knows no jesting.

Social Solidarity

Article Twenty. Islamic society is one of solidarity. The Messenger of Allah, be Allah's prayer and peace upon him, said:

> *What a wonderful tribe were the Ash'aris! When they were overtaxed, either in their location or during their journeys, they would collect all their possessions, and then would divide them equally among themselves.*

This is the Islamic spirit which ought to prevail in any Muslim society. A society which confronts a vicious, Nazi-like enemy, who does not differentiate between man and woman, elder and young ought to be the first to adorn itself with this Islamic spirit. Our enemy pursues the style of collective punishment of usurping people's countries and properties, of pursuing them into their exiles and places of assembly. It has resorted to breaking bones, opening fire on women and children and the old, with or without reason, and to setting up detention camps where thousands upon thousands are interned in inhuman conditions. In addition, it destroys houses, renders children orphans and issues oppressive judgements against thousands of young people who spend the best years of their youth in the darkness of prisons. The Nazism of the Jews does not skip women and children, it scares everyone. They make war against people's livelihood, plunder their moneys and threaten their honor. In their horrible actions they mistreat people like the most horrendous war criminals.

Exiling people from their country is another way of killing them. As we face this misconduct, we have no escape from establishing social solidarity among the people, from confronting the enemy as one solid body, so that if one organ is hurt the rest of the body will respond with alertness and fervor.

Article Twenty-One. Social solidarity consists of extending help to all the needy, both materially and morally, or assisting in the execution of certain actions. It is incumbent upon the members of the Hamas to look after the interests of the masses the way they would look after their own interests. They must spare no effort in the implementation and maintenance of those interests, and they must avoid playing with anything that might effect the future generations or cause damage to their society. For the masses are of them and for them, their strength is [ultimately] theirs and their future is theirs. The members of Hamas must share with the people its joys and sorrows, and adopt the demands of the people and anything likely to fulfill its interests and theirs. When this spirit reigns, congeniality will deepen, cooperation and compassion will prevail, unity will firm up, and the ranks will be strengthened in the confrontation with the enemy.

The Powers Which Support the Enemy
Article Twenty-Two. The enemies have been scheming for a long time, and they have consolidated their schemes, in order to achieve what they have achieved. They took advantage of key elements in unfolding events, and accumulated a huge and influential material wealth which they put to the service of implementing their dream. This wealth [permitted them to] take over control of the world media such as news agencies, the press, publication houses, broadcasting and the like. [They also used this] wealth to stir revolutions in various parts of the globe in order to fulfill their interests

and pick the fruits. They stood behind the French and the Communist Revolutions and behind most of the revolutions we hear about here and there. They also used the money to establish clandestine organizations which are spreading around the world, in order to destroy societies and carry out Zionist interests. Such organizations are: the Freemasons, Rotary Clubs, Lions Clubs, B'nai B'rith and the like. All of them are destructive spying organizations. They also used the money to take over control of the Imperialist states and made them colonize many countries in order to exploit the wealth of those countries and spread their corruption therein.

As regards local and world wars, it has come to pass and no one objects, that they stood behind World War I, so as to wipe out the Islamic Caliphate. They collected material gains and took control of many sources of wealth. They obtained the Balfour Declaration and established the League of Nations in order to rule the world by means of that organization. They also stood behind World War II, where they collected immense benefits from trading with war materials and prepared for the establishment of their state. They inspired the establishment of the United Nations and the Security Council to replace the League of Nations, in order to rule the world by their intermediary. There was no war that broke out anywhere without their fingerprints on it:

> ... *As often as they light a fire for war, Allah extinguishes it. Their efforts are for corruption in the land and Allah loves not corrupters.* Sura V (Al-Ma'ida—the Tablespread), verse 64

The forces of Imperialism in both the Capitalist West and the Communist East support the enemy with all their might, in material and human terms, taking turns between themselves. When Islam appears, all the forces of Unbelief unite to confront it, because the Community of Unbelief is one.

> *Oh ye who believe! Take not for intimates others than your own folk, who would spare no pain to ruin you. Hatred is revealed by [the utterance of] their mouth, but that which their breasts hide is greater. We have made plain for you the revelations if you will understand.* Sura III, (Al-Imran), verse 118

It is not in vain that the verse ends with God's saying: "If you will understand."

PART IV. OUR POSITION VIS-À-VIS THE ISLAMIC MOVEMENTS

Article Twenty-Three. The Hamas views the other Islamic movements with respect and appreciation. Even when it differs from them in one aspect or another or on one concept or another, it agrees with them in other aspects and concepts. It reads those movements as included in the framework of striving [for the sake of Allah], as long as they hold sound intentions and abide by their devotion to Allah, and as along as their conduct remains within the perimeter of the Islamic circle. All the fighters of Jihad have their reward.

The Hamas regards those movements as its stock holders and asks Allah for guidance and integrity of conduct for all. It shall not fail to continue to raise the banner of unity and to exert efforts in order to implement it, [based] upon the [Holy] Book and the [Prophet's] Tradition.

> *And hold fast, all of you together, to the cable of Allah, do not separate. And remember Allah's favor unto you how ye were enemies and He made friendship between your hearts so that ye became as brothers by His grace; and (how) ye were upon the brink of an abyss of fire, and He did save you from it. Thus Allah makes clear His revelations unto you, that happily ye may be guided.* Sura III (Al-'Imran), verse 102

Article Twenty-Four. Hamas will not permit the slandering and defamation of individuals and groups, for the Believers are not slanderers and cursers. However, despite the need to differentiate between that and the positions and modes of conduct adopted by individuals and groups whenever the Hamas detects faulty positions and modes of conduct, it has the right to point to the mistake, to denigrate it, to act for spelling out the truth and for adopting it realistically in the context of a given problem. Wisdom is roaming around, and the Believer ought to grasp it wherever he can find it.

> *Allah loves not the utterance of harsh speech save by one who has been wronged. Allah is ever Hearer, Knower. If you do good openly or keep it secret, or give evil, lo! Allah is forgiving, powerful.* Sura IV (Women), verses 147-148

The National (Wataniyya) Movements in the Palestinian Arena

Article Twenty-Five. [Hamas] reciprocated its respect to them, appreciates their condition and the factors surrounding them and influencing them, and supports them firmly as long as they do not owe their loyalty to the

Communist East or to the Crusader West. We reiterate to every one who
is part of them or sympathizes with them that the Hamas is a movement
of Jihad, or morality and consciousness in its concept of life. It moves forward with the others, abhors opportunism, and only wishes well to individuals and groups. It does not aspire to material gains, or to personal
fame, nor does it solicit remuneration from the people. It sets out relying
on its own material resources, and what is available to it, [as it is said] "afford them the power you can avail yourself of." [All that] in order to carry
out its duty, to gain Allah's favor; it has no ambition other than that.

All the nationalist streams, operating in the Palestinian arena for the
sake of the liberation of Palestine, may rest assured that they will definitely
and resolutely get support and assistance, in speech and in action, at the
present and in the future, [because Hamas aspires] to unite, not to divide;
to safeguard, not to squander; to bring together, not to fragment. It values
every kind word, every devoted effort and every commendable endeavor. It
closes the door before marginal quarrels, it does not heed rumors and bi-
ased statements, and it is aware of the right of self-defense.

Anything that runs counter or contradicts this orientation is trumped
up by the enemies or by those who run in their orbit in order to create con-
fusion, to divide our ranks or to divert to marginal things.

> *O ye who believe! If an evil-liver bring you tidings, verify it, lest ye smite
> some folk in ignorance and afterward repent of what ye did.* Sura XLIX (al
> Hujurat, the Private Apartments), verse 6

Article Twenty-Six. The Hamas, while it views positively the Palestinian
National Movements which do not owe their loyalty to the East or to the
West, does not refrain from debating unfolding events regarding the Pales-
tinian problem, on the local and international scenes.

These debates are realistic and expose the extent to which [these devel-
opments] go along with, or contradict, national interests as viewed from
the Islamic vantage point.

The Palestine Liberation Organization

Article Twenty Seven. The PLO is among the closest to the Hamas, for it
constitutes a father, a brother, a relative, a friend. Can a Muslim turn away
from his father, his brother, his relative or his friend? Our homeland is
one, our calamity is one, our destiny is one and our enemy is common to

both of us. Under the influence of the circumstances which surrounded the founding of the PLO, and the ideological invasion which has swept the Arab world since the rout of the Crusades, and which has been reinforced by Orientalism and the Christian Mission, the PLO has adopted the idea of a Secular State, and so we think of it. Secular thought is diametrically opposed to religious thought. Thought is the basis for positions, for modes of conduct and for resolutions. Therefore, in spite of our appreciation for the PLO and its possible transformation in the future, and despite the fact that we do not denigrate its role in the Arab-Israeli conflict, we cannot substitute it for the Islamic nature of Palestine by adopting secular thought. For the Islamic nature of Palestine is part of our religion, and anyone who neglects his religion is bound to lose.

> *And who forsakes the religion of Abraham, save him who befools himself?*
> Sura II (Al-Baqra—the Cow), verse 130

When the PLO adopts Islam as the guideline for life, then we shall become its soldiers, the fuel of its fire which will burn the enemies. And until that happens, and we pray to Allah that it will happen soon, the position of the Hamas towards the PLO is one of a son towards his father, a brother towards his brother, and a relative towards his relative who suffers the other's pain when a thorn hits him, who supports the other in the confrontation with the enemies and who wishes him divine guidance and integrity of conduct.

Your brother, your brother! Whoever has no brother, is like a fighter who runs to the battle without weapons. A cousin for man is like the best wing, and no falcon can take off without wings.

Article Twenty-Eight. The Zionist invasion is a mischievous one. It does not hesitate to take any road, or to pursue all despicable and repulsive means to fulfill its desires. It relies to a great extent, for its meddling and spying activities, on the clandestine organizations which it has established, such as the Freemasons, Rotary Clubs, Lions, and other spying associations. All those secret organizations, some which are overt, act for the interests of Zionism and under its directions, strive to demolish societies, to destroy values, to wreck answerableness, to totter virtues and to wipe out Islam. It stands behind the diffusion of drugs and toxics of all kinds in order to facilitate its control and expansion.

The Arab states surrounding Israel are required to open their borders to the Jihad fighters, the sons of the Arab and Islamic peoples, to enable them to play their role and to join their efforts to those of their brothers among the Muslim Brothers in Palestine.

The other Arab and Islamic states are required, at the very least, to facilitate the movement of the Jihad fighters from and to them. We cannot fail to remind every Muslim that when the Jews occupied Holy Jerusalem in 1967 and stood at the doorstep of the Blessed Aqsa Mosque, they shouted with joy:

Muhammad is dead, he left daughters behind.

Israel, by virtue of its being Jewish and of having a Jewish population, defies Islam and the Muslims.

Let the eyes of the cowards not fall asleep.

National and Religious Associations, Institutions, the Intelligentsia, and the Arab and Islamic Worlds
Article Twenty-Nine. Hamas hopes that those Associations will stand by it on all levels, will support it, adopt its positions, boost its activities and moves and encourage support for it, so as to render the Islamic peoples its backers and helpers, and its strategic depth in all human and material domains as well as in information, in time and space. Among other things, they hold solidarity meetings, issue explanatory publications, supportive articles and tendentious leaflets to make the masses aware of the Palestinian issue, the problems it faces and of the plans to resolve them; and to mobilize the Islamic peoples ideologically, educationally and culturally in order to fulfill their role in the crucial war of liberation, as they had played their role in the defeat of the Crusades and in the rout of the Tartars and had saved human civilization. How all that is dear to Allah!

Allah has decreed: Lo! I verily shall conquer, I and my messengers. Lo! Allah is strong, Almighty. Sura LVIII (Al-Mujadilah), verse 21

Article Thirty. Men of letters, members of the intelligentsia, media people, preachers, teachers and educators and all different sectors in the Arab and Islamic world, are all called upon to play their role and to carry out their duty in view of the wickedness of the Zionist invasion, of its penetration into many countries, and its control over material means and the media, with all the ramifications thereof in most countries of the world.

Jihad means not only carrying arms and denigrating the enemies. Uttering positive words, writing good articles and useful books, and lending support and assistance, all that too is Jihad in the path of Allah, as long as intentions are sincere to make Allah's banner supreme.

> *Those who prepare for a raid in the path of Allah are considered as if they participated themselves in the raid. Those who successfully rear a raider in their home, are considered as if they participated themselves in the raid.* (Told by Bukhari, Muslim, Abu Dawud and Tirmidhi)

The Members of Other Religions: The Hamas Is a Humane Movement

Article Thirty-One. Hamas is a humane movement, which cares for human rights and is committed to the tolerance inherent in Islam as regards attitudes towards other religions. It is only hostile to those who are hostile towards it, or stand in its way in order to disturb its moves or to frustrate its efforts.

Under the shadow of Islam it is possible for the members of the three religions: Islam, Christianity and Judaism to coexist in safety and security. Safety and security can only prevail under the shadow of Islam, and recent and ancient history is the best witness to that effect. The members of other religions must desist from struggling against Islam over sovereignty in this region. For if they were to gain the upper hand, fighting, torture and uprooting would follow; they would be fed up with each other, to say nothing of members of other religions. The past and the present are full of evidence to that effect.

> *They will not fight you in body safe in fortified villages or from behind wells. Their adversity among themselves is very great. Ye think of them as a whole whereas their hearts are diverse. That is because they are a folk who have no sense.* Sura 59 (al-Hashr, the Exile), verse 14

Islam accords his rights to everyone who has rights and averts aggression against the rights of others. The Nazi Zionist practices against our people will not last the lifetime of their invasion, for "states built upon oppression last only one hour, states based upon justice will last until the hour of Resurrection."

Allah forbids you not those who warred not against you on account of religion and drove you not out from your houses, that you should show them kindness and deal justly with them. Lo! Allah loves the just dealers. Sura 60 (Al-Mumtahana), verse 8

The Attempts to Isolate the Palestinian People

Article Thirty-Two. World Zionism and Imperialist forces have been attempting, with smart moves and considered planning, to push the Arab countries, one after another, out of the circle of conflict with Zionism, in order, ultimately, to isolate the Palestinian People.

Egypt has already been cast out of the conflict, to a very great extent through the treacherous Camp David Accords, and she has been trying to drag other countries into similar agreements in order to push them out of the circle of conflict.

Hamas is calling upon the Arab and Islamic peoples to act seriously and tirelessly in order to frustrate that dreadful scheme and to make the masses aware of the danger of coping out of the circle of struggle with Zionism. Today it is Palestine and tomorrow it may be another country or other countries. For Zionist scheming has no end, and after Palestine they will covet expansion from the Nile to the Euphrates. Only when they have completed digesting the area on which they will have laid their hand, they will look forward to more expansion, etc. Their scheme has been laid out in the *Protocols of the Elders of Zion*, and their present [conduct] is the best proof of what is said there.

Leaving the circle of conflict with Israel is a major act of treason and it will bring curse on its perpetrators.

Who so on that day turns his back to them, unless maneuvering for battle or intent to join a company, he truly has incurred wrath from Allah, and his habitation will be hell, a hapless journey's end. Sura 8 (al-Anfal—Spoils of War), verse 16

We have no escape from pooling together all the forces and energies to face this despicable Nazi-Tatar invasion. Otherwise we shall witness the loss of [our] countries, the uprooting of their inhabitants, the spreading of corruption on earth and the destruction of all religious values. Let everyone realize that he is accountable to Allah.

Whoever does a speck of good will bear [the consequences] and whoever does a speck of evil will see [the consequences].

Within the circle of the conflict with world Zionism, the Hamas regards itself the spearhead and the avant-garde. It joins its efforts to all those who are active on the Palestinian scene, but more steps need to be taken by the Arab and Islamic peoples and Islamic associations throughout the Arab and Islamic world in order to make possible the next round with the Jews, the merchants of war.

We have cast among them enmity and hatred till the day of Resurrection. As often as they light a fire for war, Allah extinguishes it. Their effort is for corruption in the land, and Allah loves not corrupters. Sura V (Al-Ma'i-dah—the Table spread), verse 64

Article Thirty-Three. The Hamas sets out from these general concepts which are consistent and in accordance with the rules of the universe, and gushes forth in the river of Fate in its confrontation and Jihad waging against the enemies, in defense of the Muslim human being, of Islamic Civilization and of the Islamic Holy Places, primarily the Blessed Aqsa Mosque. This, for the purpose of calling upon the Arab and Islamic peoples as well as their governments, popular and official associations, to fear Allah in their attitude towards and dealings with Hamas, and to be, in accordance with Allah's will, its supporters and partisans who extend assistance to it and provide it with reinforcement after reinforcement, until the Decree of Allah is fulfilled, the ranks are over-swollen, Jihad fighters join other Jihad fighters, and all this accumulation sets out from everywhere in the Islamic world, obeying the call of duty, and intoning "Come on, join Jihad!" This call will tear apart the clouds in the skies and it will continue to ring until liberation is completed, the invaders are vanquished and Allah's victory sets in.

Verily Allah helps one who helps Him. Lo! Allah is strong, Almighty. Sura XXII (Pilgrimage), verse 40

PART V. THE TESTIMONY OF HISTORY

Confronting Aggressors Throughout History

Article Thirty-Four. Palestine is the navel of earth, the convergence of continents, the object of greed for the greedy, since the dawn of history. The Prophet, may Allah's prayer and peace be upon him, points out to that fact in his noble hadith in which he implored his venerable Companion, Ma'adh ibn Jabl, saying:

> O Ma'adh, Allah is going to grant you victory over Syria after me, from Al-Arish to the Euphrates, while its men, women, and female slaves will be dwelling there until the Day of Resurrection. Those of you who chose [to dwell in one of the plains of Syria or Palestine will be in a state of Jihad to the Day of Resurrection].

The greedy have coveted Palestine more than once and they raided it with armies in order to fulfill their covetousness.

Multitudes of Crusades descended on it, carrying their faith with them and waving their Cross. They were able to defeat the Muslims for a long time, and the Muslims were not able to redeem it until their sought the protection of their religious banner; then, they unified their forces, sang the praise of their God and set out for Jihad under the Command of Saladin al-Ayyubi, for the duration of nearly two decades, and then the obvious conquest took place when the Crusaders were defeated and Palestine was liberated.

> Say (O Muhammad) unto those who disbelieve: ye shall be overcome and gathered unto Hell, an evil resting place. Sura III (Al-Imran), verse 12

This is the only way to liberation, there is no doubt in the testimony of history. That is one of the rules of the universe and one of the laws of existence. Only iron can blunt iron, only the true faith of Islam can vanquish their false and falsified faith. Faith can only be fought by faith. Ultimately, victory is reserved to the truth, and truth is victorious.

> And verily Our word went forth of old unto Our Bordmen sent [to warn]. That they verily would be helped. And that Our host, they verily would be the victors. Sura 38 (Al-saffat), verses 171-3

Article Thirty-Five. Hamas takes a serious look at the defeat of the Crusades at the hand of Saladin the Ayyubid and the rescue of Palestine from their domination; at the defeat of the Tatars at Ein Jalut where their spine was broken by Qutuz and Al-Dhahir Baibars, and the Arab world was rescued from the sweep of the Tatars which ruined all aspects of human civilization. Hamas has learned from these lessons and examples, that the current Zionist invasion had been preceded by a Crusader invasion from the West; and another one, the Tatars, from the East. And exactly as the Muslims had faced those invasions and planned their removal and defeat, they are able to face the Zionist invasion and defeat it. This will not be difficult for Allah if our intentions are pure and our determination is sincere; if the Muslims draw useful lessons from the experiences of the past, and extricate themselves for the vestiges of the [western] ideological onslaught; and if they follow the traditions of Islam.

EPILOGUE

The Hamas Are Soldiers

Article Thirty-Six. The Hamas, while breaking its path, reiterates time and again to all members of our people and the Arab and Islamic peoples, that it does not seek fame for itself nor material gains, or social status.

Nor is it directed against any one member of our people in order to compete with him or replace him. There is nothing of that at all.

It will never set out against any Muslims or against the non-Muslims who make peace with it, here or anywhere else. It will only be of help to all associations and organizations which act against the Zionist enemy and those who revolve in its orbit.

Hamas posits Islam as a way of life, it is its faith and its yardstick for judging. Whoever posits Islam as a way of life, anywhere, and regardless of whether it is an organization, a state, or any other group, Hamas are its soldiers, nothing else.

We implore Allah to guide us, to guide through us and to decide between us and our folk with truth.

Our Lord! Decide with truth between us and our folk, for Thou are the best of those who make decisions. Sura VII (Al-A'raf—the Heights), verse 89

Our last call is: Thanks to Allah, the Lord of the Universe.

Source: From Rafael Yisraeli, in Y. Alexander and H. Foxman, eds., *The 1988-1989 Annual on Terrorism* (The Netherlands: Kluwer Academic Publishers). http://www.acpr.org.il/.

APPENDIX E

STATISTICS

All facts below, except GDP, are from the CIA World FactBook *or the Department of State. GDP and per capita GDP are from the International Monetary Fund, except when otherwise noted. GDP is in U.S. dollars. Per capita GDP is in current international dollar.*

Country: Afghanistan
Area: 249,935 sq. miles
Comparison: slightly smaller than Texas
Population: 32,738,376 (2008 estimate)
GDP: $12.85 billion
Per capita GDP: $782.607
Capital city: Kabul
Major religious groups:
  · Sunni Muslim: 80 percent
  · Shia Muslim: 19 percent

Country: Bahrain
Area: 274 sq. miles
Comparison: about 4 times the size of Washington, DC
Population: 718,306, including 235,108 non-nationals (2008 estimate)
GDP: $19.675 billion
Per capita GDP: $33,988.358
Capital city: Manama
Major religious groups:
  · Shia and Sunni Muslim: 81.2 percent
  · Christian: 9 percent

Country: Egypt
Area: 386,000 sq. miles
Comparison: approximately equal to Texas and New Mexico combined

Population: 81,713,520 (2008 estimate)
GDP: $158.255 billion
Per capita GDP: $5,904.492
Capital city: Cairo
Major religious groups:
  · Muslim (mostly Sunni): 90 percent
  · Other: 1 percent

Country: Iraq
Area: approximately 168 sq. miles
Comparison: about the size of California
Population: 28,221,180 (2008 estimate)
GDP: $93.8 billion (*CIA World FactBook*— official exchange rate)
Per capita GDP: $4,000 (2008 estimate— *CIA World FactBook*)
Capital city: Baghdad
Major religious groups:
  · Sunni Muslim: 32-37 percent
  · Shia Muslim: 60-65 percent
  · Christian or other: 3 percent

Country: Iran
Area: 636,295 sq. miles
Comparison: slightly larger than Alaska
Population: 65,875,224 (2008 estimate)
GDP: $382.328 billion
Per capita GDP: $11,209.463

Capital city: Tehran
Major religious groups:
  · Sunni Muslim: 9 percent
  · Shia Muslim: 89 percent

Country: Israel
Area: approximately 8,019 sq. miles
Comparison: about the size of New
  Jersey
Population: 7,112,359, including about
  187,000 Israeli settlers in the West Bank,
  about 20,000 in the Israeli-occupied
  Golan Heights, and fewer than 177,000
  in East Jerusalem (2008 estimate)
GDP: $188.746 billion
Per capita GDP: $28,245.079
Capital city: Jerusalem
Major religious groups:
  · Jewish: 76.4 percent
  · Muslim: 16 percent
  · Arab Christians: 1.7 percent
  · Other Christian: 0.4 percent

Country: Jordan
Area: approximately 35,637 sq. miles
Comparison: slightly smaller than
  Indiana
Population: 5.86 million (2009 Depart-
  ment of State estimate)
GDP: $19.124 billion
Per capita GDP: $5,171.567
Capital city: Amman
Major religious groups:
  · Sunni Muslim: 92 percent
  · Christian: 6 percent

Country: Kuwait
Area: 6,880 sq. miles
Comparison: slightly smaller than New
  Jersey
Population: 2,596,799, including
  1,291,354 non-nationals (2008 estimate)
GDP: $159.730 billion
Per capita GDP: $40,943.252
Capital city: Kuwait
Major religious groups:
  · Sunni Muslim: 70 percent
  · Shia Muslim: 30 percent

Country: Lebanon
Area: 4,015 sq. miles
Comparison: about 0.7 times the size of
  Connecticut
Population: 3,971,941 (2008 estimate)
GDP: $28.024 billion
Per capita GDP: $12,063.217
Capital city: Beirut
Major religious groups:
  · Muslim: 59.7 percent
  · Christian: 39 percent

Country: Libya
Area: approximately 679,362 sq. miles
Comparison: slightly larger than Alaska
Population: 6,173,579, including
  166,510 non-nationals (2008 estimate)
GDP: $108.475 billion
Per capita GDP: $14,593.915
Capital city: Tripoli
Major religious groups:
  · Sunni Muslim: 97 percent

Country: Oman
Area: approximately 82,031 sq. miles
Comparison: slightly smaller than
  Kansas
Population: 3,311,640, including
  577,293 non-nationals (2008 estimate)
GDP: $56.318 billion
Per capita GDP: $26,094.938
Capital city: Muscat
Major religious groups:
  · Ibadhi Muslim: 75 percent
  · Other (mostly other Muslims and
    Hindu): 25 percent

Country: Pakistan
Area: 310,527 sq. miles
Comparison: about twice the size of Cal-
  ifornia
Population: 172,800,048 (2008 estimate)
GDP: $160.897 billion
Per capita GDP: $2,756.710
Capital city: Islamabad
Major religious groups:
  · Sunni Muslim: 75 percent
  · Shia Muslim: 20 percent

Country: Palestine Territories
Area:
- **Gaza Strip:** 138 sq. miles
- **West Bank:** 2,262 sq. miles
Comparison:
- **Gaza strip:** slightly more than twice the size of Washington, DC
- **West Bank:** slightly smaller than Delaware
Population:
- **Gaza Strip:** 1,551,859
- **West Bank:** 2,461,267
    Note: in addition, there are about 187,000 Israeli settlers in the West Bank and fewer than 177,000 in East Jerusalem.
GDP: $11.95 billion
Per capita GDP: $2,900
Capital city: claimed East Jerusalem
Major religious groups:
- **Gaza Strip:**
    - Muslim (predominantly Sunni): 99.3 percent
    - Christian: 0.7 percent
- **West Bank:**
    - Muslim (predominantly Sunni): 75 percent
    - Jewish: 17 percent
    - Christian and other: 8 percent

Country: Qatar
Area: 4,427 sq. miles
Comparison: about the size of Rhode Island and Connecticut combined
Population: 824,789 (2008 estimate)
GDP: $116.851 billion
Per capita GDP: $86,669.622
Capital city: Doha
Major religious groups:
- Muslim: 77.5 percent
- Christian: 8.5 percent

Country: Saudi Arabia
Area: 829,995 sq. miles
Comparison: slightly more than one fifth of the United States
Population: 28,146,656, including 5,576,076 non-nationals (2008 estimate)
GDP: $528.322 billion
Per capita GDP: $24,119.993

Capital city: Riyadh
Major religious groups:
- Muslim: 100 percent

Country: Sudan
Area: 967,500 sq. miles
Comparison: slightly more than one quarter the size of U.S.
Population: 40,218,456 (2008 estimate)
GDP: $62.189 billion
Per capita GDP: $2,335.259
Capital city: Khartoum
Major religious groups:
- Sunni Muslim: 70 percent
- Christian: 5 percent

Country: Syria
Area: about 71,498 sq. miles
Comparison: slightly larger than North Dakota
Population: 19,747,586; in addition, about 40,000 people live in the Israeli-occupied Golan Heights—20,000 Arabs (18,000 Druze and 2,000 Alawites) and about 20,000 Israeli settlers (2008 estimates)
GDP: $44.492 billion
Per capita GDP: $4,668.417
Capital city: Damascus
Major religious groups:
- Sunni Muslim: 74 percent
- Other Muslim: 16 percent
- Christian: 10 percent

Country: Turkey
Area: 301,383 sq. miles
Comparison: slightly larger than Texas
Population: 71,892,808 (2008 estimate)
GDP: $798.863 billion
Per capita GDP: $13,447.441
Capital city: Ankara
Major religious groups:
- Muslim: 99.8 percent
- Christian and Jew: 0.2 percent

Country: United Arab Emirates
Area: 30,000 sq. miles
Comparison: about the size of Maine

Population: 4,621,399 (2008 estimate—note that this is based on the results of a 2005 census that included a significantly higher estimate of net immigration of non-citizens than previous estimates)
GDP: $269.956 billion
Per capita GDP: $39,076.520
Capital city: Abu Dhabi
Major religious groups:
  • Muslim: 96 percent (Shia, 16 percent)
  • Hindu and Christian: 4 percent

Country: Yemen
Area: 203,796 sq. miles
Comparison: slightly larger than twice the size of Wyoming
Population: 23,013,376 (2008 estimate)
GDP: $27.562 billion
Per capita GDP: $2,404.412
Capital city: Sanaa
Major religious groups: (no given percentages)
  • Muslim
  • Jewish, Christian and Hindu

ENDNOTES

Chapter 1: The Middle East: A Central Hub of World Affairs

1. Alfred Thayer Mahan, *The Influence of Sea Power upon History, 1660-1783* (Charleston, SC: BiblioBazaar, 2007). This book was originally published in 1890 and was studied carefully by the United States, Great Britain and, as mentioned, Germany's Kaiser Wilhelm II.
2. Princeton University and the University of Chicago all have departments of "Near Eastern" studies.
3. Flavius Josephus, *The Jewish War* (London: Penguin Books, 1970), p. 370 and footnote on p. 454.
4. See photos of these reliefs on the "Arch of Titus" page of the *Encyclopaedia Romana* website, available online at http://penelope.uchicago.edu/~grout/encyclopaedia_romana/romanurbs/archtitus.html (accessed February 2008).
5. Josephus, *The Jewish War*, p. 370.

Chapter 2: Israel and the Palestinians

1. Marvin Lowenthal, ed. and trans., *The Diaries of Theodor Herzl* (London: Dial Publishers, 1956). See "Theodor Herzl," Wikipedia.com, http://en.wikipedia.org/wiki/Theodor_Herzl.
2. Allenby was himself a devout Christian with strong sympathy for the Jews. His ceremonial entry into the Walled City was on foot because, as he said, "I will not ride on the cobblestones where my savior carried his Cross."
3. Golda Meir, quoted in *The Times* (London), June 15, 1969.
4. Alan Dershowitz, *The Case for Israel* (Hoboken, NJ: John Wiley & Sons, 2004).
5. Azzam Pasha, cited in Benny Morris, *Righteous Victims: A History of the Zionist-Arab Conflict, 1881-2001* (New York: Vintage Books, 2001), p. 219.
6. "Latest Population Figures for Israel (2009)," Jewish Virtual Library. http://www.jewishvirtual library.org/jsource/Society_&_Culture/newpop.html.
7. Donna Rosenthal, *The Israelis: Ordinary People in an Extraordinary Land* (New York: The Free Press, 2003).
8. Gamal Abdel Nasser, cited in Dershowitz, *The Case for Israel*, p. 142.
9. "The Six-Day War: Israel Overcomes Existential Threat," AIPAC, June 2007. http://aipac.org/ Pub lications/AIPACAnalysesMemos/AIPAC_Memo-_Israel_Overcomes_Existential_Threat_ in_1967.pdf.
10. The Hamas Charter, translation by the Mideast Media Research Institute, February 2006. http://www.mfa.gov.il/MFA/MFAArchive/1980_1989/THE percent20CHARTER percent20OF percent20ALLAH-percent20THEpercent20PLATFORMpercent20OFpercent20THEper cent20ISLAMIC.
11. Ibid.
12. Dennis Ross on Fox News, April 21, 2002.
13. Earlier, the Saudi foreign minister had insisted that he would not enter the conference by the main entrance if the Israelis also used that entrance. Olmert agreed to lessen Prince Saud al-Faisal's discomfort by entering the hall through a service entrance.
14. "In Quotes: U.S. Election Reaction," BBC News, November 5, 2008. http://news.bbc.co.uk/2/ hi/americas/us_elections_2008/7710020.stm.

Chapter 3: Syria and Lebanon

1. Freedom House, "Freedom in the World," annual report, 2008. http://www.freedomhouse.org /template.cfm?page=415&year=2008.

2. Lord Shaftesbury and Gertrude Bell, cited in Daniel Pipes, *Greater Syria: The History of an Ambition* (New York: Oxford University Press, 1990), p. 19.

3. Ibid., p. 163.

4. Sulayman al-Assad, cited in Barry Rubin, *The Truth About Syria* (New York: Palgrave Macmillan, 2007), p. 33.

5. One of the best accounts of the slicing up of the Middle East at the end of World War I is David Fromkin, *A Peace to End All Peace: The Fall of the Ottoman Empire and the Creation of the Modern Middle East* (New York: Avon Book, 1986).

6. Hafez al-Assad, cited in Pipes, *Greater Syria*, p. 130.

7. Guy Taylor, "After the Damascus Spring," *Reasonline,* February 2007. http://www.reason.com/news/show/118380.html.

8. Robin Wright, *Dreams and Shadows: The Future of the Middle East* (New York: The Penguin Press, 2008), p. 231.

9. Barry Rubin, "Why Syria Matters," MERIA, vol. 10, no. 4, December 2006. http://meria.idc.ac.il/journal/2006/issue4/jv10no4a2.html.

10. Barry Rubin, *The Truth About Syria* (New York: Palgrave Macmillan, 2007), p. 7.

11. The author was involved in efforts to secure Terry Anderson's release, founding in 1986 the Journalists' Committee to Free Terry Anderson. Anderson returned to Beirut in 1996 and interviewed Hezbollah leader Hassan Nasrallah. The turbaned Shiite leader refused to say whether he thought the kidnapping of foreigners was right or wrong. (See Robin Wright, *Dreams and Shadows*, p. 176.)

12. Hassan Nasrallah, cited in Wright, *Dreams and Shadows*, p. 173.

13. Amal Saad-Ghorayeb, *Hizbu'llah: Politics, Religion* (London: Pluto Press, 2002), p. 161.

14. Ibid., p. 162.

15. Ibid., p. 173.

16. I visited Haifa during the 2006 war and saw one civilian apartment that had been almost entirely demolished by a Hezbollah rocket. All of the rockets were filled with ball bearings and designed to cause the maximum injury and death to humans within range of their impact point.

Chapter 4: Egypt and Jordan

1. The Battle of the Nile was the occasion for one of the best-known poems in American elementary and high schools from about 1850 to 1950, "Casablanca" (The boy stood on the burning deck . . .), by British poet Felicia Dorothea Hemans (1793-1835).

2. Source unknown; taken from "Ismail Pasha," Wikipedia.org. http://en.wikipedia.org/wiki/Ismail_Pasha.

3. "The Prospect for Democracy in the Middle East: A Conversation with Saad Eddin Ibrahim," *Logos: A Journal of Modern Science and Culture,* 2005. http://www.logosjournal.com/issue_4.2/ibrahim_interview_printable.htm.

4. Walter Laqueur and Barry Rubin, eds., *The Israel-Arab Reader: A Documentary History of the Middle East Conflict* (New York: Penguin Books, 2008), p. 19.

5. Ahron Bregman and Jihan El-Tahri, *The Fifty Years War: Israel and the Arabs* (London: Penguin Books and BBC Books, 1998), p. 91.

6. Howard M. Sachar, *A History of Israel from the Rise of Zionism to Our Time* (New York: Alfred A. Knopf, 1996), p. 645.

7. Asher Susser, *Jordan: Case Study of a Pivotal State* (Washington, DC: Washington Institute for Near East Policy, 2000), p. 54.

8. Ibid., p. 55.

9. Michael B. Oren, "Six Days of War: June 1967 and the Making of the Modern Middle East," MacroHistory and World Report, Oxford University Press, 2002. http://www.fsmitha.com/review/r-oren.html.

Chapter 5: The Persian (but Really Arabian) Gulf

1. The abolition of the slave trade in Great Britain was a lifelong passion of a group of British evangelicals led by William Wilberforce, MP. Though slavery itself was not abolished until 1833 (just days before Wilberforce himself died), Britain's Royal Navy actively patrolled the oceans of the

world, from 1806 until 1860, freeing in the process an estimated 150,000 Africans. Many of the freed slaves were aboard Arab corsair vessels intercepted in the Persian Gulf.

2. "Kuwait," Wikipedia.org, 2007-2009 data, http://en.wikipedia.org/wiki/Kuwait; "Quality of Living Global City Rankings 2009," Mercer Global Quality of Living Survey," Mercer Consulting Services, http://www.mercer.com/referecencecontent.htm?idContent+1128060.

3. David Pollock, *Kuwait: Keystone of U.S. Gulf Policy* (Washington, DC: The Washington Institute for Near East Policy, 2007), p. 11.

4. Ibid., p. 35.

5. "2009 Index of Economic Freedom: Bahrain," The Heritage Foundation, 2009 data. http://www.heritage.org/index/country/bahrain.

6. "List of Countries by GDP (Nominal) Per Capita," Wikipedia.org, data from "World Economic Outlook Database—April 2009," International Monetary Fund. http://en.wikipedia.org/wiki/List_of_countries_by_GDP_(nominal)-per_capita.

7. Noam Cohen, "Al Jazeera Provides an Inside Look at the Gaza Conflict," *International Herald Tribune,* January 11, 2009. http://www.iht.com/articles/2009/01/11/technology/jazeera.php.

8. Ali A. Allawi, *The Occupation of Iraq: Winning the War, Losing the Peace* (New Haven, CT: Yale University Press, 2007), p. 276.

9. Yoav Stern, "Al-Jazeera Admits to 'Unethical Behavior' over Kuntar Party," Haaretz, February 1, 2009. http://www.haaretz.com/hasen/spages/1009383.html.

10. You can see the video online at http://www.youtube.com/watch?v=mAXoDHy3_Ek. See also Teresa Watanabe, "Islam Fatally Flawed, Says Voice from Corona via Al Jazeera," *Los Angeles Times,* March 13, 2006, http://www.articles.latimes.com/2006/mar/13/local/me-sultan13.

11. "Trafficking in Persons Report, 2008," U.S. Department of State. http://www.state.gov/g/tip/rls/tiprpt/2008/105383.htm.

Chapter 6: Iraq

1. "California's Traffic Safety Report Card," California Office of Traffic Safety, 2008 data. http://www.ots.ca.gov/OTS_and_Traffic_Safety/Report_Card.asp.

2. The Coalition involved in the initial invasion comprised the U.S., the U.K., Poland and Denmark. Subsequently, military units from a range of countries participated in maintaining security within Iraq—including Micronesia, Palau and the Solomon Islands. As the Coalition occupation lasted into its second and third year, however, many countries, under domestic political pressure, began withdrawing their national units.

3. Dexter Filkins, "Exiting Iraq, Petraeus Says Gains Are Fragile," *The New York Times,* August 21, 2008.

4. A poster was torn down from a wall in Baghdad by a British private, kept for decades by his daughter and then sent to well-known Middle East reporter Robert Fisk. http://www.information clearinghouse.info/article6377.htm.

5. Samir al-Khalil, *Republic of Fear: The Politics of Modern Iraq* (Berkeley, CA: University of California Press, 1989), p. 6.

6. Ibid.

7. April Glaspie, cited in "Excerpts from Iraqi Document on Meeting with U.S. Envoy," *The New York Times,* September 22, 1990. http://chss.montclair.edu/english/furr/glaspie.htm.

8. April Glaspie, responses to questions from journalists as she leaves the U.S. Embassy in Baghdad on July 29, 1990. http://www.whatreallyhappened.com/WRHARTICLES/ARTICLES/april.html.

9. Dilip Hero, "Gulf War 2," *Dictionary of the Middle East* (New York: Macmillan, 1998), p. 99.

10. The lower figure is from the report of the Project for Defense Alternatives, 2003, http://www.conw.org/pda/03/0vm8.htm#N-93_.

11. Condoleezza Rice, cited in Elisabeth Bumiller, *Condoleezza Rice: An American Life* (New York: Random House, 2007), p. 140.

12. Ibid., pp. 142-143.

13. Ibid., p. 154.

14. Doug Feith, cited in Michael R. Gordon and General Bernard E. Trainor, *Cobra II: The Inside Story of the Invasion and Occupation of Iraq* (New York: Random House 2006), p. 15.

15. Bumiller, *Condoleezza Rice: An American Life*, p. 174.
16. Ibid., p. 197.
17. Ibid., p. 198.
18. Gordon and Trainor, *Cobra II: The Inside Story of the Invasion and Occupation of Iraq*, p. 484.
19. Bumiller, *Condoleezza Rice: An American Life*, p. 244.
20. Ibid., p. 240.
21. Ibid.
22. Barack Obama, cited in Josh Rogers, "Obama: Iraq Troop Surge Isn't Working," NHPR, July 20, 2007. http://www.nhpr.org.node/13507.
23. Michael O'Hanlon and Jason H. Campbell, "The State of Iraq: An Update," December 22, 2007. http://brookings.edu/opinions2007/1222_iraq_ohanlon.aspx.
24. "U.S. December Death Toll in Iraq Second-lowest of War," CNN World, Breaking News, December 31, 2007. http://www.edition.cnn.com/2007/WORLD/meast/12/31/iraq.main/index.html.
25. Barack Obama, cited in Mark Silva, "Obama: Iraq Surge Good 'Beyond Dreams,'" The Swamp, September 4, 2008. http://www.swamppolitics.com/news/politics/blog.2008/09/obama_iraq_surge_beyond_dreams.html.
26. ABC News, March 17, 2009. http://www.abcnews.go.com/Video/playerIndex?id=7095998

Chapter 7: Iran

1. Hakim Abu'l Qasim Ferdowsi, cited in Sandra Mackey, *The Iranians* (New York: Penguin Books, 1998), p. 63
2. Ibid., p. 62.
3. Ibid., p. 107.
4. Ibid., p. 82.
5. Ibid., p. 81.
6. Ibid., p. 208.
7. Amir Taheri, *The Persian Night* (New York: Encounter Books, 2009), p. 175.
8. Madeleine Albright, cited in "Mohammed Mossadegh," Onpedia.com. www.onpedia.com/encyclopedia/mohammed-mossadegh.
9. Mackey, *The Iranians*, pp. 224-225.
10. Ayatollah Ruhollah Khomeini, cited in Mackey, *The Iranians*, p. 226.
11. Ibid., pp. 247-248.
12. For an excellent account of the American failure to anticipate the collapse of pro-Western rule in Iran, see Gary Sick, *All Fall Down: America's Tragic Encounter with Iran* (New York: Penguin Books, 1985). For Sadat's call to the shah, see especially pp. 59-60.
13. Taheri, *The Persian Night*, p. 4.
14. Mackey, *The Iranians*, p. 306.
15. Taheri, *The Persian Night*, p. 38.
16. Ayatollah Ruhollah Khomeini, cited in Taheri, *The Persian Night*, p. 88.
17. Ibid., p. 102.
18. Mahmoud Ahmadinejad, cited in Aresu Eqbali, "Ahmadinejad: Holocaust Was Made Up," Mail and Guardian Online, August 28, 2006. http://www.mg.co.za/article/2006-08-28-ahmadinejad-holocaust-was-made-up.
19. Mahmoud Ahmadinejad, cited in "President Misquoted over Gays in Iran: Aide," Reuters, October 10, 2007. http://www.reuters.comarticleworldNewsidUSBLA05294620071010.

Chapter 8: Saudi Arabia and Beyond

1. It is worth noting that in the same poll, the U.S. came in only eighteenth, whereas the top scorers were Sweden, Norway and Iceland. http://a330.g.akamai.net/7/330/25838/2008102 1185552/graphics.eiu.com/PDF/Democracy percent20Index percent20208.
2. A. Guillaume, *The Life of Mohammed: A Translation of Ibn Ishag's Sirat Rasul Allah* (Karachi, Pakistan: Oxford University Press), p. 106.
3. N. J. Dawood, trans., *The Koran*, with parallel Arabic text (London: Penguin Books, 2000), p. 597.
4. Malise Ruthven, *Islam in the World* (New York: Oxford University Press, 2006), p. 37.

5. Dede Korkut, M.D., *The Medical Case of Mohammed* (Enumclaw, WA: WinePress Publishing, 2001).

6. Charles R. Crane, cited in Robert Lacey, *The Kingdom: Arabia and the House of Saud* (New York: Avon Books, 1981), p. 230.

7. A person can convert to Islam by the simple process of reciting the *shahadah* ("there is no God but Allah and Mohammed is his prophet") three times in the presence of another Muslim.

8. Dore Gold, *Hatred's Kingdom: How Saudi Arabia Supports the New Global Terrorism* (Washington, DC: Regnery Publishing, 2003), p. 101.

9. Ibid., p. 102.

10. Ibid., p. 111.

11. Abdullah Azzam, cited in Lawrence Wright, *The Looming Tower: Al-Qaeda and the Road to 9/11* (New York: Alfred A. Knopf, 2006), p. 95.

12. Osama bin Laden, "Declaration of War Against the Americans Occupying the Land of the Two Holy Places," 1996, Osama bin Laden's Jihad and Text of Fatwahs and Declaration of War, MidEast Web. http://www.mideastweb.org/osamabinladen1.htm.

13. Osama bin Laden, "Text of World Islamic Front's Statement Urging Jihad Against Jews and Crusaders," *Al-Quds al-Arabi* (London), February 23, 1998, p. 3. http://www.mideastweb.org/osama binladen2.htm.

14. Sheikh Adel Al-Kalbani, cited in "Interview with Sheikh Adel Al-Kalbani," BBC in Arabic, May 2, 2009. http://www.memritv.org/clip/en/2102.htm.

15. Sheikh Salah al-Sheikh, cited in Gold, *Hatred's Kingdom*, p. 210.

16. International Criminal Court, ICC Press and Media, March 3, 2009. http://www.icc-cpi.int/NR/exeres/OEF62173-05ED-403A-80C8-F15EE1D25BB3.htm.

17. "Leading Sunni Sheikh Yousef Al-Qaradhawi and Other Sheiks Herald the Coming Conquest of Rome," The Middle East Research Institute, December 6, 2002, special dispatch no. 447. http://www.memri.org/bin/articles.cgi?Area=sd&ID=SP44702.

Appendix B: United Nations General Assembly Resolution 181

1. See Official Records of the General Assembly, Second Session Supplement No. 11,Volumes I-IV.

2. At its hundred and twenty-eighth plenary meeting on 29 November 1947 the General Assembly, in accordance with the terms of the above resolution, elected the following members of the United Nations Commission on Palestine: Bolivia, Czechoslovakia, Denmark, Panama, and Philippines. This resolution was adopted without reference to a Committee.

3. The following stipulation shall be added to the declaration concerning the Jewish State: "In the Jewish State adequate facilities shall be given to Arabic-speaking citizens for the use of their language, either orally or in writing, in the legislature, before the Courts and in the administration."

4. In the declaration concerning the Arab State, the words "by an Arab in the Jewish State" should be replaced by the words "by a Jew in the Arab State."

5. On the question of the internationalization of Jerusalem, see also General Assembly resolutions 185 (S-2) of 26 April 1948; 187 (S-2) of 6 May 1948, 303 (IV) of 9 December 1949, and resolutions of the Trusteeship Council (Section IV).

ACKNOWLEDGMENTS

I would like to thank several people who have contributed, by their advice or contacts, to this book. I need to emphasize that any mistakes or omissions in the text are entirely my own responsibility and not the fault of the very helpful assistance I received from many people.

Before going on a reporting trip to Syria and Lebanon, I received some excellent contacts from Mayada Ani Logue. I should recognize in Lebanon the helpful comments and contacts of Said Abu Izzedin, as well as those of Marwan Bedas, who pointed out many important aspects of Beirut. Also in Lebanon, a long-time friend, Habib Malik, was both hospitable and very informative.

In Israel, the list of friends and contacts goes back many years, but I would like to mention a long-time friend, Dmitry Radyshevsky, whose hospitality and counsel I have long enjoyed.

Nafez Nazzal, living in the Palestine Authority territories, is also a long-time friend and has provided wise insights into the Palestinian situation for many years.

I have had stimulating and informative conversations in recent years with myriad friends in the Washington, DC, area on many aspects of the reality in the Middle East.

At Regal Books, I would like to thank Senior Editor Steven Lawson for his courtesy, helpfulness and, above all, patience as this book has been written and gone to press.

My literary agent, John Eames, deserves great thanks for spotting the opportunity of writing this book.

Finally, I am indebted to my wife for her support and help during the writing of this book.

INDEX